Understanding justice

An introduction to ideas, perspectives and controversies in modern penal theory

Second edition

CRIME AND JUSTICE
Series editor: Mike Maguire
Cardiff University

Crime and Justice is a series of short introductory texts on central topics in criminology. The books in this series are written for students by internationally renowned authors. Each book tackles a key area within criminology, providing a concise and up-to-date overview of the principal concepts, theories, methods and findings relating to the area. Taken as a whole, the *Crime and Justice* series will cover all the core components of an undergraduate criminology course.

Published titles

Understanding youth and crime
Sheila Brown

Understanding crime data
Clive Coleman and Jenny Moynihan

Understanding white collar crime
Hazel Croall

Understanding justice (second edition)
Barbara A. Hudson

Understanding crime prevention
Gordon Hughes

Understanding violent crime
Stephen Jones

Understanding community penalties
Peter Raynor and Maurice Vanstone

Understanding criminology (second edition)
Sandra Walklate

Understanding justice

An introduction to ideas, perspectives and controversies in modern penal theory

Second edition

Barbara A. Hudson

Open University Press

Open University Press
McGraw-Hill Education
McGraw-Hill House
Shoppenhangers Road
Maidenhead
Berkshire
SL6 2QL
United Kingdom

Email: enquiries@openup.co.uk
World wide web: www.openup.co.uk

and
Two Penn Plaza
New York, NY 10121-2289, USA

First Published 1996
Reprinted 1997, 1998, 1999, 2000
First published in this second edition, 2003
Reprinted 2004

Copyright © Barbara A. Hudson, 2003

A catalogue record of this book is available from the British Library

ISBN   0 335 21037 6 (hb) 0 335 21036 8 (pb)

Library of Congress Cataloguing-in-Publication Data
Hudson, Barbara, 1945 -
    Understanding justice : an introduction to ideas, perspectives, and controversies in modern penal theory / Barbara A. Hudson. –
    2nd ed.   p.   cm. (Crime and justice)
Includes bibliographical references and index.
ISBN 0-335-21037-6 – ISBN 0-335-21036-8 (pbk.)
    1. Punishment.   2. Criminal law – Philosophy.   I. Title.   II. Crime and justice (Buckingham, England)

K5103.H83 2003
364. 6'01–dc21   2002030371

Typeset by Type Study, Scarborough
Printed and bound in Great Britain by Biddles Ltd, King's Lynn, Norfolk

Contents

Series editor's foreword   viii
Acknowledgements   x

1   **Perspectives on punishment**   1
    Defining modern penology   1
    The goals of punishment   3
    Punishment and society: the social role and characteristics of
        penal systems   6
    Punishing effectively: the criminological tradition   10
    Transgressing crime and punishment: abolition and
        deconstruction   12
    Summary   13

Part one: The goals of punishment: the juridical perspective

2   **Utilitarian approaches**   17
    Introduction   17
    Deterrence   18
    Evaluating the deterrent effects of punishment   21
    Individual deterrence   24
    Reform/rehabilitation   26
    Criticisms of rehabilitative penalties   28
    Prevention through incapacitation   31
    Problems with prevention   33
    Conclusion   36

3   **Retribution**   38
    Introduction   38
    Modern retributivism: the just-deserts movement   39
    Proportionality and seriousness   43

Retribution and the justification of punishment 46
Deterrence and retribution in distribution 52
Summary and conclusion 54

4 Hybrids, compromises and syntheses 56
Introduction 56
Desert and deterrence: crime reduction within limits 57
Desert and rehabilitation: reform with rights 62
Targets and restraints: syntheses of utilitarian and
retributive theories 66
Conclusion 73

5 Restorative justice: diversion, compromise or replacement
discourse 75
Introduction 75
Definition, principles and models 77
The range and limits of restorative justice 83
Retribution, rights and restorative justice 88
Conclusion 92

Part two: Punishment and modernity: the sociological perspective

6 Punishment and progress: the Durkheimian tradition 95
Introduction 95
Durkheim: punishment and solidarity 97
Durkheim's sociology of law: critical evaluation 102
Weber: bureaucracy and rationality 104
Durkheimian and Weberian themes: some contemporary
applications 108
Punishment and culture: contemporary formulations 109
Conclusion 111

7 The political economy of punishment: Marxist approaches 112
Introduction 112
Key concepts in Marxist sociology 113
Punishment and the labour market 115
Why prison? 118
Ideology and the control of surplus populations 121
The challenge of feminism 128
Conclusion: the legacy of Marxism 130

8 The disciplined society: Foucault and the analysis of penality 132
Introduction 132
Foucault's disciplinary penality 133
Delinquency and normalization 137
Critique and controversy 142

Periodicity 143
Overgeneralization 144
Partiality 146
Functionalism 148
Politics 149
Summary and conclusion: Foucault's legacy 150

9   Understanding contemporary penality 153
Introduction: punishment and contemporary culture 153
Governmentality, risk and actuarialism 157
Penal policy as problem-solving 164
The mass imprisonment society 168
Summary and conclusions: punishment in the twenty-first
century 171

Part three: Towards justice?

10   The struggle for justice: critical criminology and critical
legal studies 175
Introduction 175
Challenges to mainstream penology 177
Abolitionism 178
Feminist jurisprudence 180
Concluding comments 184

Postscript: Beyond modernity: the fate of justice 187
Introduction 187
Human rights and the politics of public safety 188
Justice and postmodernity 190

Glossary of key terms 193
Suggestions for further reading 195
References 197
Index 212

Series editor's foreword

Understanding Justice, the first edition of which appeared in 1996, was the first book in Open University Press' successful Crime and Justice series. Indeed, the quality of this book was one of the main reasons that the series became so quickly established as a key resource in universities teaching criminology or criminal justice, especially in the UK but increasingly also overseas. The author, Barbara Hudson, is internationally renowned in the field of penal theory, and her book set the pattern for a series of short but intellectually challenging introductory textbooks on important areas of debate in criminology, criminal justice and penology. The aim in every case has been to give undergraduates and graduates both a solid grounding in the relevant area and a taste to explore it further. Although aimed primarily at students new to the field, and written as far as possible in plain language, the books are not oversimplified. On the contrary, the authors set out to 'stretch' readers and to encourage them to approach criminological knowledge and theory in a critical and questioning frame of mind.

Professor Hudson has now substantially revised and updated the text, including two new chapters on key developments in penological thinking over the last few years: the rapid growth of interest in restorative justice; and the rich new vein of criminological and sociological writing on the major shifts in modes of punishment (or 'penality') which appear to be taking place in 'late modern' western democracies. The book, however, continues to give full weight to the views of earlier social theorists, as well as to juridical perspectives on punishment. It provides a substantial discussion of fundamental philosophical questions about the principles and goals of, and justifications for, punishment. It also outlines and critically analyses the pioneering contributions of major sociological writers, from Marx, Weber and Durkheim to Foucault, in explaining why particular types or modes of punishment (such as capital punishment and imprisonment) become prominent in different kinds of societies at different times in history.

The final two chapters take us to the cutting edge of current sociological and penal debates, to which Hudson herself has been a major contributor. She introduces key concepts such as governmentality, risk and actuarialism, and surveys the (largely depressing) current penal landscape, characterized by the grouping of offenders into risk categories and by increasingly harsh and exclusionary penal measures, including massive increases in imprisonment. In seeking alternative directions, she emphasizes the critical importance of holding on to the concept of 'justice', outlining the particular contributions of feminists, abolitionists and advocates of restorative justice. Overall, the strength of the book stems from the unusual ability of a highly knowledgeable author to compress a wide range of sophisticated theoretical writing and debate into a short and accessible text, without either grossly over-simplifying arguments or assuming too much initial knowledge on the part of the readers.

Other books previously published in the Crime and Justice series – all of whose titles begin with the word 'Understanding' – have covered criminological theory (Sandra Walklate – now also in a second edition), crime data and statistics (Clive Coleman and Jenny Moynihan), youth and crime (Sheila Brown), crime prevention (Gordon Hughes), violent crime (Stephen Jones), community penalties (Peter Raynor and Maurice Vanstone) and white collar crime (Hazell Croall). Others in the pipeline include texts on prisons, policing, social control, sentencing and criminal justice, race and crime, psychology and crime, risk and crime, and crime and social exclusion. All are major topics in university degree courses on crime and criminal justice, and each book should make an ideal foundation text for a relevant module. As an aid to understanding, clear summaries are provided at regular intervals, and a glossary of key terms and concepts is a feature of very book. In addition, to help students expand their knowledge, recommendations for futher reading are given at the end of each chapter.

Mike Maguire
Professor of Criminology and Criminal Justice, Cardiff University

Acknowledgements

I would like to thank Mike Maguire for inviting me to do this book, and for helpful comments during its production. Thanks are also due to the editorial staff at the Open University Press for their patience and support. I am also grateful to various friends and colleagues for encouraging me in the belief that this book will be useful, and to students at the University of Northumbria at Newcastle, whose questions, comments and criticisms have done much to shape the form and content of the book. The final section owes much to discussions with Andrew von Hirsch, Kathleen Daly and Joe Sim, and to an all too brief time as visiting scholar to the Jurisprudence and Social Policy Program, University of California, Berkeley, which gave me the time and inspiration to sort out what I really think about current developments in penal policy and theory.

As ever, thanks to Harry and Adam, without whom I would never finish anything.

Acknowledgements for the second edition

Participation in the colloquium on restorative justice, organized by the Centre for Penal Theory and Penal Ethics, Cambridge University, and in the seminar on risk, crime and justice held at John Jay College of Criminal Justice, New York, has helped with the preparation of the two new chapters, 5 and 9. Students in the sentencing seminars at my present university, the University of Central Lancashire, have provided lively and challenging discussion. Special thanks are due to my colleagues Helen Codd and David Scott, for their encouragement and support.

chapter one

Perspectives on punishment

Defining modern penology
The goals of punishment
**Punishment and society: the social role and the characteristics of penal
     systems**
Punishing effectively: the criminological tradition
Transgressing crime and punishment: abolition and deconstruction
Summary

Defining modern penology

The aim of this book is to introduce the main ideas, disciplines and perspectives that are found in modern Western penology. By 'penology' is
meant the study of punishment for crime, and by 'modern' is meant from
the time of the industrial revolution onwards.

This usage of both 'punishment' and 'modern' is narrower than that of
everyday conversation. 'Punishment' is a word widely used in relation to
anything that is painful: we talk of a 'punishing' schedule of work, a
'punishing' exercise regime, even a 'punishing' diet; we talk of punishment
by parents of children, or by teachers of pupils. The punishment that is the
subject matter of penology, however, does not encompass everything that
is painful or demanding, and does not encompass all kinds of control or
discipline of one person by another. It means penalties authorized by the
state, and inflicted by state officials, in response to crime. Punishment in
this sense is usually distinguished from other kinds of pain and deprivation,
and from the wider concept of 'social control', by listing its essential
features. A frequently used set of five criteria was suggested by the philosopher Flew (1954), with a sixth, suggested by Benn and Peters (1959),
often being added:

1 it must involve an evil, an unpleasantness to the victim;
2 it must be for an offence, actual or supposed;

3 it must be of an offender, actual or supposed;

4 it must be the work of personal agencies;

5 it must be imposed by authority conferred through or by the institutions against the rules of which the offence has been committed.

A sixth criterion . . . is that the pain or unpleasantness should be an essential part of what is intended and not merely a coincidental or accidental outcome.

(Hudson 1987: 2)

These criteria distinguish 'punishment' from other kinds of unpleasantness – for example divine retribution, the pangs of conscience, having to be at school or at work when one would rather be elsewhere – by specifying that the pain must be inflicted by one or more persons on another person and that it must be the essential purpose of the pain-causing activity. Being at work on a sunny day might feel like 'punishment', but punishment is not the aim of work. This difference between deliberate punishment and situations that are unpleasant is partly covered by the sixth criterion, but is further clarified by Nigel Walker's additional criterion, that

It is the belief or intention of the person who orders something to be done, and not the belief or intention of the person to whom it is done, that settles the question whether it is punishment.

(Walker 1991: 3)

Even with this added criterion, however, the definition of 'punishment' arrived at would include more than that form of punishment that is the subject of penology. We must add that the offence for which it is inflicted must be a criminal offence, and that the rules and institutions of criterion 5 are the criminal law and the penal system. The punishment with which penology is concerned, then, is punishment for crime, pronounced by the judiciary and administered by penal institutions such as prisons and the probation service. Other types of 'punishment' – for example, of pupils by teachers, or of criminals by vigilantes and lynch mobs – are excluded.

'Modern' is also used in a more specific sense than in everyday usage. It is taken to designate the time, from about 1700–1750 onwards, when Western societies ceased to be feudal and land-based, and became industrial, urbanized and constitutional. The social institutions with which we are familiar began to emerge at this time – parliamentary government; constitutional monarchy; factory-based employment; universal education; and extension of the right to vote first to all property owners, and eventually to all men and women over the minimum qualification age. The penal systems with which we are familiar also emerged during this era. Modernity is characterized by the rise of scientific and rational thought, the declining influence of religious and traditional authority, and a belief that human life can be enriched, and social problems can be solved, by the application of science. Some social theorists claim that this period of modernity is now over (Beck 1992). If this is so, then we can expect considerable implications for conceptions of justice and systems of punishment.

The goals of punishment

Why should offenders be punished? This apparently simple question has several possible answers: because they deserve it; to stop them committing further crimes; to reassure the victim that society cares about what has happened to him/her; to discourage other people from doing the same thing; to protect society from dangerous or dishonest people; to allow offenders to make amends for the harm they have caused; to make people realize that laws must be obeyed. Each of these reasons, and others one could easily imagine, are plausible justifications for imposing punishment on offenders. These are the kinds of consideration judges and magistrates have in mind when they pass sentences, and at first glance they may seem such obvious, common-sense reasons for punishing criminals that it is surprising that they are the subject of a large body of scholarly writing and generate much argument.

Difficulties arise, however, because these reasons may conflict. Generally, such conflicts are between reasons based on preventing crime (either by the same offender doing it again, or by potential offenders), and the idea that punishment is because the offender 'deserves it'. Furthermore, there is a perennial and unavoidable tension between protecting the rights of offenders not to be punished more than they deserve, and protecting the rights of the public not to be victims of crime.

The reasons for punishment listed above fall into two groups, those which are concerned with preventing future crimes, and those which are concerned with punishing already committed (or past) crimes (von Hirsch 1985). Those theories which see the goal of punishment as to prevent future crime are sometimes referred to as *utilitarian* (Hart 1968; Walker 1991) because they are derived from Utilitarian political-moral philosophy; or as *consequentialist* (Braithwaite and Pettit 1990), because they justify punishment by its anticipated future consequences; or as *reductivist* (Cavadino and Dignan 1992) because their aim is the reduction of crime. These ideas will be discussed in more detail in Chapter 2. Past-oriented theories are usually known as *retributivist*, because their aim is to exact retribution from offenders for their crimes. Central to retributivist perspectives is the idea that the purpose of judicial punishment is to place moral blame on the offender for the offence s/he has committed, and that the future conduct of the offender or other members of his/her society is not a proper concern of punishment. Retributive theories will be discussed in Chapter 3.

Debates between the advocates of past- and future-oriented punishment philosophies have been around as long as societies and systems of punishments have been around. Variants of both approaches are found in the writings of the ancient Greeks, in the teachings and laws of the major religions, in the flowering of political and moral philosophy in the Renaissance and Enlightenment periods, and new formulations of both perspectives continue to be produced. Contemporary debates will be reviewed in Chapter 4.

The debate between the various philosophies of punishment will never be resolved because all the reasons for punishing offenders listed above are functions which members of a society look to their penal system to fulfil. People expect punishment to discourage potential offenders from offending at all and actual offenders from offending again; victims feel better if their misfortunes are reflected in a sentence being passed on the offender; citizens feel protected if dangerous offenders are removed from circulation; people who do not transgress the criminal law feel aggrieved if those who do transgress seem to get away without punishment; there is a sense of injustice if penalties are unconscionably harsh and if defendants are not given a fair trial.

In practice, penal codes and the judges and magistrates who implement them in the courts seek to balance the various reasons for imposing punishment, all of which are accepted as proper goals for the penal system to pursue. From time to time, however, one or other of the ideas becomes dominant, and penal codes are written or altered to prioritize one penal goal at the expense of others. Since the institution of modern penal systems, there have been successive 'fashions' in penal theory: at various stages in the development of penal codes in modern industrial societies, the alternative justifications for punishment have enjoyed differing degrees of relative influence. The earliest penal codes of modern Western societies prioritized deterrence of potential offenders above the other aims; reform and rehabilitation of actual offenders have been fashionable aims during the nineteenth century and for most of the twentieth; in the last quarter of this century, there has been a widespread disillusion with the rehabilitative aim and a return to public protection and to punishment according to desert. All the penal goals are represented in the actual codes and practices of Western societies, but the balance between them changes.

Because goals may conflict, penal codes generally prescribe which is to have priority, and it is this question of priority which has been the major source of theoretical and policy debate.

In a penal system with utilitarian/reductivist/consequentialist goals, there could be clashes between, for example, protection or deterrence, and reform of individuals. It may be thought that deterring potential offenders and protecting the public from crime requires long prison sentences, whereas reforming the actual offender may be better served by community penalties such as probation. This argument is often heard between the advocates of increased and decreased prison use, the former claiming that 'prison works' and the latter maintaining that 'prison does not work'. What the 'more imprisonment' lobby claims is that prison works to keep people who might commit more offences off the streets, and that it might put some people off the idea of committing crime; the 'reduce imprison-ment' lobby claims that prison is not generally successful in making people who have been sent there into better, more law-abiding citizens. The argu-ment is not really about the effectiveness of imprisonment as such, but about the relative priority which should be accorded to deterrence, protec-tion or reform.

There also arise conflicts between reductivism in any form, and desert-based retributivism. For example, if a person is assessed as likely to commit a further offence, should s/he be punished more severely than someone who commits the same offence but is not assessed as likely to reoffend? Conversely, should someone who commits an offence and has a record of previous offences be punished more severely than someone committing the same offence for the first time? In other words, what priority should be given to the current offence, as opposed to someone's record, both previous and prospective?

These are perennial dilemmas for penal policy and practice, and all that penal theory can do is to elucidate the principles of each approach, and point out the dilemmas – both ethical and practical – of alternative approaches.

This juxtaposing of reductivist and retributivist theories of punishment may seem something of a false dichotomy because, it may be argued, the purpose of defining some sorts of behaviour as crime is surely to reduce their occurrence. If the purpose of criminal law is to prevent or curtail the actions that society regards as harmful enough to be criminalized, then by definition judicial punishment, as the system of penalties for transgressing the criminal law, must share this goal of reducing crime. If we wish to encourage a certain type of behaviour, we do not make it the subject of a criminal law and provide penalties for its commission. If we would like more members of society to do something – join the armed forces, or look after their elderly neighbours, for example – we run media campaigns emphasizing its importance and merit, we increase or introduce payments, we award medals. It is when we want to discourage something – theft, killing, assaults, incitement to racial hatred – that we make it a 'crime'. There are, of course, other forms of behaviour which society or particular social groups might want to discourage – taking a day's unofficial holiday after the New Year festivities, bearing children outside marriage, eating meat – but although these may be disapproved behaviours, they are not crimes. If we try to distinguish 'crimes' and other forms of disapproved behaviour by characteristics of the actions themselves (being harmful to other people, for example), we would soon find ourselves in difficulties. The way criminologists and others usually distinguish between crimes and other forms of disapproved conduct is to say that crimes are those kinds of conduct which are proscribed by the criminal law, and for which there is provision for state punishment.

State, or judicial, punishment, then, is the mechanism of enforcement for the criminal law, the purpose of which is to discourage the behaviours which it specifies. The whole point of criminal law, then, and the system of punishments through which it is enforced, is to prevent crime. If we ask the question 'Why have a system of punishment at all?', then, most people would answer 'To prevent crime' as though it were self-evident, a 'truth by definition'. When we are giving an answer to this question, we are proposing a *general justifying aim* for punishment. This does not, however, help us answer questions such as 'How much punishment should there be for certain types of offences/offenders?' or 'What types of punishment should there be?'. These are *principles of distribution*, and it is important to distinguish the two types of principles. We also need to be clear when rationales for punishment such as rehabilitation, deterrence or retribution are being suggested as justifying principles, and when as principles of distribution (Hart 1968). In Chapter 4, some contemporary formulations will be suggested which attempt to resolve the arguments between the various positions by adopting reductivism as the justifying principle and retribution as the principle of distribution. Chapter 5 introduces restorative justice, which has become increasingly important in criminal justice practice. Debates about its role, its limits and its relationship with other principles of punishent are reviewed.

Punishment and society: the social role and the characteristics of penal systems

The principles of punishment referred to above are generally discussed by moral philosophers and philosophers of law. Punishment has also, however, been great interest to sociologists and historians. While philosophers and legal theorists have developed theories about and argued about the different justifications for punishment, sociologists and historians have been concerned with the ways in which the different ideas have come and gone in penal fashion, the ways in which penal codes and penal policies have shown the relative influence of the different philosophies. They have shown us that there are many factors other than the truth or reasonableness of the ideas themselves which affect their incorporation into actual penal practices.

Sociologists have been concerned to demonstrate the relationship between the ways in which societies are organized – the economic system, the social stratification system – and the kinds of penal system they develop.

Social scientists take as their subject the *penality* characteristic of different societies at different times. By 'penality' is meant the complex of ideas (about proper punishment, about effective punishment), institutions (laws, policies and practices, agencies and buildings), and relationships (who has the power to say who is punished, whose ideas count, what is the relationship of those who punish and are punished to the rest of society) involved in the punishment of offenders (Garland and Young 1983: 14; Cavadino and Dignan, 1992: 58).

The involvement of sociologists and historians with punishment has been concentrated on two major questions: what punishments are *like*, and what they are *for*.

Looking at the nature of punishment, the most influential sociological analysis has been that showing the transition from penalties inflicted on the body (execution, torture and mutilation, as well as less drastic physical punishments such as the stocks) to those directed at the mind and the character (labour and penance in eighteenth- and nineteenth-century prisons, education and therapy in twentieth-century prisons), punishments which are designed to produce not the physically incapacitated citizen but the right-thinking citizen (Foucault 1977). Sociologists have also demonstrated the social organization that takes place inside prisons – the inmate groupings, the power relationships that develop – providing a sociology of prisons alongside the more abstract and theoretical sociology of imprisonment and punishment more generally (e.g. Goffman 1961). That the defining characteristic of modern punishments is their disciplinary nature, and that the most predictable effect of imprisonment on offenders is institutionalization, are important ideas developed in these sociologies, important ideas which have been incorporated into much subsequent sociological-penological thinking.

Sociological analysis of the role of punishment in modern society started with the same issue as that of the Utilitarian philosophers mentioned in the previous section. As feudal, land-based societies changed into industrial, urbanized modern society, and as autocratic kings gave way to constitutional monarchies or republics, criminal law and punishment became encompassed by the general question of what should be the role and limits of the power of government. The principal idea to emerge was *social contract theory*, according to which the existence of 'society', as opposed to a group of mutually predatory individuals, depends on the existence of a contract (tacit, unwritten) between citizens and government, such that some degree of individual freedom is surrendered in return for government protection against harm from others. There are variants in the social contract theories that developed in the seventeenth and eighteenth centuries, but all incorporate this essential idea. The best-known British versions of social contract theory are those of Hobbes (1962), who in his book *Leviathan* argued that mutual obligation did not exist prior to the constitution of a sovereign state, and that rebellion against the state cannot be justified, and Locke (1924), who argued that principles of morality and mutual obligation can be derived from nature and thus exist prior to the formation of states, and states can therefore be challenged or overthrown if they fail to uphold these principles. Another well-known version of social contract theory is that of Rousseau (1973). 'Man is born free but is everywhere in chains' is probably one of the most-quoted phrases from modern philosophy. In fact, it is not a call to rebellion, but an observation, and in his book on the social contract he asks why, under what conditions, people are willing to surrender their freedom to governments.

As sociology developed as a separate discipline, with a distinctive approach from political economy and moral philosophy, thinkers such as Émile Durkheim saw law as the only available source of moral authority in modern society. Durkheim saw the criminal law and the system of punishment as the way in which society expressed its rules and values: the moral boundaries were defined and maintained by the pronouncement of penalties for crimes.

Durkheim's work is thus addressed primarily to the question of what law is for, what is the function of law and punishment. In his analysis of different kinds of power, the German sociologist Max Weber addressed the question of what law is, or should be, like in modern society. He showed the importance of law as a system of rules, consistently applied, with authority vested in persons only when they are acting in an appointed role. Thus, judges can only pronounce sentence when sitting in a duly constituted court; as private citizens (doing the shopping, walking the dog) they have no more power than anyone else to penalize someone they may come across committing an offence. Weber's description of the characteristics legal systems must display to command respect in modern societies finds a contemporary echo in questioning of the degree of *legitimacy* granted by a population to its penal system – the degree to which the criminal justice and penal systems of a country are felt by the majority of its citizens to be fair and reasonable, to be staying within proper limits in their exercise of power. Contemporary sociologists of punishment talk of a 'crisis of legitimacy' (Cavadino and Dignan 1992: Chapter 1), and concern with issues such as 'disparity' in sentencing (giving different sentences for similar offences) echoes Weber's emphasis on the importance of rule-governed rationality in modern legal systems.

Durkheim and Weber see the role of law and punishment as being important for the cohesion of society as a whole; another tradition, that of Marxist sociology, sees punishment and criminal law as being in service of the needs of capital, and as repressing those who do not accept capitalist discipline. This analytic tradition comes from looking at changes in the nature of punishments in relation to changes in economic organization and other social characteristics, and noticing that there does seem to be significant correlation between developments in penality and in other social spheres.

A second important strand in this 'sociology of repression' has derived from looking at the official rationales given (by legislators, policy-makers and influential figures of the time) for the purposes of punishment, and comparing these with what actually happens. For example, if the official rationale for punishment is reform of offenders, but the forms of punishment which are developed most are those that seem least effective in reforming offenders, does this mean that the 'real' goal of punishment is something else, and reform is only a gloss adopted by politicians and penal professionals to make their policies and practices publicly acceptable? This dissonance between the supposed goal of reform and the actual outcome of punishments making people worse has been most frequently commented upon in relation to prisons. If prisons do not in fact reform people, it is suggested, but nevertheless people continue to be imprisoned, then the 'real' goal of punishment must be something other than reform. While some sociologists have accordingly identified other 'real' functions of prisons in particular and punishment in general (e.g. Mathiesen 1974; 1990; Reiman 1979), others have objected to the 'functionalism' of this argument. Functionalism, in sociology, is a perspective which suggests that social forms and institutions do not survive if they do not perform some useful function for society, and it is a general criticism of this approach to prisons and punishment that it falls too easily into either functionalism or economic determinism. Critics of this 'hidden functions' approach to penality argue that prisons really do not work, but that we have failed to come up with more effective alternatives (e.g. Ignatieff 1983).

The sociological perspective on punishment will be explored in Part Two of this book. Chapter 6 will look at the Durkheimian and Weberian reflections on punishment and on law more generally, exploring Durkheim's emphasis on law as the source of social stability and cohesion in modern industrial societies, and Weber's characterization of the forms that authority, and institutions exercising authoritative power, must take if they are to serve the needs of modern industrial society.

In Chapter 7, the Marxist tradition will be examined, and examples of more recent writings which start from the basic Marxist premise of law and punishment as being given their essential role and character by the economic system, will be discussed. While the emphasis of Chapter 6 will be on the function of punishment in reinforcing social solidarity, Chapter 7 will focus on the repressive functions of punishment.

Chapter 8 will look at the so-called 'post-Marxist' sociologies of punishment. This body of work takes for granted the relationship between penal systems and the economic systems of the societies in which they exist, and also accepts the importance of penal systems as techniques of repression. However, the analysis of power to be found in the works of 'post-Marxists' such as Michel Foucault is rather different from that in orthodox Marxist works. There is also a much more concrete engagement with the specific exercise of power and repression in the actual practices of punishment, than can be found in the more abstract writings of orthodox Marxists.

Chapter 9 examines work published during the late 1990s and early 2000s which analyses the nature of contemporary penality. Themes of governmentality and actuarialism have been used to illustrate penal trends in late modernity, and Garland's powerful analysis of the 'cultural preconditions' of these trends provides a comprehensive and illuminating account of the penality of our times.

Punishing effectively: the criminological tradition

The perspectives on punishment mentioned so far have all been highly theoretical. Jurisprudence and the philosophical tradition are concerned with the *ought* of punishment – what ought to be the goals of punishment, what ought to be the values embodied in and upheld by the criminal law – and little will be encountered by way of discussion of the actual practices of punishment. The sociological perspective is concerned with the *is* of punishment – what punishment really is for, what the true nature of modern penal systems is – again, this is description at a highly abstracted and theorized level. Such sociological description often claims to be revealing the 'deeper structures' of penal systems (Cohen 1984), and although actual policies and practices may be referred to, they are offered as examples, chosen to illustrate the analyst's general characterization of the penal systems under examination. In other words, in reading writers such as Melossi, Cohen or Foucault, one finds references to certain sorts of punishment, which they see as representative of the defining developments in modes of punishment of particular stages of social development; one does not find a full, descriptive account of penal institutions, policies and practices.

There is another stream of penology which is much less abstract, and has more pragmatic aims. As philosophical penology sets itself the task of showing what punishment should be for, and as sociology sets itself the task of revealing what punishment really is like, the criminological tradition sets itself the apparently more modest task of suggesting punishment strategies to match the goals set by others, be they philosophers or, more usually, legislators.

This is 'technicist penology', as opposed to the 'social analysis of penality' (Garland and Young 1983), which is simply aimed at helping those with the power to punish to put their ideas into practice. Technicist penology is a principal strand of so-called administrative or mainstream criminology (Cohen 1981; Young 1988). Administrative or technicist penology and criminology accept, rather than question, the aims of punishment espoused by the state. The problems they seek to resolve are second-order questions such as what type of prison regime will serve the needs of reform, or public protection, or retribution; how prisons can be managed so as to minimize disorder and maximize security; what kind of non-custodial penalties will satisfy the penal aims of protection, retribution and rehabilitation. They also address themselves to the values which law is supposed to encompass, such as fairness and consistency, but the focus is on whether the correct legal processes are followed, and they pay little attention to the outcomes of criminal justice and penal processes.

Administrative criminology and penology can be critical in the sense of finding existing systems and practices wanting. Without debating the aims of punishment, or revealing the true functions of penal systems, or questioning the extent of the state's punitive repression, it is possible to point out that, for example, certain existing prison regimes make riots more likely, or that changes in rates and length of imprisonment may make prisons harder to govern or less successful in reforming offenders. Such penology may appear to criticize, but it is not critical in the sense of wanting to bring about any profound change in the state's penal strategies.

Technicist penology merges with mainstream criminology in that the advice it offers is often based on the beliefs of mainstream criminology about the causes of crime and the nature of people who commit crimes. Ideas about the gradation of punishments which were the foundation of so-called 'classical criminology' of the eighteenth century were thus based on the idea that crime was rational behaviour, an idea which is in favour again now, whereas the 'positivist criminology' of the nineteenth century and the first two-thirds of the twentieth was based on ideas of people's behaviour as being determined by circumstances or by psychological or physiological predisposition. Contemporary ideas about additional imprisonment, or refusal of parole, for prisoners likely to reoffend, as well as suggestions about how to help people refrain from reoffending while dealing with them by community penalties such as probation, all derive from current criminological notions about the causes of crime.

Much of this technicist and administrative penology proceeds without reference to the philosophical or sociological debates. If these are reflected at all, it is to the extent that the currently fashionable justifications for punishment, or sociological insights which prove useful for the technicist project, are incorporated by being taken for granted.

Technicist penology, and the administrative criminology to which it is so closely related, are contingent upon the juridical-philosophical discourse in that their project is to devise strategies for the implementation of penal aims, or to test their effectiveness. If the dominant penal aim changes, then so do the topics of the main body of technicist penology.

Another criminological approach to punishment, however, derives more from the sociological tradition than from the legal-philosophical. This body of writing on punishment starts from the assumption that the functions of punishment are what the Marxists say they are, or that the characteristics of punishment are as Foucault described, and proceeds to more detailed and specific investigations of these aspects of punishment.

From the Marxist analysis of punishment as part of the repressive apparatus of the state, for example, have come studies of the link between punishment and inequality, found in the work of Box (1987) and others. The class analysis of Marxism has been reformulated to encompass other dimensions of oppression, notably those of gender and race. The work of writers such as Carlen (e.g. 1983; 1988) on the penal repression of women, and Headley (1989) and Sabol (1989) on race and criminal justice, are examples of such investigations. These writers will be mentioned in Part Two (Chapters 6–9) as demonstrating refinements or applications of the 'master theories' under examination, but, again, more comprehensive coverage of their work will be found in the companion volumes in this series.

Transgressing crime and punishment: abolition and deconstruction

Whatever their disagreements on the most important goals of punishment, the real or rhetorical functions of punishment for the state, the nature of punishment, the most effective and efficient ways to punish, the strategies needed to reduce class, gender or race oppression in punishment, all the approaches to punishment mentioned so far assume that Western societies will – and should – continue to have criminal laws and penal codes. They assume, in other words, the continued existence of state punishment as the normal response to crime.

There are penologists, however, who question the necessity or desirability of punishment; there is an (albeit fairly small) abolitionist tradition. Abolitionists differ from each other in what it is they wish to abolish (Steinhert 1986). Most people associate the term 'abolitionism' with the abolition of particular forms of punishment. The death penalty has been the focus of abolitionist campaigns by penologists and penal reformers, and of course there are Western countries – most notably the USA – where the death penalty still exists. In western European countries which no longer use the death penalty, abolitionism most often means campaigns to abolish imprisonment. Although few abolitionists would dispute the need for some criminals to be confined in institutions for public protection, they would argue that the number of truly dangerous offenders is very small, and that such individuals should therefore be treated as exceptional cases. Prison as a normal response to run-of-the-mill crime could and should be abolished, they argue – see, for example, Mathiesen (1974; 1990), for offenders generally, and Carlen (1990), for women offenders.

Other abolitionists would go somewhat further. They would select the objective of compensating victims of crime as the most important task of criminal justice, and propose that instead of a system which is focused on the offender, and whose objective is his/her punishment, the system should be focused on the victim, with the objective of recompense and reconciliation between offender and victim. The restorative justice movement thus seeks to abolish not just imprisonment, but punishment as the usual response to crime (see, for example, Christie 1982; de Haan 1990).

Other abolitionists go even further, and question the whole concept of crime, and therefore of the necessity or justification for punishment. Events which we now consider as crimes, they would argue, are better conceived as problematic events, which may require a variety of responses, such as reparation, restitution, reconciliation of the parties, or perhaps improvement of the social circumstances of the 'offender' (Hulsman and Bernat de Celis 1982).

Another radical challenge to the traditional perspectives on punishment has come from legal theorists who challenge the authority of law on which the right to punish depends. Critical legal theorists have questioned the liability to punishment of people who do not enjoy a fair share of the rights and privileges which are meant to be protected by law. Others, especially feminist legal theorists, have called into question the claims of law to protect the rights and reflect the interests of all sections of society. The presuppositions of law, they claim, are not equal and race- and gender-neutral, but in fact male, white and middle-class (Smart 1989; Kerruish 1991; Hudson 1993).

These abolitionist challenges to punishment, and deconstructionist challenges to law, are reviewed in Part Three, along with some contemporary proposals for punishment systems which go beyond the parameters of traditional theories and current legislation and practice.

Summary

What is evident from this brief overview of the topics to be covered in this book is that the subject of punishment is complex, and that it has inspired a rich body of philosophical, sociological and criminological literature. Punishment is of profound theoretical and practical importance. Crime is something which affects the quality of life of all citizens, and so its reduction would be of great benefit. Hence the appeal of reductivist theories, and of technicist penology. The quality of our civilization is also gauged by how we treat those whom we define as wrongdoers or outsiders, and so we all share the responsibility to be just and humane in our response to crime. Law's moral authority derives from its claims to fairness and equality, to represent the general good against sectional interests, and thus the sociological depiction of its true nature, and the penology which draws on those insights, is equally important. Finally, since punishment is, after all, the deliberate imposition of pain and deprivation by the state on individuals, it behoves society to ensure that this imposition is kept within proper limits, and is inflicted only for proper purposes.

part one

The goals of punishment: the juridical perspective

chapter two

Utilitarian approaches

Introduction
Deterrence
Evaluating the deterrent effects of punishment
Individual deterrence
Reform/rehabilitation
Criticisms of rehabilitative penalties
Prevention through incapacitation
Problems with prevention
Conclusion

Introduction

Punishment is unpleasant for those on whom it is inflicted. It is also expensive: the costs of running courts, prisons, probation services, attendance centres, of collecting fines, are enormous. Why, then, do modern societies do so much punishing? If two wrongs, as it is commonly said, do not make a right, why add the pain of punishment to the pain already caused by the offence? The victim has already suffered from the crime; why make the offender suffer, too?

As mentioned in the previous chapter, 'To prevent crime' or 'To reduce the amount of crime' seems an obvious answer to the question 'Why punish?'. In this chapter, we shall look at the different reductivist aims and discuss the strengths and the weaknesses of each. The questions that we will raise are the extent to which objections to reductivist penal strategies are objections on grounds of effectiveness or objections in principle, and whether objections are against particular reductionist aims or against reductionism in general.

It is possible to be a reductionist without being a Utilitarian (Cavadino and Dignan 1992: 33), and we shall be pointing out which aspects of reductionism are and are not derived from Utilitarianism. Most influential forms of crime-reduction penal theory in modern times have, however, been linked with the theories of the eighteenth- and nineteenth-century Utilitarian thinkers. Utilitarianism combines moral and political philosophy in that it is concerned both with arriving at a definition of 'the good' and with establishing a foundation for the role of government and the basis of political obligation in the modern state. The theory was most systematically expounded by Jeremy Bentham (1748–1832). It proposes that 'the good' is not some abstract metaphysical property, such as harmony with the will of God, but human happiness, and that therefore the role of government is to promote the sum of human happiness, minimizing the amount of human suffering. In relation to punishment, this means that the pain suffered by the offender is only justified if more pain (stemming from more crime) is thereby avoided.

Avoidance of further crime can be achieved by deterring potential criminals, by reforming actual criminals, or by keeping actual or potential offenders out of public circulation. Variants of Utilitarian penology have stressed one or the other of these tactics, or have pursued 'eclectic' strategies which allow for all three goals. All three are consistent with popular expectations of the role of punishment:

> Most people have no difficulty in identifying its [punishment's] utility. For them it is the reduction of the frequency with which people infringe the rules which make for a contented society. It contributes to this by deterring the offender from reoffending, discouraging others from following his example, or putting him where he cannot offend any longer. It is this sort of utility that is the justification offered by utilitarians – Protagoras, Grotius, Beccaria, Bentham, Mill, Wootton.
> (Walker 1991: 6)

Deterrence

To Utilitarians such as Bentham, punishment is 'mischief', which can only be justified if the harm that it prevents is greater than the harm inflicted on the offender by punishing her/him. Unless punishment will deter further crime, then it is adding to, rather than subtracting from, the sum of human suffering:

> If we could consider an offence which has been committed as an isolated fact, the like of which would never recur, punishment would be useless. It would only be adding one evil to another. But when we consider that an unpunished crime leaves the path of crime open, not only to the same delinquent but also to those who may have the same motives and opportunities for entering upon it, we perceive that punishment inflicted on the individual becomes a source of security to all. That punishment which considered by itself appeared base and

repugnant to all generous sentiments is elevated to the first rank of benefits when it is regarded not as an act of wrath or vengeance against a guilty or unfortunate individual who has given way to mischievous inclinations, but as an indispensable sacrifice to the common safety.

(Bentham, *The Principles of Penal Law*, in von Hirsch and Ashworth 1992: 63)

Bentham distinguishes, as do contemporary deterrence theorists, between *individual* and *general* deterrence, that is, between deterring someone who has offended from offending again, and deterring potential offenders from offending at all. He sees three strategies for deterring an individual from reoffending:

1 By taking away from him the physical power of offending.
2 By taking away the desire of offending.
3 By making him afraid of offending.

while general deterrence is achieved by using punishment as an example to others:

The punishment suffered by the offender presents to every one an example of what he himself will have to suffer, if he is guilty of the same offense.

(ibid.)

The first two means of individual deterrence are now more usually known as *prevention* or *incapacitation* and *reform* or *rehabilitation*, and will be discussed under those sub-headings. Deterrence as a penal strategy is usually taken to mean discouraging reoffending, or offending by hitherto lawabiding citizens, through fear of the potential punishment, and this usage is followed here.

The first major penologist of the modern constitutional state was an Italian, Cesare Beccaria, who in 1764 published *Dei delitti e delle pene* (Beccaria 1963). Beccaria proposed a graduated system of penalties, with punishments appropriate to the crime, reminiscent of the 'tariff' of contemporary penal policy. The main aim of his system was general deterrence.

Before the installation of constitutional governments in most of western Europe in the eighteenth and nineteenth centuries, penalties were arbitrary, dependent on the whims of monarchs or the local nobles to whom they delegated authority to punish. There was very little proportionate gradation of penalties, with capital punishment available for everything from murder and high treason to fairly minor theft (as reflected in the old saying 'one might just as well be hanged for a sheep as a lamb').

Beccaria's proposed penal code is termed 'classicist', not just in the sense that his book was, and is, 'a classic', but in that it derives from the so-called classical philosophy of the eighteenth-century movement known as the 'Enlightenment'. Enlightenment thought stressed the importance of human reason, in opposition to medieval ideas such as the divine right of kings, divine revelation and the one true interpretation of the Scriptures. In common with other Enlightenment thinkers, Beccaria argued that institutions of government – including the penal system – ought to be such as to command the rational adherence of citizens. Rational citizens, he said, would only agree to such powers to punish as would benefit them by promoting their physical safety and security of property through reduction of crime. The theory thus contains within it a limitation on the severity of punishments, since the state would not be constitutionally authorized to impose more severe penalties than were necessary to prevent crime.

Beccaria's model of the criminal is an individual with free choice, who should be deterred by anticipation of the punishment if s/he does commit a crime. His system allows for no consideration of circumstances, personal characteristics and so on – once a crime has been committed, the due penalty must be imposed. This is echoed in contemporary calls for 'swift and sure punishments', heavier penalties to weight the odds in such a way that potential offenders will decide that the hoped-for gain from an offence is not worth the certain punishment. Contemporary 'tariff' approaches, calling for the punishment to fit the crime, not to suit the needs and circumstances of the offender, are accordingly referred to as neo-classicist.

Bentham's Utilitarian deterrent scheme also contains a limitation on punishment, in that the principle of maximizing happiness and minimizing pain prescribes that the pain of punishment must be less than the relief from pain achieved by crime reduction. A contemporary approach, which will be discussed in more detail later, and which contains a formula very similar to Bentham's 'felicific calculus', is the 'decrementalism' of Braithwaite and Pettit (1990). They urge the progressive reduction of penalty levels to the point at which there is a demonstrable, consequent, increase in crime. This would surely have found favour with Bentham as a way of operationalizing his stricture that the pain of punishment should not exceed the crime reduction thereby achieved.

Another deterrent approach is to fix draconian punishments. Like the laws promulgated by Draco for Athens in 621 BC, such a penalty system would be so severe as to put most rational people off committing crimes, even with only a remote likelihood of being caught and punished. Without the limitations of Utilitarianism's stricture that the pains inflicted by the penalty must not exceed the pain avoided through crime reduction, there is nothing in deterrence theory from which may be derived criteria for limiting punishment. Utilitarianism has a bias towards frugality in punishment, because the pain inflicted by the punishment is certain and in the present, whereas the pain avoided through deterrence is only hoped for in the future, but non-Utilitarian deterrence theories have no in-built limitation on the severity of punishments. Near-Draconian ideas are advocated by the so-called 'get tough' lobby in contemporary Western societies, a lobby which is particularly influential in the USA and in England and Wales.

Even though they may have deterrent value, very severe punishments for any but the most serious offences are generally thought unacceptable in terms of the human rights of offenders in modern Western societies. A compromise between generally draconian sentences and more moderate penal schedules is use of the 'exemplary sentence', a sentence more severe than that usually given for a particular offence, and designed to give the message that the offence in question is being taken especially seriously at that moment.

Evaluating the deterrent effects of punishment

The immediately obvious difficulty with deterrence is how we can know how severe penalties have to be to make people decide against crime. The key notion here is *reciprocity*: we can, to some extent, presume that people who think much as we do will be put off by the prospects of punishments that would deter ourselves. This 'reciprocity of perspectives' is fundamental to social theory and social policy (Schutz and Luckman 1974). How can we ever assess the impact of policies, how can we theorize about social behaviour, how can we, indeed, interact with each other in everyday life, unless we can assume that, given the same circumstances and biography, others would act as we do?

It is perhaps plausible to assume that with the kinds of crime we can imagine ourselves committing in circumstances that characterize many offenders, we can devise a schedule of penalties which would have reasonable deterrent effect. Most of us can imagine situations in which we might be tempted to steal, to return provocation with assault, to exceed the speed limit, and so forth. This line of reasoning has been followed in Scandinavia, where the idea of general deterrence has been better supported than in other Western countries (Andenaes 1974). Deterrent strategies have been adopted for offences such as driving with excess alcohol. Mandatory short prison sentences have existed in Sweden, Norway and Finland, on the assumption that most reasonable people would prefer to refrain from alcohol or take a taxi rather than risk imprisonment. Similar tactics have begun to be used in the UK, where imprisonment for driving with excess alcohol is far more common than it used to be.

Even with 'normal' offences, however, reciprocity of perspectives can only be a working hypothesis: it is impossible to know with any certainty that what would deter me, would deter anyone else. There has, over the years, been little systematic research into offenders' attitudes, but the popularity among professionals such as probation officers, and social workers involved with young offenders, of 'cognitive therapies', suggests that rather than offenders having different psychological characteristics from non-offenders, it may be their attitudes and beliefs about crime and its likely costs and benefits, that are different (Blagg and Smith 1989). If true, this is obviously a considerable problem for deterrence strategies, with their reliance on similarity of reasoning among offenders and non-offenders.

More problematic still for a penal strategy of deterrence are impulsive offences, where acts do not arise out of rational premeditation, but out of particular circumstances and relationships between particular individuals. Most murders and many assaults are of this nature.

Even if some sort of 'deterrence calculus' for at least the kinds of crime of material gain that seem to arise from rational deliberation could be established as a system of penalties, any consequent deterrent effects would be very difficult to measure. The amount of crime is notoriously difficult to establish. Official statistics relate how many crimes are reported to the police, how many people are arrested and cautioned or charged, how many people are sentenced, but it is impossible to know how much unreported, unrecorded crime there is (Bottomley and Pease 1986). It is even more difficult to know if crime is increasing or decreasing: apparent increases in crime may in fact be increases in reporting and/or detection rates, rather than increases in actual criminal behaviour. In recent years, changes in insurance regulations, so that claims are not met unless losses are reported to the police, are thought to have influenced the rates of recorded burglaries and car thefts, while increased consciousness, especially feminist consciousness, has affected recording rates of domestic violence and sexual offences. How much of the statistical increase in 'date rape', for example, is due to women's heightened awareness that such behaviour is rape? How much of the increase in child sexual abuse is due to increased willingness to believe children when they talk about the things that happen to them? If it is so difficult to know how much crime has actually occurred, how could we possibly expect to know how much crime would have occurred in the absence of sentences fixed at certain levels of severity?

If crime rates, and changes in them, could be measured with reasonable accuracy, it would still be difficult to be sure that any reduction in crime was due to deterrent penalties. Driving with excess alcohol, mentioned above as one of the targets for deterrent sentencing, is a good illustration. It is undoubtedly true that sentences for this offence have been more interventionist, with more prison sentences, more probation with conditions of attendance at alcohol education projects, and fewer fines or discharges, in recent years in England and Wales. Other countries, such as the Netherlands, have followed the Scandinavian example of giving more prison sentences. It seems to be the case that the incidence (as revealed, for example, by the percentage of police stops over periods such as Christmas and the New Year that lead to positive breathalyser readings) of driving with excess alcohol has declined, and police say that only a 'hard core' of recalcitrant drink-drivers remains. Whether this change in drivers' behaviour is due to the increased sentences, however, is not certain. Tougher sentencing has been accompanied by extensive moral education campaigns, with hard-hitting television advertisements showing the consequences of drink-driving, so that there seems to have been a change in public consciousness about the activity, rather than, or as well as, a fear of tougher penal consequences. The effect of tougher sentences on levels of public disapproval of crimes themselves, rather than fear of punishment, is relatively unresearched, and such evidence as exists is far from conclusive (Walker and Marsh 1988).

Studies of the effects of sentencing levels on crimes other than driving with excess alcohol do not support a conclusion that deterrent sentencing strategies are successful in reducing crime rates, either generally or in relation to specific crimes. Among Western countries, those with the most severe penalty scales tend to have the highest crime rates. This is especially true of the USA, where those states which have retained the death penalty do not have lower murder rates than those which have not. More generally, the death penalty has not prevented rates of violent crime being the highest of all the advanced Western societies. There is some evidence for 'marginal deterrence', for the effect of tough penalties not in reducing the crime rate, but in deterring some of the more aggravated forms of crime (Beyleveld 1979). It has been claimed, for example, that the existence of capital punishment or very long prison sentences, while perhaps not reducing the volume of armed robbery, deters armed robbers from actually using firearms.

Deterrent penalties can only be effective, moreover, if potential offenders know about them. Imposing long prison sentences on drug couriers from poor countries (often female) presumes a level of knowledge of the sentencing practices of English courts among the people, often with little or no knowledge of the English language, that is scarcely plausible (Hudson 1993).

After undertaking the most comprehensive review to date of studies of the deterrent effects of punishments, Beyleveld (1979: 136) concludes that

> there exists no scientific basis for expecting that a general deterrence policy, which does not involve an unacceptable interference with human rights, will do anything to control the crime rate. The sort of information needed to base a morally acceptable general policy is lacking. There is some convincing evidence in some areas that some legal sanctions have exerted deterrent effects. These findings are not, however, generalizable beyond the conditions that were investigated. Given the present state of knowledge, implementing an official deterrence policy can be no more than a shot in the dark, or a political decision to pacify 'public sentiment'.

It might seem more feasible to go for short-term deterrence of especially prevalent or harmful crimes through 'exemplary sentences', rather than to follow a comprehensive general deterrence strategy. The 1991 Criminal Justice Act, in leaving the idea of 'seriousness' of offences, and their consequent penalties, to judicial interpretation rather than specifying tariffs in some sort of sentencing scale, allows for local circumstances to be taken into account. Spates of certain crimes and public disquiet about the levels of particular sentences are examples of 'local circumstances' intended by the legislation. The evidence for the crime reduction effects of exemplary sentences, however, is not encouraging. A well-known instance in England is the 20-year custodial sentence passed on a 'mugger' in Birmingham in 1973, which did not halt the rise in muggings after the widespread reporting of the sentence (von Hirsch and Ashworth 1992: 58). Another prominent example is the so-called Great Train Robbery in 1963, when 30-year sentences led to prison escapes, but no noticeable reduction in the robbery rate.

Individual deterrence

Individual and general deterrence are more easily distinguished in theory than in practice, as a penalty framed to deter potential offenders will be undergone by actual offenders. True individual deterrence would require sentences of indeterminate length, with the content tailored to the individual offender, and the degree of disparity thus involved would generally be unacceptable. It would also conflict with general deterrence, since offenders might hope to manipulate the associated assessment procedures to convey the impression that a small amount of punishment would deter them from future crime. What is usually meant by individual deterrence is a strategy where individual offenders receive a taste of what will happen if they reoffend.

The 'taste of custody' is the most obvious example of this kind of individual deterrence. In England and Wales 'short, sharp shock' regimes were tried in detention centres for young offenders in the early 1980s. This was a short sentence served in an institution with no educational aims, with a regime based on military-style drills and strict discipline. Canadian and US probation orders often include a period of 'shock incarceration' at the beginning of the sentence, to show offenders what will happen next time. In the 1980s 'boot camps' became popular in the USA, and have been introduced into England and Wales (*Guardian*, 2 June 1994). These are similar to the detention centres, based on the training regimes of US marines. Boot camps are for non-violent first offenders, so their use as an alternative to non-custodial sentences is clearly aimed at deterrence, rather than imposing punishment proportionate to the offence.

There is no evidence that these toughened penalties are more effective in preventing reoffending than they are in bringing about reductions in the overall crime rate. 'Reoffending' is a vague term, but most recent studies measure reconviction, often within two years of the end of a previous sentence. By this measure, prison is no more effective in deterring reoffending than other penalties, and the more severe regimes such as boot camps are no more successful than less severe facilities.

As well as these doubts about the effectiveness of deterrent sentencing strategies, there are moral objections. Three objections are frequently made by retributivists to deterrence (and other utilitarian strategies, such as reform and prevention): first, that it allows for the punishment of the innocent; second, that it allows for punishment in excess of what is deserved in proportion to the harm done by the offence; and third, that it allows for punishment for offences which may possibly be committed in the future, rather than for offences which have actually been committed.

The first objection is that if the aim of punishment is to remind all the members of society what the penalties for offences are, and thereby to deter potential offenders, what is important is the ceremonial pronouncement of sentences and their reporting, and whether the person is in fact guilty or innocent is immaterial.

Deterrence theorists might answer this in two ways. First, they could argue that since the object is to prevent crime, the sentences should never need to be imposed, and if they are imposed, this will be so rare as to make the unmerited suffering of wrongly convicted persons a price worth paying for the amount of crime prevented. Draconian penalties (like the availability of the death penalty for many offences in pre-nineteenth-century England) tend to exist in societies with low probability of detection and conviction, and so the amount of pain actually inflicted is not as great as objectors suggest. A second pragmatic defence would be that if members of a society believed that being innocent would not prevent them from being punished, there would be no reason for refraining from crime; therefore deterrent efficacy is dependent on punishments only being inflicted on the guilty.

Apart from these practical defences, consequentialists often invoke the 'definitional stop' (Hart 1968). The very definition of punishment, they argue, requires that it is suffering inflicted for an offence, and thus imposing penalties on the innocent, whatever crime reduction effects it may have, does not fall within the definition of punishment, and so is precluded by a theory of deterrent *punishment*. Contemporary retributivists say they find this unconvincing, and that Utilitarians do not include statements about guilt and innocence among their principles of distribution (see, for example, von Hirsch and Ashworth 1992: 55). While it is true that Bentham's list of 'cases where the application of punishment would be groundless' does not mention punishment of the innocent, it seems clear that he is using the definitional stop himself by defining punishment as 'pain consequent upon the act'.

To the second objection, that deterrence allows for punishment in excess of that deserved by the act, the defence is more equivocal. The objection only has force, of course, if one believes that punishment should be in proportion to the harm of the act, but even without being a thoroughgoing retributivist one can concede that the common sense of fairness would suggest some intuitive connection between the seriousness of an act and its punishment. As mentioned above, Bentham's formulation does suggest that because the pain of punishment is certain and the avoidance of crime is not, penal systems should be very cautious about the severity of penalties. This is a recommendation, however, not a theoretically secured principle.

More promising is the argument of some contemporary deterrence advocates that since such evidence as can be cited in support of deterrence supports marginal rather than overall deterrence, the spread of penalties between those for the least and most serious crimes needs to be distinct (Posner 1985). If overall crime rates cannot be reduced but one could reasonably hope to deter robbers from using firearms, or burglars from harming householders, there needs to be a significant difference between the available penalties for robbery and armed robbery, burglary and aggravated burglary. Deterrence thus shares the limitation that will be encountered in connection with retributivism – that it provides for the ranking of offences according to harmfulness, but has little guidance to offer on fixing the severity level of the overall penalty scale.

The third objection seems to me to be the strongest, and to apply to most utilitarian theories. It is, of course, of the nature of forward-looking penalties that they are concerned with offences that the offender has not (yet) committed, and may never have committed regardless of the penalty. The sense of (commensurate) justice is offended by inflicting on someone, as a warning, the penalty provided for a more serious offence than the current offence, even if this infliction is only for a short period.

Reform/rehabilitation

Bentham's second mode of inducing an offender to refrain from reoffending, taking away the desire to offend, is the aim of reformist or rehabilitative punishment. The objective of reform or rehabilitation is to reintegrate the offender into society after a period of punishment, and to design the content of the punishment so as to achieve this.

The prerequisites for the development of reformative or rehabilitative penal strategies were two. First, there was a social-economic impetus, provided by the increasing need for labour brought about by the industrial revolution, to reintegrate offenders into the community rather than to keep them out of the community by severe sentences. Second, there was the growth of the human social sciences, which admitted the idea of criminal behaviour as caused by psychological or environmental factors susceptible to change. Reform/rehabilitation is therefore associated with 'modernism' and 'positivism', which, most simply, means belief in the possibility of change and improvement through the application of science to human behaviour, as well as to enterprises such as public health and engineering.

The words 'reform' and 'rehabilitation' are favoured by different authors, and are sometimes used interchangeably. My own preference is to use 'reform' for the nineteenth-century development of regimes designed to

effect change in individuals through educative and contemplative techniques, and to use 'rehabilitation' to signify the more individualistic treatment programmes that became established during the twentieth century
(Hudson 1987). Reform could logically stand alongside deterrence because
it operates through the will of the individual, but rehabilitation, in the way
the term is intended in post-Second World War formulations and critiques,
has an image of the offender not as acting from free will, but as responding to forces (either internal or external) exerting pressure upon him/her
(Bean 1976; von Hirsch 1976).

Reform became a prime concern of the penal system in the late eighteenth and into the nineteenth century, when the demands for labour were
such that penalties which would equip offenders with the desire to work,
and the necessary self-discipline to work in a factory, were developed.
Although nowadays penal reformers try to discourage the use of imprisonment on the grounds of its tendency to make people worse rather than
better, it must be remembered that when imprisonment changed from
being a means primarily for holding people awaiting trial or deportation,
or for inducing compliance with payment orders, to being primarily a
mode of punishment, it was being introduced as an alternative to death or
transportation, not as an alternative to probation or community service.
Death or transportation removes offenders permanently from the workforce, while older punishments such as the stocks do nothing to increase
their ability or willingness to be productive as well as law-abiding citizens.
The difference between deterrence and reform or rehabilitation is that the
former is only concerned with whether or not the offender commits a
further crime, whereas the latter aims to make her/him a better and more
productive person.

The prisons that were built in the nineteenth century in most Western
countries, and which were established in the major industrial cities of
Britain, were designed to reform as well as to incarcerate. By a combination of work and contemplation, the modern 'penitentiary' was built on
the model of the monastery. Individual cells afforded space for solitary
reflection (penance), whereas workshops provided the necessary instruc-
tion and discipline (the work ethic). Alternative designs provided for more
or less isolation of prisoners from each other, but the essential mix of work
and penance was common to all the prisons that were built at that time.
One of the most famous prison designs was that of Bentham himself, the
'panopticon', which allowed the warder positioned in a central control
circle to see into all the cells along wings radiating from the centre (the
panopticon is discussed more fully in Chapter 7). Although the panopticon
was never built exactly to Bentham's specifications – either of architecture
or regime – the big Victorian prisons such as Strangeways, Wormwood
Scrubs and Pentonville are close enough to give us a very clear idea of the
strategy envisaged. By the close of the nineteenth century, reform had
become the primary official aim of the penal system in England and Wales
as well as in many other Western industrialized countries. One manifestation

of this philosophy is that prisons came to bear plaques at their entrance proclaiming that their purpose was to assist inmates to lead a 'good and useful life'.

Reform in the nineteenth century was unsophisticated and undifferentiated: all prisoners in a prison were subject to the same regime. As the human sciences of psychology, physiology and sociology developed, however, these were brought into service, and the modern discipline of criminology developed in service of the state's correctional efforts (Young 1988). As this criminological project of reforming offenders through the application of science grew, offenders began to be classified into various types, and diagnosis and treatment supplemented, and in some jurisdictions supplanted, work and penance (Garland 1985).

Just as deterrence had its foundational text in Beccaria's work, the seminal text in the development of positivist criminology was Cesare Lombroso's *L'uomo delinquente* (*Criminal Man*), published in 1876. This set out a typology of criminals, of which the best known is the 'atavistic' born criminal, who is at a lower evolutionary stage, less morally developed, than non-criminals. Although this notion of atavism may sound risible to us now, the idea of the born criminal, the criminal type, persists, and each generation seems to produce a new form of biological criminal determinism. In recent decades theories of criminality have been linked with the possession of an extra X chromosome, mesomorphic body shapes, extra amounts of testosterone, and, perenially in the popular mind, 'shifty eyes'.

Lombroso's evolutionary theory was succeeded by the more sophisticated typology of Enrico Ferri, who divided criminals into three types: the born criminal; the insane criminal; and the person who, in different circumstances, would not have been criminal at all (Ferri 1917). This broadening of ideas about the causes of crime to psychological and social factors led to the development of rehabilitation as we think of it today, with its combination of psychotherapeutic techniques and help with circumstances such as addictions, debt and unemployment.

Criticisms of rehabilitative penalties

It is this idea of crime as 'caused' by psychological or physiological predisposition, or by social factors such as poverty, unemployment or coming from certain types of family, that has called forth the most argument about reform/rehabilitation as a penal aim. Proponents argue that not to recognize the influence of such factors makes punishment impersonal and, by assuming all crime to be the result of a freely taken decision, imputes to offenders greater culpability and responsibility than is often the case (see, for example, Lacey 1988; Hudson 1993). On the other hand, opponents of rehabilitative punishment claim that the deterministic view of human behaviour held by positivist reformists treats people as less than fully human, morally rational citizens (Duff 1986).

This objection has most force when rehabilitation in its strongest form is being considered. In post-war years, a view of crime as the result of psychological problems or social deprivation depicted offenders as 'pathological', in need of treatment (Wootton 1963). Crime was seen as a disease to be cured, and it is this 'treatment model' which is the target of the criticisms of the modern retributivists (see, for example, von Hirsch and Maher 1992). Seeing crime as determined rather than willed denies the moral integrity of the offender, it is argued; it deals with him/her in a patronizing, infantilizing way, or, as some rather more lurid statements of the moral defects of rehabilitationism put it, as animals to be trained (Walker 1991; von Hirsch 1993). The 'cure' for crime, under the treatment model, is to change the personality of the offender, and in taking away the likelihood of choosing to do wrong, taking away the capacity for moral choice at all.

A celebrated statement of this moral integrity objection to rehabilitation is C. S. Lewis's attack on psychological techniques, in which he describes the process of rehabilitation as the coerced change of personality according to the edicts of Freud, a process which does not end until either the offender is indeed changed, or has learned to act as if s/he has been changed (Lewis 1971).

As well as the 'assault on personality' involved in rehabilitation, Lewis refers to its link with the indeterminate sentence. If the object of punishment is not to mark the offence that has been committed, but to make the offender unlikely to commit a further offence, then the duration of punishment is logically linked not to the seriousness of the past offence, but to assessments of the offender's progress towards harmlessness. In jurisdictions such as California in the 1960s, where the treatment approach was pursued more wholeheartedly than in most places, sentences were left open-ended within very broad limits. The length of sentence to be served would be fixed not by the judge at the conclusion of a trial, but by the prison administrators. In England and Wales, and elsewhere, such extreme indeterminacy did not obtain, but elements of indeterminacy were provided through parole. The time served by two offenders convicted of the same crime could thus differ by several years, according not to the circumstances of the crime but to progress on rehabilitative programmes. As Lewis suggests, prisoners could 'cheat' by participating in programmes in which they had no belief, by expressions of remorse they did not feel, and of intentions to refrain from crime to which they had no commitment.

It is certainly the case that some techniques used in the name of rehabilitation were grossly intrusive with respect to the moral integrity, personality and civil liberties of offenders. Behaviourist techniques such as aversion therapy, chemical reduction of aggression or libido, even psychosurgery, were used in the name of treatment – techniques which would be condemned as 'cruel and unusual' if they were acknowledged as punishment, but were more readily defended if they were supposedly for the offenders' own good (Kittrie 1973; Hudson 1987).

Defenders of rehabilitation have pointed out that neither the indeterminate sentence nor these drastic treatment techniques are indispensible to rehabilitation. In fact, they would argue, such elements of the worst interpretations of the rehabilitative aim are inimical to rehabilitation. No one is likely to become a better citizen if s/he is not a fully consenting participant in the programmes being offered (Cullen and Gilbert 1982; Rotman, 1990). Such practices are more properly deterrent than rehabilitative: compliance is being induced through fear of the sentence being longer, fear of being subject to even more invasive therapies, and fear of the length or content of punishment.

As with deterrence, there has been much criticism of rehabilitation on the grounds that it is ineffective. This was most influentially voiced in a much quoted article by Martinson (1974). He baldly stated that 'nothing works': no treatment programme works very successfully in preventing reoffending, no programme works better than any other. Although he tried to correct this extreme pessimism later, his acknowledgement that some programmes work sometimes, for some types of offender, received far less attention than his earlier pronouncement. English commentators such as Brody (1976) criticized Martinson's original conclusions, and further evaluations were more optimistic, but penal pessimism took widespread hold nevertheless.

'Nothing works' pessimism has recently given way to a resurgence of 'something works', limited optimism, especially since the widespread innovation in probation and juvenile justice programmes in the 1980s (Pitts 1992). Intensive intermediate treatment, the probation day centres that followed the 1982 Criminal Justice Act, have targeted serious repeat offenders, and claim reasonable degrees of success (Raynor 1988; Blagg and Smith 1989). Rehabilitation work in prisons, especially in units such as the Barlinnie Special Unit and Grendon Underwood, has demonstrated success with several well-known, previously violent, persistent offenders. Alcohol and addictions programmes, and more recently the sex-offender programmes, that have been developed in prisons and by the probation service, similarly have achieved success with the kinds of offender usually thought of as the most likely to continue offending.

What is certainly the case is that success cannot be guaranteed, and that there is no single programme that has proved successful with all kinds of offenders. It is equally true that until very recently, criminal justice professionals most committed to rehabilitation – probation officers and juvenile justice workers – have done little to develop measures of success or to publicize their effectiveness (Hudson 1993). Again, we find similar problems as arise in relation to deterrence. To make success a certainty or near-certainty, rehabilitation would have to use such extreme techniques as would be unconscionable, especially for routine offenders. 'Mind-bending' drugs, aversion therapy and the like conjure up 'Brave New World' scenarios. The case of Alex, the young man in Anthony Burgess's *Clock-work Orange*, who is subjected to aversion therapy and, deprived of the possibility of violence even in self-defence, becomes a victim, portrays the fears of objectors such as Lewis. Less extreme, but equally intrusive, is the total control society depicted by Cohen (1979), in which people who have been caught up in the social control net, particularly youths, are shown as having almost every moment of their lives filled with pro-grammes and surveillance. These portrayals of rehabilitative control sys-tems show rehabilitation's essential dilemma: if it strives for guaranteed effectiveness, rehabilitation must resort to fear of further intrusion (deter-rence) or physical restraint through chemistry, psychotherapy or tech-nology such as electronic surveillance – in other words, it ceases to be rehabilitation and becomes prevention. Rehabilitation must leave the possibility of failure open, and it therefore is able to offer a defence against the moral infantilism objections of one set of critics, but only if it is pre-pared to restrict itself to the pursuit of limited effectiveness, thus making it vulnerable to the other critics.

Another objection, expressed by Hart (1968), points to the definitional illogicality of rehabilitation as a general justifying aim. If the overall aim of punishment is to prevent reoffending, he points out, then it must be desir-able for people to commit crimes – otherwise there would be no one to rehabilitate. Since this is absurd – the whole point of making something subject to criminal law is to prevent or reduce its occurrence – rehabili-tation cannot serve as a general justifying aim. This is an unanswerable argument, and so rehabilitation, if it is to be a penal aim, must be either a subsidiary aim, or an aim of distribution rather than justification. This theme will be taken up in Chapter 4.

Prevention through incapacitation ✦

Deterrence and rehabilitation both carry a necessary possibility of being unsuccessful, because whether or not potential offenders offend, or actual offenders reoffend, is up to them. Freedom of choice remains, and there-fore the possibility of offending remains. However draconian the penalty scale, someone may still decide that the costs are worth the satisfaction to be gained from the offence, or the low probability of detection makes the risks worth while; however well educated and well adjusted the offender becomes, the work ethic may be rejected, or the pressures from criminal associates may be irresistible.

If general deterrence and individual rehabilitation are difficult to achieve, it perhaps seems a plausible goal to protect potential victims from further crime by known offenders through physical incapacitation, either by rendering criminals physically harmless, or by removing them from circulation. Prevention of reoffending by amputation, by death, or by life imprisonment are incapacitative punishments, which render it impossible (or very difficult) for the offender to reoffend. The death penalty is the most obviously certain incapacitative punishment. Its claims to effectiveness as a deterrent for murder are doubtful – it is impossible, for instance, to tell from murder rates which US states retain the death penalty and which do not (Walker 1991) – but a murderer who is executed obviously cannot kill again. Similarly, when law and order conservatives say that 'prison works', what they mean is that criminals cannot commit crimes when they are incarcerated, except against other prisoners.

In the 1990s, two incapacitive policies gained great political and public popularity: selective incapacitation and the so-called 'three strikes' penalty. Both begin from the perception that a relatively small number of offenders commit a relatively large amount of crime.

Conventional criminological wisdom maintains that most offenders commit one offence and do not reoffend. Furthermore, labelling theory, which has been extremely influential in the development of work with (particularly young) offenders, holds that rather than reducing the likelihood of reoffending, the intervention of the criminal justice system tends to increase it, and the more severe the punishment, the greater the impact on the offender in the direction of reoffending (Blagg and Smith 1989). This is because being labelled a criminal by the courts places handicaps in pursuing a non-criminal lifestyle (it is more difficult to get a job with a criminal record, and non-criminals may not wish to associate with the criminal), and because the offender comes to think of him/herself as a criminal, with crime the only available 'career'. This thinking has influenced the development of cautioning schemes, whereby first offenders are given an official warning by police rather than being taken to court, and schemes such as intermediate treatment and intensive probation which aim to keep offenders in the community rather than in prison. Some offenders, however, will not go through the normal processes of growing out of crime, or may be arrested or convicted when they are already too far into their criminal lifestyle, and the appeal of selective incapacitation is that if these likely reoffenders could be identified and the public protected against them, then those offenders who would be unlikely to reoffend could be dealt with in minimum-intervention ways which would be unlikely to make them worse.

Selective incapacitation promises the following benefits: that the amount of crime will be reduced by removing from circulation those who would otherwise commit many offences; that the amount of crime will be further reduced by not excessively punishing those whose reoffending probabilities would be increased rather than decreased by severe punishment; and that state expenditure can be kept down by not punishing the majority of offenders more than is useful in crime reduction terms.

Positivist criminology offered the possibility of distinguishing those criminals who are likely to reoffend (Ferri's born criminals and insane criminals), and most jurisdictions provide for incarceration of the criminally insane for longer than the usual 'going rate' for the particular offence. The more difficult problem, however, has been identifying which criminals who are not classified as insane are likely to reoffend.

Police officers often claim that there are a small number of 'hard-core villains' in their area whose removal from circulation would have a dramatic impact on the local crime rate. The Rand Corporation in the USA undertook a large-scale study aimed at coming up with predictive factors which would give this kind of anecdotal knowledge a more systematic basis, and it is this study which gave impetus to adoption of incapacitative policies (Greenwood 1983). This research claimed to be able to reduce the robbery rate in California by about 15 per cent, by identifying factors which were statistically correlated with reoffending. These factors include a bad employment record, addiction, and a criminal record as a juvenile, factors which have been found by statistical studies to be characteristics of populations of offenders, and have also been found to be associated with repeat offending in studies of the criminal 'careers' of groups of persistent offenders.

Versions of incapacitative policies using these or similar risk-of-reoffending factors link them to imposition of sentences of different lengths according to reoffending assessment (see, for example, Wilson 1975), or to decisions about granting of parole. The UK Home Office uses a risk-of-reconviction assessment for parole decision-making in England and Wales, and this has also been adopted by some probation services in deciding what sort of sentence to recommend in reports to the courts.

Problems with prevention

Like deterrence and rehabilitation, incapacitation also provokes the familiar objections of effectiveness and moral principle. Until recently, the effectiveness rates of reoffending predictions have not been impressive. The best-known English study, by criminologists at the Cambridge Institute of Criminology, assessed which of a group of seven-year-olds would have been convicted of an offence by the age of 14, and which would still be offending at age 21 (West and Farrington 1973). This study identified factors which are widely accepted to influence the likelihood of becoming delinquent (such as poor school records, and parents or older brothers being involved in crime), but even so, only half of those predicted to be delinquent actually were.

Measuring the success of reoffending predictions is inevitably difficult. First, one cannot know whether people who are not reconvicted have or have not reoffended. Second, there is the problem of separating the correctness of the prediction from the effect of being predicted. Evaluations of parole reconviction predictions show about 11 per cent fewer reconvictions within two years of parole than the prediction assessment would suggest

(Hann *et al.* 1991). Does this show that the reoffending prediction was wrong in 11 per cent of cases, or does it reveal a beneficial effect of being paroled? Comparisons of imprisonment and community sanctions have the same problem: are differences in reconviction due to differences in the impact of the punishment, or to initial differences in the personal circumstances and/or offending histories of the persons being punished?

For the public, concern with reoffending prediction centres on 'false negatives', individuals who are predicted as posing little risk of reoffending, and who are therefore paroled or given a community punishment, and then reoffend. This is also an issue in relation to the granting of remands on bail rather than in custody. There have been some notorious cases of people released from imprisonment or confinement in a secure hospital, who have committed further violent crimes, and there has also been the so-called 'bail bandit' campaign, with police authorities drawing attention to the numbers of (mostly young) offenders committing offences while on bail (Williams 1993).

Of more concern theoretically, however, are the so-called 'false positives', people who are wrongly predicted as being likely to reoffend. If two people are convicted of the same offence, and one person is predicted as likely to reoffend and the other as unlikely, and the former is therefore given a longer prison sentence than the latter, it is possible to know whether or not the person who is at liberty reoffends, but not whether the person who is incarcerated would have reoffended had s/he been at liberty. The person predicted to reoffend and therefore given a long prison sentence or, even more drastically, executed or incapacitated through mutilation or chemical control, can never prove whether s/he would or would not have reoffended if given the opportunity. It is impossible to know, therefore, the extent of overprediction.

There have been one or two 'natural' or accidental experiments, when offenders who had been predicted as posing a danger to the public if at liberty, were reclassified and so released earlier than envisaged at sentence. These 'experiments' have arisen because institutions were closed or damaged by fire, as in the Patuxent or Baxstrom incidents. These incidents, though often quoted, are not very significant because the inmates had already served long terms in the institutions and were perhaps beyond the age when they posed a great threat of further violence; nevertheless, either within their new institutions or after release, they did not reoffend more than the other inmates of the institutions to which they were reclassified. A more important instance, perhaps, is that discussed by Kozol *et al.*, when sexual offenders were released by court decisions, against the advice of clinical experts, after diagnosis but before the recommended treatment. The opportunities for evaluation of positive classifications of dangerousness may be unscientific and haphazard, but the results do not give grounds for belief that prediction is sufficiently accurate for policy-makers to be confident that the number of 'false positives' is low (Walker 1985).

Critics of preventive sentencing assert that the offender has a right not to be punished more than s/he deserves for the current offence, because of predictions of dubious accuracy. The offender, in other words, has a right to be protected from being a false positive; the law-abiding public, on the other hand, has a right to be protected against false negatives, against people being punished relatively leniently because of assumptions that they will not offend again (Bottoms and Brownsword 1983). One answer to this dilemma was given by the Floud Committee, which looked at the question of the ethics and effectiveness of preventive sentencing. The Committee argued that there can never be a situation where the rights of offenders and potential victims are in exact equilibrium; the impossibility of totally accurate prediction means that there will always be some risk to offenders of being needlessly incapacitated, and some risk to the public of being mistakenly exposed to criminal victimization. As long as an individual has not committed an offence, they say, s/he should be given the benefit of a presumption of harmlessness; the community of potential victims must bear the risk of an offence. Once a serious offence has been committed, however, the presumption of harmlessness is forfeit, and the risk of reoffending should be taken more seriously than the risk of unnecessary punishment (Floud and Young 1981).

Even if predictions were known to be reasonably accurate, preventive sentencing would still involve punishing people not just for the offence they have committed, but for crimes they may commit in future. Does this conflict with notions of justice? If punishment were entirely based on risk of reoffending, then it could be that someone who has committed a very harmful offence would get a less severe punishment than someone who has committed a lesser offence. Murder, for example, is the offence with the lowest recidivism rates – although, of course, it could be argued that this is because murderers are usually either executed or serve long prison terms and so do not have the opportunity of reoffending. Most offences of serious violence, however, arise out of particular circumstances and relationships between victim and offender, and in any case, most people would argue that even if a murderer is unlikely to reoffend even if unpunished, the crime itself is so serious that it is only appropriately acknowledged by a severe punishment. This comes close to the position of the retributivists, as will be shown in Chapter 3. The offences with the highest recidivism rates, however, are the common-or-garden dishonesty offences and the less serious sex offences.

One attempt to reconcile ideas of deserved punishment and protection from reoffending is *categorial incapacitation* (Cohen 1983; von Hirsch 1985). According to this idea, presumptive sentencing bands should be fixed by desert (for example, one to three years for burglary, three to six years for robbery), and, within these bands, those offenders who are predicted as likely to reoffend would receive the maximum permissible sentence, with lesser terms for those assessed as posing less risk. Another way of achieving categorial incapacitation, much used in Western penal systems, is through parole. In England and Wales, prison sentences are pronounced by the trial judge, with terms reflecting the seriousness of the offence. Remission is then automatic for less serious offences provided it is not lost because of disciplinary offences while in prison, but parole for the more serious offences depends on prediction of risk of reoffending.

A contemporary interpretation of something like the Floud Committee's recommendations is the 'three strikes' principle. Given the inaccuracy of predicting which offender among a group with a similar number of previous convictions is likely to reoffend, this principle says that once people have committed three or more imprisonable offences, they have demonstrated risk to the extent that they lose all presumption of future harmlessness. Third-time offenders should therefore be given long sentences of imprisonment to protect the public against their predations. This 'three strikes and you're out' principle, so named after one of the rules of the game of baseball (a player has three chances to make a hit, and can miss or mishit the ball twice, but if the third strike is not good, the player is out of the game), would avoid selective prediction while affording protection for the public from people who have proved themselves dangerous.

'Three strikes' and selective incapacitation are proposed preventive add-ons to a basically retributive penalty scale. Other penal systems combine prevention and rehabilitation, using criminological knowledge to divide offenders into the corrigible and the incorrigible, giving rehabilitative assistance to the corrigible and preventive incarceration to the incorrigible. The penal strategy of *social defence* pursued in France and Italy, and other continental European countries to a greater or lesser extent, uses this bifurcated approach (Ancel 1987). The strategy is clearly derived from the criminological positivism of Ferri and those who followed him. Although they would probably reject this positivism, probation officers follow the same logic if they recommend some offenders as suitable for probation, on grounds linked with estimates of future behaviour, but not others.

Conclusion

The problem with incapacitative and rehabilitative sentencing is that they could lead to more severe sentencing for less serious offences, if people are to be sentenced according to their future prognosis rather than their current offence. Deterrence policies can lead to more severe sentencing of similar crimes at different times – an exemplary sentence now and then to make potential offenders think again. If this seems unjust, then the claims of retribution are making themselves heard. The key divide is between those who think that the essential function of criminal law is to reduce offending and that the practice of punishment must always be looking forward, concerned not with the offending that has already happened, but with that which may be prevented from happening in the future, and those approaches – to be discussed in Chapter 3 – according to which the amount and nature of punishment must always be firmly linked to criminal behaviour that has already occurred.

chapter three

Retribution

Introduction
Modern retributivism: the just-deserts movement
Proportionality and seriousness
Retribution and the justification of punishment
Deterrence and retribution in distribution
Summary and conclusion

Introduction

As well as 'To prevent crime', the other answer to the question 'Why should offenders be punished?' that springs readily to the lips is 'Because they deserve it'. The theory that punishment is justified because it is deserved is retributivism, in its various forms. Retribution means 'to give in return for', and 'to punish suitably' (*Chambers Twentieth Century Dictionary*, 1983 edition), and these two elements of the definition are the key features of retributive theories of punishment: that punishment should be in return for crimes past rather than in anticipation of crimes future; and that the punishment should be suitable for the crime – the severity of punishment should be commensurate to the seriousness of the crime for which it is inflicted:

> The 're' in 'reward', 'repayment' and 'retribution' points to the past, and suggests that it must be *reflected* in what is being done now. There must be some sort of equivalence.
>
> (Walker 1991: 69)

Retributive penal systems have existed throughout history. Best known, perhaps, is the *lex talionis* of biblical times – an eye for an eye, a tooth for a tooth, a life for a life. This system seeks equivalence between the punishment and the crime, such that the offender should forfeit that which the victim has lost. Although support for such equivalence persists, most contemporary Western societies do not exact talionic punishments. Many people in societies which do not have capital or corporal punishments, however, continue to think that the only appropriate punishment for the taking of a life is the forfeiture of a life, so that violent crime should be matched by physical punishment.

This chapter will examine the main ideas, strengths and weaknesses of retributivism, concentrating particularly on contemporary formulations.

Modern retributivism: the just-deserts movement

For most of the twentieth century, until about 1970, although there had been individuals who continued to advocate retributive principles, retribution was generally thought of by criminologists as simple vengeance, as a rather unprogressive basis for punishment, especially compared to rehabilitation. During the 1970s, however, old retributivist ideas were revived, new formulations were put forward, and penologists who had been dismissive of retribution changed their minds and became adherents (Honderich 1984). By the 1980s the new retributionist theory of 'just deserts' had become the most influential penal theory.

In the 1970s, liberals in the USA were disturbed by the excesses of rehabilitative sentencing, and alarmed by the 'get-tough' incapacitative agenda which was being put forward by conservatives. Under indeterminate sentencing schemes, especially in jurisdictions such as California, how long an offender served in prison was decided by the Adult Authority (the equivalent of the Parole Board in England and Wales), which considered how much the offender had 'improved' (psychologically, socially) and what was his/her likelihood of reoffending, rather than being decided by the trial judge with reference to the actual crime committed. This meant that prisoners convicted of non-violent property offences could serve longer sentences than violent offenders, particularly if they insisted that they were rational and not in need of treatment. Investigations into a series of prison riots, most notably the Attica riots, revealed that not knowing the date of release, and the perceived unfairness of the lack of relationship between offence and punishment, were among the main grievances of prisoners (American Friends Service Committee 1972). Civil rights and prisoners' rights groups, therefore, demanded sentencing reforms to introduce tariffs of determinate sentences, graded according to the seriousness of crimes.

Other criticisms of existing practices concerned judicial discrimination against minority ethnic groups, the unemployed and the unconventional, allowed by the wide discretion in a rehabilitation-orientated system where the punishment was meant to fit the chances of the offender reoffending, rather than the circumstances of the crime (Frankel 1973). For female offenders, judicial discretion and judicial paternalism were held to produce a situation of 'double jeopardy', in which women were liable to punishment for the crime they had committed, and also for offending against stereotyped ideals of feminine behaviour (Edwards 1984 *inter alia*). The retributivist idea of punishing the crime, not the person, therefore had obvious attractions for those seeking an end to abuse of judicial discretion.

Other opponents of rehabilitative sentencing practices argued that the development of non-custodial sanctions that rehabilitative thinking had encouraged meant too many criminals 'getting away with it', and the 'get tough movement' argued for tough, certain penalties which would deter and, for those who were not deterred, incapacitate (van den Haag 1975; Wilson 1975).

Rehabilitative penalties, then, were held by left-wingers to be oppressive and over-intrusive (Cohen 1979; 1985; Austin and Krisberg 1981), and by the right to be soft and ineffective. Apart from the nature of the penalties themselves, the wide disparities in sentences given for the same offence that resulted from giving priority of concern to the circumstances of the offender, were held to be bringing judiciaries into disrepute, and to be perceived as unfair by offenders themselves. This concern with disparity resulting from the discretion of criminal justice professionals was one of the strongest themes of the 'back-to-justice movement' that was pursued with great vigour in England and Wales and other western European countries. Justice-movement arguments became especially influential in the field of juvenile justice (Giller and Morris 1981).

The new retributivism that was articulated in a series of influential books published during the course of the 1970s was therefore an important development in penal theory, and quickly gained adherents among liberal and radical theorists and criminal justice professionals. *Struggle for Justice* (American Friends Service Committee 1972) was a civil-libertarian investigation of the state of American prisons in the wake of the Attica riots, as was *The American Prison Business* (Mitford 1974), while *Criminal Sentences* (Frankel 1973) and *We Are the Living Proof* (Fogel 1975) were written by well-known lawyers. The most authoritative and philosophically elaborated version of the new retributivism appeared in 1976, with the publication of the report of the Committee for the Study of Incarceration, published under the title *Doing Justice* (von Hirsch 1976).

Like all retributivist approaches, the primary principle of new retributivism is that punishment should be commensurate to the seriousness of the offence. Instead of the equivalence of talionic systems, however, the modern version interprets commensurate as *proportionate*. What is required is that there should be a schedule of punishments in which the most serious is reserved for the most serious offences, and that penalties should be graduated throughout the scale according to offence seriousness. This is often known as *tariff* sentencing: for every crime there is a price to pay. Put into practice, it usually involves a 'presumptive sentence' for the various crimes, or grades of seriousness, with a band above and below this within which actual sentences can be imposed, depending on the circumstances of the offence. Thus, the presumptive sentence for burglary or offences designated of similar seriousness might be five years' imprisonment, with actual sentences ranging from three to five years where the circumstances of the particular case are less serious than the 'typical' incident, and from five to seven years where they are more serious.

Possible future offences do not come into the reckoning at all. Punishment should be to the extent that it is deserved by the offence already committed, and estimates of the likelihood of further offences should not influence the sentence passed, or the amount of punishment actually undergone. Previous convictions are allowed some influence, however, in that most deserts writers would support reductions in sentence for first offenders. This is because 'desert' is derived from the seriousness of the offence and from the culpability of the offender. Thus, however serious the crime, an accidental or coerced act would not carry the penalty of a freely chosen, fully willed action; the *mens rea*, the intentionality that is important in Western legal systems, is incorporated into the idea of punishment being imposed to the extent that it is deserved. It may be plausible for defendants to argue, deserts theorists allow, that a first offender might not realize the consequences of her/his actions, might not realize the impact on victims, but this mitigation would become less plausible for repeat offences.

The reasoning for this advocacy of the punishment for a crime matching the extent that it is deserved by the wrongness of the act, is that such proportionality reflects the nature of punishment. Deserts theorists thus point out that the difference between punishment and other impositions or deprivations which are in many respects similar, is that punishment conveys blame for wrongdoing. The difference between a fine and a tax, for example, is that the former implies blame for wrongdoing, while the other does not – the good citizen will pay her taxes, the bad citizen will incur fines. Blame attaches to offenders because they have done wrong; it is therefore right that the extent of blameworthiness incurred by commission of the crime is reflected in the severity of the resulting punishment.

If punishment is thereby envisioned as society's means of apportioning blame on offenders, then the prohibition against punishing the innocent is more firmly anchored than it is with utilitarian theories of punishment. Whether or not one assumes Bentham and other Utilitarians to be limited by the 'definitional stop', it is arguable that if punishing someone – whether innocent or guilty – every now and then secured a general reduction in crime, then for a non-utilitarian reductionist there would be no problem, the object of punishment would be achieved, while for the Utilitarian there would be no problem provided the reduction in social harm because of the reduction in crime was greater than the harm to the punished. The Utilitarian might say that this was not (by definition) punishment, but might nevertheless see it as a desirable social practice, in need of renaming rather than abolishing.

This theoretical possibility and actual practice of imposition of something which could be said to be definitionally not-punishment, but which was experienced by those on whom it was inflicted as punitive, explains the allegiance to the 'justice model' of many radical theorists and, in particular, professionals such as juvenile justice workers, in the late 1970s and 1980s. Following the 1969 Children and Young Persons Act, social workers had developed projects which recruited children and teenagers who were assessed as being 'at risk' of delinquency but who might not actually have committed any crime or any but the most trivial misdemeanour. Court judgments assigning these young people to the care or supervision of social workers or probation officers were obtained using welfare legislation, under clauses providing for those 'in need of care and protection'. Critics of these 'prevention-of-delinquency' interventions into the lives of young people argued that they represented gross curtailment of their civil liberties, and were in any case more likely to encourage rather than discourage crime and delinquency in those subjected to them (Thorpe *et al.* 1980). Similar developments occurred, and similar criticisms were made, in the USA and elsewhere (Austin and Krisberg 1981), and led those concerned with juveniles to call for 'minor penalties for minor crimes', and to support 'justice-model' changes to legislation and to professional practice. In England and Wales the 1982 Criminal Justice Act restricted the discretionary powers of social workers and emphasized 'due process', basing decisions on hard facts about the offences young people had committed rather than subjective assessments of their welfare needs. Juvenile justice social workers also started to limit entry to their centres and projects to so-called 'heavy-end' offenders, young people who had committed serious or several offences and were deemed at risk of custodial sentences, rather than those who were deemed to be at risk of committing a first or second offence.

These developments in social workers' response to juveniles were followed by similar developments in probation with regard to older youth and to adult offenders. Before 1982, probation had been considered an 'alternative' to a sentence, with the result, among other things, that onerous or restrictive conditions in probation orders were not allowed. The 1982 Criminal Justice Act made provision for compulsory attendance at day centres as part of the conditions of probation orders, and the years since have seen the development of far more demanding forms of supervision in probation orders, with much more focus on the actual crimes committed rather than on the personal-social difficulties of offenders. These changes to the nature of non-custodial sanctions have also taken place in the USA and other countries, where 'intensive probation' has become far more common than the old-fashioned social casework approach. The Criminal Justice Act 1991 further clarified this trend towards recognition of probation and other non-custodial sanctions as 'punishment' rather than help or treatment, by designating them as *punishment in the community*, to be used to inflict restrictions on liberty proportionate to the offence which occasioned the sentence.

Many US states, the US Federal Sentencing Commission, Australia, Canada, Sweden and other European countries, introduced desert-based sentencing schemes during the 1980s (Ashworth 1989). In the 1991 Criminal Justice Act in England and Wales, and in some places such as Sweden, proportionality of penalty severity to offence seriousness was stated as a principle, without the legislation containing an actual schedule of offences ranking their seriousness and specifying the commensurate penalties. Elsewhere, in several US states for example, this ranking of offences and prescribing of penalties was undertaken. In thinking about these sentencing schedules, we encounter two of the main dilemmas that retributivists face when translating their ideas into actual deserts schemes.

Proportionality and seriousness

First, there is the problem of how to rank offences in terms of seriousness. Whose views of seriousness are to count? In some jurisdictions, for example California, judges' and prison administrators' views appear to be the ones which counted, because the presumptive sentences adopted were averages of sentences that had already been passed. In England and Wales, judges' views are also the views that count. During the 1970s and 1980s, the Court of Appeal delivered a series of guideline judgments which discussed not only the individual case that had been the subject of appeal but also classes of similar cases. Thus an appeal against a sentence for burglary was the occasion for pronouncements about the 'going rate' for burglary, with examples of when a burglary might be seen as more or less serious than the typical case. Guideline judgments were also issued for rape, social security fraud and other kinds of case, and these judgments were circulated to other judges who, through the training activities of the newly established Judicial Studies Board, were informed that their task in a particular case was to decide which of the guideline categories of offence the case matched and to sentence accordingly. For some commentators, this amounted to a 'tariff' of sentences for the different crimes (Thomas 1979) although others disagreed (Ashworth 1983).

Another approach was to appoint a sentencing commission, which deliberated the relative seriousness of offences, and in some cases commissioned research into public opinion on the subject. This was done in Minnesota, whose resulting sentencing guidelines have widely been commended as being the most nearly based on desert of any actual sentencing system. The Minnesota sentencing guidelines are represented by a grid with two axes, the horizontal axis showing previous convictions and the vertical axis showing the offence type. In determining sentence, a judge has to locate the appropriate cell on the grid for the particular offender being sentenced, the cell where the offence severity ranking and the number of previous criminal convictions intersect. Each cell on the grid contains a presumptive prison term in months, which would be the normal term for a standard case of that type. A band below and above the presumptive sentence is also given, indicating the range within which the sentence should fall in the actual case. For example, an aggravated burglary (seriousness level VII), where the offender has three previous convictions, carries a presumptive term of 49 months, and a range of 45–53 months. The choice of actual sentence within this band would depend on aggravating and mitigating factors in the case. What has led to the praise by just-deserts liberals of the Minnesota grid is that the line between prison and alternative sentences is not a diagonal, but a stepped line, which allows some offences to be punished without imprisonment no matter how often the offender has been convicted previously. Offences where the combined seriousness and criminal history score falls below the line are presumed to warrant imprisonment, but those above the line are presumed to warrant an alternative, non-custodial sentence. (The actual grid is reproduced in Hudson 1987: 76–7; Tonry 1995: 156.)

However, even in jurisdictions which tried as diligently as did Minnesota to find some widely held assessment of seriousness, without some principled basis the views that are enacted in the sentencing schedule will be those of the people who are empowered to enact the legislation or guidelines, and to make the actual judgments in court. These may be judges – in the English example, Appeal Court judges formulate the guidelines and Crown Court judges interpret them – or politicians – in some American states, sentencing schedules are legislated, and judges in court are obliged to follow them exactly, and legislators may subsequently alter them at will. In commenting on amendments to the California Determinate Sentencing Laws, for example, the criminologist Zimring (1976) pointed to the 'eraser hazard' which allows politicians in that state (and others with similar procedures) armed with only a pencil and an eraser, to raise the tariffs in response to pressures from public opinion or the media, or in order to out-tough other politicians.

Some deserts theorists have engaged at a theoretical level with this problem, and have suggested that seriousness should be assessed according to the *harm of the living standard* of the victim, brought about by the crime (von Hirsch and Jareborg 1992). By this they mean something wider than the sense of standard of living that is usual in everyday speech, which generally refers only to a person's income and level of consumption. For von Hirsch and Jareborg (1992: 222), living standard 'refers to the quality of persons' existence, embracing not only material support and amenity but other noneconomic capabilities that affect the quality of a person's life'. They suggest four kinds of interest which may be intruded upon by crime: physical integrity; material support and amenity; freedom from humiliation and degrading treatment; and privacy and autonomy. Assessment of crime seriousness would involve identifying which of these interests had been affected by the act, and to what extent. To judge extent, they suggest four different levels of living standard: subsistence; minimal well-being; adequate well-being; and enhanced well-being. A crime that affected an interest to the degree that it was no longer sufficient for subsistence would therefore be ranked as more harmful or serious than one which allowed the victim only adequate well-being. For example, a burglary which resulted in the removal of a television set from the victim's home would reduce her level of well-being but not threaten her subsistence, whereas an arson attack which destroyed her home and everything in it would reduce her to subsistence level and would therefore be ranked as more serious. Von Hirsch and Jareborg make the point that these intrusions into interests should refer to a standard victim – in the case of the destruction of a home, we should have in mind neither a victim who is so wealthy as to have several other homes to which s/he could immediately go, nor the victim who is so unusually disadvantaged as to have neither insurance, nor friends or relatives, nor recourse to any other assistance.

A simpler approach to the question of offence seriousness is that taken in England and Wales in the 1991 Criminal Justice Act. This describes just three broad divisions of seriousness: so minor that a fine or discharge is sufficient; serious enough to warrant a community punishment; so serious that only a prison sentence is appropriate. There is probably widespread social agreement about the most and least serious offences, but difficulties arise if attempts are made to grade offences finely, particularly offences of medium seriousness. Most people, in other words, would have no difficulty in assessing murder as more serious than shoplifting, but might have difficulty in assessing whether burglary is more or less serious than embezzlement. Whether the concept of harm to living standard, or any other candidate for an objective basis for ranking offences, could be sufficiently elaborated and adopted into practice, or whether one is satisfied with less sophisticated rankings such as the serious enough/so serious threshold, the second problem of proportionate sentencing systems then arises: the question of cardinal proportionality.

Ranking offences according to seriousness and then establishing a scale of penalties of commensurate severity achieves *ordinal proportionality*, but gives little guidance on *cardinal proportionality*, the overall severity of penalty scales. Put simply, the problem is that deserts theory can help with the graduation of punishments within the most severe and least severe points, but can do nothing to tell us what those anchoring points should be. What has happened in practice is that in jurisdictions with traditions of relatively lenient punishment, such as Sweden and Minnesota, the introduction of deserts guidelines has provided moderate penalty scales, whereas in places with severe traditions, such as New Mexico or Indiana, the schedules are predictably severe (von Hirsch 1990).

The overall severity of a scale of punishments depends on what it provides as its most severe penalty. If imprisonment is the most severe penalty available, then ordinal proportionality will provide for shorter terms of imprisonment, or non-custodial penalties, for lesser offences. If, further, the length of imprisonment provided for the most severe categories of offence is moderate, then the use of short sentences and non-custodial penalties will be reached quite soon as the seriousness scale is descended.

This moderate scale was recommended by von Hirsch and his colleagues on the Committee for the Study of Incarceration, which proposed that there should be no sentences of over five years except for certain murders (von Hirsch 1976). For serious offences, which are 'intentional and unprovoked offences that cause grave injury to the victim', the proposal is imprisonment for a period between 18 months and three years, or three to four years for repeat offences (von Hirsch 1976). Most people, in all but the most moderate of jurisdictions, would find these terms quite inadequate, so lenient as to be non-commensurate, for crimes of serious physical violence: the point is not whether you or I agree or disagree with the proposals, but that deserts theory contains no principle which would tell us that those are indeed properly commensurate sentences. If the penalty for the most serious offences is death, then long terms of imprisonment are ordinally proportionate penalties for less serious offences, the situation that obtains in many states in the USA. Again, deserts theory offers no principle which would rule out the death penalty, and its advocates have stated their dislike of it, rather than arguing its incompatibility with notions of desert and commensurability: 'We have made one significant but intentional omission: the death penalty. A civilised state, we feel, should not have this vile sanction at all' (von Hirsch and Ashworth 1992: x).

Retribution and the justification of punishment

In spite of these problems with grading offence seriousness and deciding the overall severity of punishments, desert has much to commend it as a principle for the distribution of punishments. It offers more secure protection from punishment for the innocent than do most other theories; it offers protection from extra punishment because of predictions of future offending, predictions which may possibly be wrong and which are generally unverifiable. Furthermore, desert's promise of reducing the scope of judicial discretion, used to punish people for their personal or social characteristics rather than for their crime, made it appeal to those who were concerned about race, gender or class bias in criminal justice. The introduction to the Minnesota guidelines (Minnesota Sentencing Guidelines Commission 1980) states that sentencing should not be influenced by race, gender or class, and this aspiration has been incorporated into the 1991 Criminal Justice Act. This commitment to race, class and gender blindness in sentencing, the commitment to consistent punishment with similar penalties for similar crimes, has been welcomed by many critics of what appeared to be discriminatory use of judicial discretion before the influence of just-deserts ideas made itself felt through sentencing reforms.

Retribution is on less firm ground, however, when it turns from the questions of who should be punished, and of how much offenders should be punished, to why offenders should be punished at all. In many versions, retributivists do not make it clear whether they are advocating their theories as principles of distribution or of general justification, or both. As will be discussed further in Chapter 4, the latest retributivist writings, those appearing in the 1990s, tend mainly to restrict themselves to advocating retribution as the basis of distribution, but there have been suggestions that retribution of itself can serve as a principle of general justification.

Most retributivists in justification (Hart 1968) emphasize the *denunciation* aspect of punishment. To pronounce a sentence is to denounce the crime; it is to make a public statement of disapproval of the behaviour that has been perpetrated. The degree of severity of a penalty announced marks the degree of disapproval of the crime. This *censure* is said by retributivists to be the core characteristic and function of punishment (Duff 1986; von Hirsch 1993). Only by announcing a proportionate penalty, they would claim, can the crime be given its proper degree of disapproval. The difficulty with this idea is that the censure is in the pronouncement of the penalty by the judge, rather than in its undergoing by the offender. How do retributivists make the further step of justifying the actual serving of the penalty? A distinction that many penal philosophers have made is between the expression of disapproval, the censure aspect of punishment, and the 'hard treatment', the pains and deprivations which are the mode through which this censure is delivered (Feinberg 1970).

Deserts writings in the 1970s and 1980s justified 'hard treatment' on the grounds that it removed advantages which the criminal had seized unfairly; punishment was argued to be necessary to restore the proper balance of social advantage and disadvantage, benefits and burdens (Finnis 1972; 1980; Murphy 1979). The offender, it was claimed, had seized an unfair advantage – property in theft or burglary, transport or excitement by taking a car, release of tension or malice in violent offences – which the law-abiding deny themselves by obeying the laws. Punishment is necessary to remove this unfair advantage.

This theory of the just basis for punishment derives from the wider theory of political obligation to be found in the writings of the social philosopher John Rawls, whose work has had a profound influence on English and American political and legal thinking. In his classic work, *A Theory of Justice*, Rawls (1972) examines the conditions which social institutions must meet if they are to command allegiance in a free society. He offers a modern version of the social contract theory mentioned in Chapter 1, looking at the advantages that people would expect in return for engaging in social co-operation, and the rules they would create for the regulation of social life. Like the pre-social 'savage' of contract theory, Rawls says that social institutions, such as formal systems of law, can only be assessed if we ask whether they follow rules that people in this pre-social state, what he calls the 'original position', would devise for themselves as a basis for co-operation. In the original position, because there would be as yet no society, individuals could not have ideas of their position relative to each other: relative social status, relative economic advantage or disadvantage, relative intelligence or stupidity, honesty or dishonesty, are ideas which derive from the experience of society, and cannot exist prior to society. Individuals would, therefore, in the original position choose rules and institutions from behind a 'veil of ignorance' (Rawls 1972: 12) as to whether in an established society they would be among the advantaged or the disadvantaged. Only principles that would be agreed by people operating behind this veil of ignorance, Rawls argued, could be considered just, because they would be the only rules that could be reached by rational agreement of free individuals. If people were aware of themselves as rich, they would choose principles which favoured the rich, and the resultant laws and institutions would be an imposition of the rich on the poor, while if they were aware of themselves as poor, they would favour laws which would promote the interests of the poor at the expense of the rich.

The only principles and social arrangements which would be freely entered into by all potential members of society, operating behind the veil of ignorance, would be those ensuring fair distribution of advantages and disadvantages, benefits and burdens, because only in this way could individuals guarantee that they would not be disadvantaged, whatever their eventual social status. Although, of course, Rawls is well aware that no one ever starts off from the original position, that we are all born into an existing society, one which, furthermore, is hierarchical and unequal, he insists that the hypothetical standpoint of the person behind the veil of ignorance is the standard from which actual social institutions should be evaluated. Considering social institutions and social rules from this vantage point of the veil of ignorance leads him to advocate the principle known as *justice as fairness*, which Rawls elaborates in his book, and which has been so attractive to modern retributivists.

Rawls argues that his principles of social justice demand fairness to each individual, and in the course of his analysis he mounts a powerful attack on Utilitarian theory. The main point of his attack is that allowing the disadvantage of one for the good of the many is not a system that would be agreed to by rational, freely choosing, individuals behind the veil of ignorance, because they could not know that they would not be the ones to be disadvantaged. His preferred principles of fairness and equal treatment, on which his general theory of political obligation is based, have been incorporated into neo-retributivism, and his refutation of Utilitarianism gave them a basis for advancing retribution as a justifying aim as well as a principle for the distribution of punishment. If Utilitarianism cannot be supported as a general principle for the ordering of social institutions, it clearly cannot be the basis for the institution of punishment.

Rawls's principle of justice as fairness, then, yielded the idea that the object of punishment is to restore the balance of advantage and disadvantage disturbed by the crime. This must be the case because, according to his ideas of the arrangements free and rational citizens would establish, the object of all social institutions must be to promote as fair a distribution of advantages as possible.

To this it has been objected that since actual society is characterized by inequality rather than fairness, and since actual laws can be shown to promote the interests of certain sections of society and to be imposed on rather than freely chosen by others, in actual societies this rationale of the removal of unfair advantage cannot impose the obligation to obey laws, and therefore the liability to punishment for the breaching of laws, on all citizens. Only if society were much more equal could punishment be justified. Several Marxists have taken this position, arguing that the notion of the restoration of the balance of advantage could only apply in an ideal society (see, for example, Murphy 1973; Paternoster and Bynum 1982). Generally, these criticisms are taken to mean that removal of unfair advantage cannot be a justification for punishment; another interpretation of the same point, however, would be that this is indeed the proper function of punishment, and if society is so unequal as to make this inapplicable, then the inequalities need to be remedied, rather than another theory of punishment being invented. If inequalities are such, in other words, as to render obligation to obey the law inoperable, then social inequality is of such an order as to imperil the rule of law, and thence the very existence of society. This is certainly an implication of Murphy's account of the impossibility of justifying punishment in present capitalist societies.

Another reply to the objection that there cannot be equal liability to punishment if rights and benefits are so unevenly distributed, is to point out that even the most disadvantaged are better off with a system of law than without it. Even the poorest members of society would want to retain the system of law because they too have an interest in protection from physical harm, from theft of the few possessions they have, and so they share the general obligation to obey actual laws because of their interest in preserving a system of law (Lacey 1988; Kerruish 1991).

For some retributivists, however, removal of unfair advantage is inadequate as a justification for punishment for reasons other than the imperfection of present-day society. Duff points out that although it may be appropriate to think in these terms for some kinds of crime, particularly property crimes, it hardly corresponds to the way law-abiding individuals think about other crimes. It may be that if someone gains a material advantage by stealing something, then not only is the victim's bundle of advantages depleted, but also people who refrain from that activity are voluntarily denying themselves the unfair advantage of possession of the money or goods involved – but this is not how we think, argues Duff, about murder, rape or similar crimes. Non-offenders cannot sensibly be said to be denying themselves the advantage of something they are never tempted to do. The 'wrongness' of rape and murder lies not in the fact that it steals a march on the law-abiding (Duff 1986: 212), but in the nature of the harm done to the victim and in the breach of society's boundaries of moral conduct. Removal of unfair advantage, then, cannot serve as a general justification for punishment, because if it is defensible at all, it is only with regard to some categories of crime.

Retributivists who regard these criticisms of the idea of unfair advantage as sufficiently strong to rule it out as the justification for punishment, but nevertheless want to see retribution as more than a principle of distribution, return to the function which is so fundamental to all forms of retributivism, the condemning of the crime. Thus Duff lays great emphasis on the censure function of punishment, and suggests that the imposition and serving of the penalty are the means of communication between the offender and society. The message of disapproval is given by the pronouncement of sentence, and received or acknowledged by the serving of the sentence (Duff 1986). On this account, punishment is seen as a penance, to be undergone as a demonstration of acceptance that the crime is indeed blameworthy; suffering the punishment allows the offender to rejoin society's moral consensus by acknowledging that s/he, too, shares or has been induced to share the view that the crime is wrong. The offender is reinstated in the community as someone who, though s/he may have committed a wrong deed, shares the normative consensus none the less. Punishment is thus portrayed as a process of moral communication, the purpose of which is to reconnect the offender with society's values (Nozick 1981).

It could be objected, however, that this communicative justification is in fact a rehabilitation theory. Coming to share society's moral beliefs and being reconnected with society are surely the two central ingredients of rehabilitation: change in attitudes and reacceptance by society. What is being put forward by writers such as Nozick and Duff looks like rehabilitation expressed in moral-philosophical discourse rather than in the discourse of psychiatry, social work or social education. The main difference, perhaps, is that this communicative retribution has no forward-looking aspects. Not only would the sentence not be set with reference to risk of reoffending, but also the punishment would be 'effective' if the offender expressed regret for the past offence, but went on to commit further crimes. Whether or not it is rehabilitation in another voice, however, the communicative theory is deficient as a general justification since it offers no reason why this moral rethinking and reconnnection with society should take place.

Rawls's work does, however, offer another possibility for a retributive justification of punishment. What the unfair advantage theory and the communicative theory have in common is their insistence on treating offenders as rational moral agents. This presumption of rationality is a cornerstone of Rawls's political theory, and it is a principle of utmost importance in all modern versions of retributivism.

As explained above, Rawls stipulates that the institutions and rules adopted by a society would be those that members, as free and equal citizens, would rationally agree. If advantages were equally distributed, then rules which forbade one citizen from transferring advantages from another citizen to him/herself would be agreed, as would rules forbidding attack: in other words, a system of criminal laws would be developed.

Since these laws would be those that protected the interests of the free and equal, rational citizen, s/he would want to see those laws upheld. The offender, as a party to this social contract, would have as great an interest as the law-abiding citizen in seeing it upheld. Punishments, as the 'by definition' sanctions attached to criminal law, then, are to be enforced because to do so is consistent with the rational will of citizens, including offenders, in order that the rule of law is upheld. Just like any other citizen, the offender has a right to live in a society where the rules that maintain the social contract are taken seriously.

This 'rule-enforcement' justification for punishment fits with the derivation of Rawls's thought in the moral philosophy of Kant, who, writing in the eighteenth century, argued that moral principles must be derived from rationality itself, not from public opinion about what may be good or bad. Kant argued that only if moral principles are based on reason can they be applicable to all members of society, because if they are derived from people's ideas about what may be good or bad at any given time or in any given society, then they will be influenced by individuals' own circumstances, and may not be generalizable to the whole society. Rawls's appeal to the original position, his criterion of the veil of ignorance test, is thus a contemporary reformulation of Kant's demand that morality be derived from rationality, not from public opinion.

The two best-known principles which Kant derives from his appeal to reason are, first, that people should always be treated as ends, never only as means; and second, that one should only do that which one could wish to be universalized. These two principles are entwined in the 'rule-following' justification for punishment, and in the retributivists' arguments with Utilitarianism. The rationally choosing citizen would not choose to live in a society where rules were never enforced, therefore must wish them to be consistently enforced, and punishing people to bring about some future state of affairs is to use them as a means to an end (less crime) rather than as an end in themselves (addressing their own moral status).

Two points are of particular importance here. One is the assumption that because a criminal may have chosen to do a wrong action, s/he is not in some way morally different from the rest of society. The theory presumes that the person could still choose right action in the future, and, more fundamentally, that breaching one particular rule does not mean that the criminal rejects the idea of the rule of law altogether. For a retributivist, someone may be a criminal but this does not make him/her an outlaw! The second point is that these arguments for retributivism – arguments which distinguish it from vengeance – rest on a model of the human as someone whose actions are the result of moral choices. There is a very strong sense of free will inherent in retributivism. Retribution is claimed to be the only principle which freely choosing individuals entering into a social contract would accept even without the rationale of unfair advantage, because it is the only system under which individuals can be certain that whether or not they are punished depends on their own actions and choices. By choosing to refrain from crime, under a retributive system, the individual can be certain of avoiding punishment: 'The criminal justice system is voluntary: you keep out of it by not committing crime' (Posner 1985: 1213).

The idea that crime is the result of free choice has been criticized, mainly by criminologists with a sociological viewpoint, aware that actions may be the result of choice, but that choices are very much constrained by circumstances (Lacey 1988; Carlen 1989; Hudson 1993). However, if one does, as retributivists do, have a model of the human being as acting out of freedom of choice, rationally balancing the costs and benefits of potential actions, then this argument for retribution as providing the best security against unwarranted punishment for those who chose to obey the law is persuasive.

As was pointed out in relation to Utilitarian theories, with rehabilitation and incapacitation individuals could be punished because someone else thinks they may commit a crime in the future, whereas deterrence does not guarantee freedom from punishment of the innocent. While, as has been shown, utilitarians can defend themselves against these criticisms, the objections do have some force. The punishment-without-crime to which people are at risk under rehabilitative or incapacitative schemes is generally extra punishment because of risk assessment, that is, punishment extra to that deserved for the crime already committed. This objection only has force, of course, if one has first conceded that the proper amount of punishment is that which is deserved by acts already carried out – otherwise the notion of 'extra' or 'unwarranted' punishment has no meaning. Theories which try to build protection against 'undeserved' punishment into consequentialist approaches are discussed in Chapter 4.

Deterrence and retribution in distribution

The relationship between retribution and deterrence is somewhat less clear than that between retribution and rehabilitation or incapacitation. Both require a graded system of penalties, retribution to achieve proportionality in punishment, and deterrence to induce restraint from aggravated forms of crime. Both are appealing to the potential criminal's reason and free choice of action, and are offering the inducement of avoiding punishment by refraining from crime. Both have deficiencies with regard to the overall severity of punishment scales: retribution because of dependence on subjective assessments of what is commensurate punishment; deterrence because it depends on subjective assessments of what is adequate to persuade people that the risks of punishment are not worth the gains of crime. So what distinguishes them?

One question that might elucidate the difference is that of the necessity of the application of punishment in every case. For deterrence, it is necessary that punishments are seen to be imposed, but must they be actually inflicted? Drawing on the kinds of justification for retributive punishment outlined above, Nigel Walker proposes that while the retributivist must logically demand that punishments imposed must actually be served (because they are deserved), the deterrence theorist need not. Public perception of punishments is what counts for deterrence; it does not matter, says Walker (1991: 30–1), if the sentenced offender is 'secretly smuggled away from the Old Bailey under another name to live in freedom on the Costa Brava'. A better-known 'hypothetical' is Kant's (1887: 198) 'last murderer'. If for some reason society is about to cease to exist, and one murderer remains in prison awaiting execution, should s/he be executed before the other members of the society escape, surrender authority or succumb to whatever catastrophe is upon them? For a Utilitarian of any kind, the answer would clearly be 'no': the execution would serve no purpose since there is no one left for her/him to endanger, and no one left to give way to temptation to murder in the belief that murderers sometimes escape execution. Only a hard-and-fast retributivist in justification, who believes that once the deserved penalty has been incurred, it must be carried out whatever the future holds, would see any necessity for the last execution. For a Kantian retributivist, to deny the last murderer her/his execution means that the society has colluded in the crime by not according it sufficient importance to carry out the punishment before leaving, and that it has failed to treat the murderer as an end, failed to respect her/his moral autonomy, by not carrying out the execution because it is no future use to society. If punishment is retrospective, then the fact that it serves no future purpose is irrelevant; but if it is forward-looking, then to impose it in circumstances where it brings about no future benefit is gratuitous violence.

Unless one believes, as Kant ultimately did, in God and something akin to the necessity of punishment in this world to forestall eternal punishment in the next, it remains difficult to be completely convinced by any of the suggestions given for retribution as a justifying principle. Most of the functions assigned to it could be as well served by compensation as by punishment. Certainly, the gravity of an offence could be as well marked by proportionality in compensation awards, and the rational rule-chooser would be as likely to agree with a rule which laid down that if s/he suffered any unfair disadvantage s/he would be compensated as with one which stated that if s/he took unfair advantage s/he would be punished.

If asked 'Why punishment and not compensation?', most retributivists would undoubtedly answer either that punishment is necessary to bring about remorse on the part of the offender (the communicative theory, which is really a form of moral rehabilitationism) or that punishment is more effective than compensation in deterring crime. Most contemporary retributivists readily admit that their principle is concerned with distribution rather than justification, and their limiting of their claims to retribution as a rule for sentencing rather than for the existence of a system of punishments at all has become clearer as the new retributivism has been refined. Both von Hirsch and Duff, for example, separate the censure and hard treatment aspects of punishment, giving to censure the function of expressing the wrongness of the act, and to hard treatment that of providing a 'prudential' reason for restraining from crime. The existence of a tariff of punishments will deter people from crime by telling them that it is wrong and that they will suffer unpleasant consequences if they commit it. Von Hirsch (1993: 13) sums up the two aspects of retributive punishment thus:

> Persons are assumed to be moral agents, capable of taking seriously the message conveyed through the sanction, that the conduct is reprehensible. They are fallible, nevertheless, and thus face temptation. The function of the disincentive is to provide a prudential reason for resisting the temptation. The account would make no sense were human beings much better or worse: an angel would require no appeals to prudence, and a brute could not be appealed to through censure . . .

Von Hirsch agrees that the institution of punishment would/should be abolished if it were not necessary for the prevention of crime, so that his general justification is consequentialist and forward-looking. He insists, however, that 'making prevention part of the justification for punishment's existence . . . does not permit it to operate independently as a basis for deciding comparative punishments' (ibid.: 17).

Summary and conclusion

This insistence on desert not just as merely a principle of distribution but as the only principle of distribution, however, is the point at which contemporary retributivism has encountered most opposition. Fixing punishments according to desert, it can be argued, does not give the courts adequate powers to punish persistent and dangerous offenders, or to respond to waves of particular crime. After the enactment of sentencing laws and guidelines in the USA which either were based on desert or at least had been influenced by desert, the departures from prescribed sentences that were upheld by appeal courts, or the raising of penalties in the sentencing schedules, led to the charge that the reforms had been 'co-opted' by the get-tough lobby (Greenberg and Humphries 1980; Hudson 1987). More recently, the 'three strikes' legislation introduced in some states, whereby a third violent crime (not necessarily involving grave violence) can lead to life imprisonment, has shown that there is a public/political demand for sentencing which looks to frequency as well as to seriousness of offending.

In England and Wales, the 1991 Criminal Justice Act, which made seriousness of the current offence by far the most important consideration in sentencing (Wasik and Taylor 1991), was soon criticized by the judiciary and by politicians as providing inadequate powers for sentencing persistent offenders. The Act was superseded by the 1993 Criminal Justice Act, which allowed more influence to previous convictions in sentencing. A subsequent provision for the building of new 'child jails' has introduced something like the three strikes principle in England. Young offenders with three convictions (which do not need to be for violent or otherwise serious offences) can be given custodial sentences, even if the seriousness of the current offence would indicate a non-custodial response.

What these examples show is that deserved retribution is not the only thing that members of advanced Western societies seek from their criminal justice systems. They also seek protection from dangerous or persistent offenders, and they seek strong action against kinds of offending that become suddenly prevalent. Critics from other vantage points seek reformative efficacy from sentencing (Matthews 1989). For retributivists in distribution, one of the principal questions posed by these criticisms, and by the failure of deserts-based systems in practice apparently to satisfy the requirements of society, is what happens when principles of desert clash with other principles. Von Hirsch (1993: 43) can admit a place of other goals (rehabilitation, protection) as 'subsidiary', but what if there are actual conflicts? If the general justification for punishment is crime reduction, does this mean that if there is conflict in actual sentencing practice between desert and reduction, then reductionist claims are more important? Can a place be found for desert that reflects the force of some of the arguments made by modern retributivists, but does not mean that the principle of distribution is being given more importance than the, surely prior, principle of general justification? Chapter 4 deals with some contemporary attempts to find compromises – both principled and pragmatic – between retributive and Utilitarian approaches to punishment.

chapter four

Hybrids, compromises and syntheses

Introduction
Desert and deterrence: crime reduction within limits
Desert and rehabilitation: reform with rights
Targets and constraints: syntheses of utilitarian and retributive theories
Conclusion

Introduction

The previous two chapters have set out the main principles of Utilitarian and retributive theories of punishment. Each has provided a critique of the other, and it is the persuasiveness of these critiques as well as the attractiveness of the arguments of both theories that has led contemporary penal theorists to seek compromises between them. These attempts to combine the best of the two approaches, guarding against the danger of insensitive or purposeless punishment if retributive principles are adopted, and against disproportionate punishment or punishment for crimes not (yet) committed, which is the danger of consequentialist theories, are the subject matter of this chapter.

The main flaw in Utilitarian theories is the lack of a limit to the amount of punishment that may be inflicted in the pursuit of crime reduction. Utilitarians make arguments in the form that unrestrained punishment would not be effective – resentment at overly severe penalties might make criminals less receptive to rehabilitative efforts, and deterrent impact might be lost if sentences were not proportionately graded, with offenders taking the attitude that they might as well be hanged for a sheep as a lamb – but these are only expectations; there is nothing in the theory itself to make disproportionate punishments unacceptable. Retributivists are surely correct when they say that there is a common sense of justice which demands at least some degree of proportionality between gravity of crimes and severity of punishments. On the other hand, punishment that does not achieve any social good is pain for its own sake, which is, or should be, morally doubtful. The case of Kant's last murderer shows the limitations of punishment without any social utility: it may be just, but it is certainly futile.

Utilitarianism, then, is weak on principles of distribution, but retribution, while making a strong principled argument on distribution, fails to provide a general justification. If people are to be punished, it is reasonable to say that they should only be punished to the extent that they deserve it, but it is also reasonable to say that unnecessary suffering – which punishment without utility is – should be avoided. Retribution is at its weakest when trying to establish why the pain of punishment is necessary, if retributivists eschew the aim of achieving some future social good. In most situations, common moral sentiments would hold that 'two wrongs don't make a right': why make an exception of punishment, and say that more pain somehow repairs the pain already caused by the offence?

Desert and deterrence: crime reduction within limits

Forms of contemporary retributivism that very clearly limit desert to a principle of distribution are one answer to this fundamental weakness of retributivism. As von Hirsch and Ashworth (1993) make clear in their critique of Braithwaite and Pettit's statement of the requirement that a penal theory needs to be able to deal with all the stages of the criminal justice process, as well as with questions such as what kinds of behaviour should be criminalized, desert theory applies only to sentencing. It is concerned with the distribution of punishment, given that a system of penal sanctions exists, and allowing that this system has been instituted for crime reduction purposes.

Must sentencing always follow retributive principles, however? Suppose desert in distribution makes the purposes which punishment is established to serve less easily achieved. Sentencers have to confront difficult decisions when, for instance, the required sentence for a crime is imprisonment or a fine, but the offender would be likely to commit further offences unless s/he received some help with addictions or psychological problems more readily offered under a probation order; when someone with a very low income would be likely to commit a further offence to raise the money to pay a fine. There are often conflicts between a short prison sentence which an offence may indicate, and the fact that this would interfere with someone's job prospects, offer no time for any treatment or therapy, and therefore make further offending more rather than less probable. Desert theorists may well argue that these dilemmas point not to the defects of desert as a principle of distribution, but to the dysfunctionality of prevailing penalty scales. Unfortunately, if they restrict themselves to arguing for desert as a principle of sentencing among sanctions once they are set, they rather deny themselves the opportunity for any input on questions of the overall nature of the penalty scale.

Whatever penalties were available, however, there would undoubtedly be some cases where principles of desert conflicted with the general purposes of criminal law and punishment. How are such cases to be decided?

Von Hirsch, Ashworth and other deserts theorists allow for Utilitarian principles to operate as *ulterior* purposes, which could be pursued once deserts constraints have been satisfied (von Hirsch 1993: 47). This would mean that sentencers should choose the penal value of a sanction according to desert, but that from among sentences of equal penal value, they could choose that which was most likely to achieve crime reduction objectives. Attendance at a probation centre and community service might be seen as sentences of equal penal value, suitable for offences which are not (in the words of the 1991 Criminal Justice Act) 'so serious' that only a prison sentence is appropriate, and the choice between them could be made on the basis of whether a crime was committed simply out of greed or disregard for society – in which case community service, with its component of work on behalf of the community, would be chosen – or whether the offence seemed to be associated with personal difficulties – in which case the probation centre, with its opportunities for counselling and social learning, would seem more apt. Probation could not, on this model, be substituted for a prison sentence if the crime was judged serious enough to warrant custody in order to provide help to the offender; nor could a prison term be substituted for a non-custodial sentence if the crime did not warrant imprisonment but the offender was thought to be dangerous or especially likely to reoffend. Exemplary sentences for general deterrence purposes would also be disallowed.

A proposal for desert to be the main principle of distribution, but for departures from desert to be allowed in exceptional cases, is contained in Robinson's (1988) 'hybrid' scheme. Robinson summarizes the dilemma succinctly: a single-purpose system is bound to be unsatisfactory, but a system which does not have a principle for prioritizing when purposes conflict, gives too much discretion to sentencers and creates disparity and possible abuse, to the detriment of respect for law. As he says, the Utilitarian principles, if used alone, would allow or compel distribution of punishment according to factors that are not thought acceptable (such as ethnicity, family or employment status) and would give insufficient prominence to factors that are thought important by most people, such as the nature of the offence. On the other hand, basing sentencing purely on desert is inefficient in crime reduction. Robinson calls, therefore, for recognition of the multiple purposes of punishment, and also for the formulation of a 'guiding principle' for use by sentencers in choosing between purposes in individual cases.

Although he differs from the deserts theorists in giving the same priority to desert and crime prevention as purposes in sentencing, Robinson's principle would have the same result in most cases: fixing the *amount* of punishment according to desert calculations, but the *method* according to Utilitarian concerns. He explains that the injustices that deserts writers have identified as stemming from unfettered utilitarian systems, are mostly injustices in amounts of punishment: one person serving a much longer prison sentence than another for a similar offence because of differences in rehabilitative progress. These could be avoided if penal equivalences were calculated for different penalties, so that judges would first determine the deserved amount, and then select the method of punishment that would be most likely to produce crime reduction effects.

Where Robinson differs from the deserts 'purists' is, first, that he arrives at this suggestion by a rather different argument from theirs. Instead of putting desert immediately as the priority requirement in distribution, his principle for the interrelationship of sentencing purposes is that none shall be followed to the extent that others are undermined. Generally, using desert to calculate the amount of punishment but crime reduction to choose the method, would satisfy both deserts and crime reduction requirements. Choosing a sentence to achieve the maximum general deterrence, or to keep the offender in prison for long enough to make sure s/he could never pose a danger to the public, might very well conflict with desert requirements in relation to the current offence. Giving one requirement overall priority, therefore, can lead to breaches of other principles. Since, as he says, effective crime control can be pursued through a variety of different methods, but desert can only be satisfied by giving the deserved amount of punishment, the principle that no requirement should be pursued to the elimination of another would produce the desert amount/crime reduction method approach to sentencing in most cases. Crime reduction objectives should be pursued, but only to the extent that they do not produce punishment which is disproportionate on desert criteria.

It may be, however, that fixing the amount of punishment according to desert sometimes not merely limits the crime reduction potential in a particular case, but renders it negligible, or makes further crime more rather than less likely. Robinson therefore allows for unacceptably low crime reduction potential to be a limit on the application of desert. Where desert requirements would lead to a sentence that is too low to offer any acceptable degree of crime prevention, Robinson's 'principle of interrelationship between purposes' would allow for the imposition of more than the deserved amount of punishment.

An approach which is somewhat similar in its reasoning to Robinson's is Norval Morris's *limiting retributivism*; but where the former's proposals would allow more severe sentences than desert requires, Morris accepts in all circumstances the constraints of desert in setting limits to the amount of punishment that can be imposed (Morris 1982). Morris differentiates himself from deserts theorists by pointing out that – at least in earlier formulations such as *Doing Justice* (von Hirsch 1976), which are less clear about crime prevention as the general justifying aim – they see the relationship between crime and punishment such that desert is the *defining* principle of punishment, whereas for him it is only the *limiting* principle.

The general purposes of punishment are indisputably utilitarian, there-fore crime reduction must be the defining principle, but he allows that pursuit of these purposes is properly limited by a sense of what is or is not reasonable punishment. Desert sets maximum limits to punishment, because of a shared sense that excessively harsh penalties, even though they may have deterrent effectiveness, are unacceptable. It also sets mini-mum limits because, even where there is no risk of reoffending, or the opportunities for offending would not be available to anyone other than the offender, a very small amount of punishment, or no punishment, would offend against the sense of what is due retribution for the offence. Morris (1992: 205) gives the example of the lenient sentence passed on the former US vice-president, Spiro Agnew, 'which, in my view, was entirely correct, for utilitarian and government practical reasons, but which certainly strained at the lower level of deserved punishment'. Desert, for Morris, gives a broad spread of maximum and minimum penalties for the various levels of offence severity. Within those limits, crime prevention purposes can act fairly freely, with the amount as well as the method of punishment being chosen for crime reduction efficacy (Ten 1987). The broadness of the limits, however, makes Morris's scheme quite different from the deserts theorists' admittance of crime reduction aims as determinant of the mode of punishment, because it opens the question of how to choose the amount of punishment within the limits.

Desert theorists would insist on penalties of equal penal value for like cases, but Morris prefers the principle of *parsimony* to that of equality. His reasoning is Benthamite: equality means that crime reduction objectives produce too much punishment. He wants the benefits of crime reduction to be gained with the minimum pain of punishment. The deterrent effects of penalties on potential offenders come from the existence of the sanction, and the public's knowledge of them. If some offenders receive the maxi-mum penalties allowed by the desert limit, and the sentences are highly publicized, then potential offenders will realize that they risk the same punishments: it is not necessary for all offenders to receive the same punishment. Morris argues from utilitarian principles of minimizing the pains of crime while inflicting the minimum possible pains of punishment, whereas his deserts-minded critics assume that equality has a high value independent of any crime reduction or overall pain reduction.

Braithwaite and Pettit put forward a rather ingenious defence of parsi-mony against the criticisms of deserts supporters. They argue that because so few offenders are actually caught and prosecuted, the goal of treating all people who have committed the same crime in similar fashion would be better served by not punishing, or by minimally punishing, those who are caught than it would by punishing them all to the limit of available penalties:

There are two states of complete criminal justice equality. One is where every guilty person is equally punished. The other is where every guilty person is granted mercy. The sociological and fiscal realities of criminal justice mean that every society is always closer to the latter state of equality (zero enforcement) than it is to the former (100 per cent punishment). If we lived in a world where 90 per cent of the guilty were punished, then the way to make the system more equitable would be to pursue the 10 per cent who were getting off. But the reality of the societies we know is the opposite. We are lucky to punish 10 per cent of the guilty, leaving 90 per cent of crimes unpunished. It follows that the more of the 10 per cent that can be extended mercy, the more equitable the criminal justice system will become. In this most fundamental sense, the principle of parsimony is a principle for maximising equality.

(Braithwaite and Pettit 1990: 197)

Morris advocates the choice of the least severe penalty that will serve some legitimate social purpose. By 'least severe', his argument about 'straining at the lower limits of desert' indicates that he means the bottom of a desert-determined band, rather than, for example, the least punishment which may be necessary to prevent the offender from reoffending. He does not, and neither does Robinson, provide much guidance about how to choose the 'legitimate social purpose'. Both tend to discount rehabilitation on grounds of immorality of penalties that seek to change the offender's nature rather than merely influencing his/her rational choices, as well as on the grounds of lack of proof of effectiveness of rehabilitative strategies, but admit both deterrence and incapacitation as legitimate purposes. Deterrence and incapacitation might suggest different penalties, although both would very often result in more severe sentences than desert. If Morris is going to allow for these crime prevention purposes within his limits, then, this would suggest that the maximum available sentences allowed under his formulation would need to be rather high. He still, however, begs the question of when deterring the individual from reoffending, physically preventing the offender from reoffending, or deterring potential offenders is to be the preferred purpose.

One simple, pragmatic approach is described by Walker (1991) as that practised by the supreme court in Victoria, Australia. The purpose to be chosen is that which is most likely to be achieved, and if no crime reduction effects are likely, then simple proportionality is the principle followed. The problem with this is that prevention is the most achievable of all the utilitarian purposes, and therefore such a system is potentially extremely harsh. This reasoning can be seen in the 'prison works' arguments put forward in England and Wales by Michael Howard, as Home Secretary introducing the 1993 Criminal Justice Act, and the provisions for 'secure training centres' for young offenders in the 1994 Criminal Justice and Public Order Act. Prison works in keeping offenders off the streets; prison does not (generally) work in reforming offenders. Choosing the purpose with the best chance of success would, therefore, mean choosing long, incapacitative prison sentences rather than shorter sentences or non-custodial sentences aimed at rehabilitation.

A variation on the Victoria approach is proposed by Ten (1987), who says that sentencers could impose the penalty which had proved effective in similar cases. There is not, however, the necessary data to demonstrate effectiveness of deterrence or rehabilitation, and so again this might be expected to lead to increased, incapacitative penalties. Robinson (1988) discusses – and dismisses – a similar strategy, at least a strategy which would be similar in its effects. One way to choose between different purposes would be to choose that which produced the most severe sentence, on the grounds that this would encompass the other objectives. He points out, however, that this would often conflict with desert requirements.

Desert and rehabilitation: reform with rights

The ideas outlined above are attempts to reconcile the limitations of deserts philosophies – that offenders should only be punished to the extent that their conduct is blameworthy – with the general purposes of punishment, namely to reduce the incidence of crime. They have emphasized deterrence as the most important utilitarian goal, but have also acknowledged prevention/incapacitation; most of them are critical, or at least sceptical, of rehabilitation.

There are writers, however, who have argued for the retention of rehabilitation as the primary aim of punishment, and who have sought to elaborate new rehabilitative strategies in the light of the persuasive critiques of 1960s-style rehabilitation made by the 'back to justice' movement. These *new rehabilitationists* have defended the values of humanitarian responses to offenders, and the optimism that offenders can change, that lay behind the development of reformative and rehabilitative elements in penal systems. They have, however, granted that deserts critics were correct to point out the oppressive features of the models operating before the sentencing reforms of the 1970s and 1980s.

It will be remembered that the most criticized aspect of the penal practices of jurisdictions such as California in the 1960s, where the rehabilitative ethos received its most extreme expression, was the indeterminacy of sentences. Terms were not fixed at trial, and the decision not only to release from prison, but also to terminate probation orders and juvenile supervision and care orders, was made by prison governors, probation officers and social workers in the light of rehabilitative progress. Defenders of the basic ideas of rehabilitative punishment claim that indeterminate sentences are by no means a necessary correlate of rehabilitation, indeed are antithetical to it (Cullen and Gilbert 1982; Hudson 1987; Rotman 1990): the preoccupation with trying to find out the likely release date, the temptation to pretend to have made more rehabilitative progress than is really the case, and resentment at refusal of early release, all get in the way of full acknowledgement of problems connected with the offending and openness to rehabilitative efforts. All the new rehabilitationists, therefore, are agreed that rehabilitation should be offered within the context of a fixed sentence; to a greater or lesser degree they are clear that this sentence should be fixed according to the seriousness of the offence.

New rehabilitationists argue that of all the penal rationales, theirs is the only one which combines crime reduction purposes with respect for the rights of the offender. General deterrence has no reference to the actual offender: it would not matter how inappropriate for an individual offender a sentence was, it would not matter what its potential impact on her/his life and prospects of future offending might be, since the sentence is directed towards other people. Deserts critics of deterrence are correct, then, in saying that this violates the Kantian–Rawlsian imperative of treating people as ends, never merely as means. Prevention/incapacitation denies people's right only to be punished for something they have done, and removes autonomy, moral and physical, by removing their possibilities of free action in the future. Individual deterrence through tactics such as the 'taste of custody', while it respects autonomy, also denies the right to be punished only for something one has already done. Rehabilitation shares with deserts the awareness that while the gains of prevention and deterrence are speculative, what is certain is that the convicted offender has committed a crime, and that the pains of punishment will fall on her/him. Punishment therefore ought to reflect the crime itself, but also ought to be appropriate to the offender as well as to the offence. As well as marking society's disapproval of the act, it should offer some potential for reducing the offender's likelihood of repeating it.

The claim of new rehabilitationists is not only that they alone offer the prospect of crime reduction (reducing the likelihood of future offending by someone who is known already to have committed an offence) while respecting the rights of the offender, but also that humane advances in penal systems have been introduced because of motivation towards rehabilitation (see especially Cullen and Gilbert 1982). Capital punishment and lengthy imprisonment may deter and will certainly incapacitate, and may well be thought to be proportionate punishments for a range of crimes by many people; rehabilitation, however, is only accomplished if criminals re-enter society, and so only rehabilitation would rule out these extreme punishments. This is argued as a matter not just of reason but also of empirical history: the advances in reducing and then abolishing capital punishment and physical torture, and of introducing more constructive regimes in prisons, were made in the era of rehabilitation. Conversely, as rehabilitation has become less fashionable, regimes in prisons have become less constructive, with more hours spent by prisoners inside their cells, and fewer workshops and educational classes.

One version of the new rehabilitationism ties it strongly to the sort of right to limited and proportionate punishment that is defended in deserts theory. For rehabilitationists, this is because of their recognition that it is only if rights are thus respected that rehabilitation can be effective (Rotman 1990). Any resentment at arbitrary release dates, at unequal and perceivedly unjust treatment, will get in the way of the receptiveness of offenders to rehabilitative programmes on offer. Rotman puts forward a 'rights-oriented' rehabilitation which concedes the offender's liability to punishment, but claims for her/him a corresponding 'right to an opportunity to return to society with a better chance of being a useful citizen and staying out of prison' (Rotman 1990: 183). This reference to the offender's right to be helped to become a better citizen is a key point in post-justice movement formulations, and is why the perspective is often referred to as *state-obligated rehabilitation*. In their defence against the onslaught of the back-to-justice lobby in the 1970s, Cullen and Gilbert argued that rehabilitation had only been tried patchily and half-heartedly, and, most important, that while there was an obligation on the part of offenders to participate in rehabilitative programmes, and sanctions in the form of refusal of parole if they did not do so, there was no similar obligation on the state to offer rehabilitative opportunities. In most prisons, certainly in the USA and in England and Wales, education, therapy, workshops, discussion groups and treatment of various kinds have been privileges not rights, and liable to curtailment in the interests of security or convenience. Prisoners can be removed from a prison where they are involved in a rehabilitative programme to one where the same facility is not available; programmes may be abandoned, workshops and classes closed, because of staff movement, security concerns, cash shortages, or political pressures for tougher regimes.

There are two versions of this state-obligated rehabilitation. One, the weaker form, is that if the state takes to itself the right to punish, it should ensure that it inflicts no more harm on the criminal than that intended when the sentence is pronounced. Thus, the intention of a prison sentence is deprivation of liberty – not loss of family ties, loss of responsibility for one's own decisions, loss of employability. The handicaps that are created by punishment, especially by imprisonment, should thus be offset by rehabilitative efforts (Gallo and Ruggiero 1991).

This version of new rehabilitationism is held by Rotman to be based on a right, acknowledged by most developed countries since the Second World War, of protection against 'cruel and unusual punishment'. Rotman argues that not to provide at least sufficient rehabilitative input to prevent the deterioration of prisoners through bad conditions, lack of contact with relatives and lack of education or work to preserve skills and employability, amounts to cruel and unusual punishment. He discusses the constitutional challenges made by prisoners in several states of the USA to the 'totality of conditions' in US prisons which because of overcrowding and lack of facilities inflict cruel and unusual punishment on inmates, and he also gives other examples of Western countries (Spain and Germany among them) where constitutional provision for respect for human rights in punishment can be held to be recognition of a 'right to rehabilitation' (Rotman 1990: 75ff.).

Cullen and Gilbert argue for rehabilitation to be an obligation on the state because this is the only way in which it could be effective; Rotman also argues that state obligation is necessary for effectiveness in helping prevent reoffending, and further that it is necessary for effectively translating constitutional principles into penal practices. A further reason for rehabilitation to be obligatory is provided by writers such as Carlen (1989) and Matthews (1989) who see rehabilitation within determinate sentences as the only penal rationale likely to lead to sanctions that could be properly reflective of the causes of crime. States have the right to punish offenders, they argue, because offenders do act out of choice; free will is a characteristic of human beings in normal societies, not just a legal fiction. On the other hand, choices are constrained by circumstances, and under certain social conditions people will turn to crime who in other social climates would remain law-abiding. Poverty, social and material inequalities, lack of psychiatric provision, drug and alcohol facilities, as well as experiences of abuse and harassment, lead people into crime. The state should thus recognize its role in crime causation, and its obligation towards crime prevention, by providing some rehabilitative elements in sanctions to help the offender refrain from further crime:

> A fundamental assumption of state-obligated rehabilitation would posit that as both offender and state might be more or less responsible for the breakdown of social relations which had resulted in crime, both had an obligation (more or less) to take action to reduce the likelihood of similar rupture in future.
>
> (Carlen 1989: 18)

The offender's part in the commission of the crime would be acknowledged by a corresponding obligation on her/him to participate in the rehabilitation on offer:

> so long as the state fulfilled its obligation to rehabilitate in a particular case the offender could be obliged to participate in any 'feasible' programme of rehabilitation or regulation (including, for instance, urine testing of drug-takers or electronic monitoring of other offenders). For *no* rehabilitative or regulatory programme would be rejected out of hand on the grounds of its being an essential violation of civil liberties or on the grounds of its being essentially lacking in feasibility. Rather, it would only be rejected on the grounds of its non-feasibility in a specific case.
>
> (ibid.: 20)

This formulation juxtaposes punishment and rehabilitation, with Carlen urging that punishment should be a 'primary aim' of sentencing only in cases where rehabilitation is irrelevant (ibid.: 20). Rehabilitation thus appears to be seen as an alternative to punishment, rather than as an aim to be achieved through mode of punishment. This version of state-obligated rehabilitation is a more thoroughgoing consequentialist, forward-looking perspective than the version advocated by Rotman, which is more of a true hybrid of utilitarian and desert approaches. If by 'punishment' Carlen and others writing from the same viewpoint mean retributive punishment, then this approach in its logic has much in common with the Australian, desert as fall-back, strategy. The main difference, of course, is that it proposes that the state's obligation towards prevention of future crime should be exercised through provision of rehabilitation rather than, for example, by provision of deterrent sentences. The argument thus rests on belief, widely shared by criminologists and sociologists, that crime rates are more influenced by social and economic policies than by penal policies (see, for example, Box and Hale 1982; Cohen 1985; Young and Matthews 1992).

These ideas are all in some way hybrids – using two principles instead of one to decide on the amount or mode of punishment – or compromises – having one primary principle, but allowing that in some cases its application should be tempered because of the claims of another principle, or because the primary principle is not appropriate. Thus desert may be compromised by the claims of deterrence or protection; rehabilitation may be compromised by its redundancy in some cases, when desert will be resorted to. They all, moreover, stay within the range of punishment goals contained in the traditional utilitarian or retributive theories. There are other ideas being put forward, however, which argue that the competing claims of the different positions can only be reconciled by appeal to some further ideal.

Targets and constraints: syntheses of Utilitarian and retributive theories

Critique of stark, arbitrary pre-modern retributive punishments gave rise to the consequentialist theories of Beccaria, Bentham and the positivists. In turn, disillusionment with rehabilitative punishments gave rise to the 'back-to-justice' movement, the re-espousal of retributive ideas in their contemporary form. The evolution of penal theory has thus followed the thesis–antithesis model of reasoning, whereby ideas call forth their opposites. One penal idea displaces another, with residues of the competing, superseded theory allowed as exceptions and compromises.

The next stage, the latest stage, is synthesis, in which some new theory appears which contains positive elements of both sides of the former argument. This type of theory invokes some new principle to be followed in all cases, not a principle for making exceptions or resolving conflicts. And while basically deserts theorists such as Robinson find accommodations with deterrence and protection, and basically rehabilitationists such as

Carlen and Cullen and Gilbert find a role for desert, other writers are putting forward ideas which go outside the bounds of the traditional justifications.

These penologists accept that compromises are always uneasy and entail the making of some important sacrifices. Desert will, in Robinson's formulation, have to be breached on those occasions when deterrence is to be given greater weight; prioritizing rehabilitation may mean that societies' retributive sentiments are left unsatisfied. Furthermore, compromises and hybrids may not satisfy the deficiencies inherent in any of the traditional justifications. The search for some other principle, which can incorporate both retributivist and utilitarian aims and insights, and can transcend their limitations, is therefore understandable and attractive.

One idea which has been put forward as a candidate overarching principle is *human rights* (Walker 1991; Cavadino and Dignan 1992). Like Utilitarians, human rights penologists believe that the competing claims of one penal goal against another can only be settled with reference to some wider political/moral theory. It is all very well to claim that desert should sometimes give way to deterrence or protection, or that rehabilitation should be offered within a desert-limited amount of punishment, but why should these claims be granted? There may be political or pragmatic arguments why one penal goal should not be pursued at the expense of all the others. For example, in the USA and in England and Wales after the passage of the 1991 Criminal Justice Act, desert policies have been undermined by political clamour for stronger punishments for persistent offenders, and so desert has given way to incapacitative strategies (Greenberg and Humphries 1980; Hudson 1995a). There is no real reason, however, why anyone who has been impressed by the strengths of deserts theorists' arguments *should* concede that there should be any cases in which desert should be disregarded in favour of any other goal in distribution of punishment, just as there is no reason, except in cases of anticipated barriers to effectiveness if deserts criteria are disregarded, why reductivists should adopt the constraints of deserved retribution. They might just as well try to defend their theory more vigorously, rather than yield to pressure to compromise. Only if some more fundamental goal which penal theory seeks to serve demands compromise, is there any principled (as opposed to pragmatic) necessity for it.

The fundamental objection to Utilitarianism as a general political theory, however, is that it allows for the sacrifice of the individual to the social good. It has been demonstrated in preceding chapters that it is extremely difficult for Utilitarians to rule out undeserved punishment (especially punishment undeserved because offences are anticipated rather than already committed, as well as punishment of the innocent, against which the definitional stop provides a stronger defence). This is because there is no principle to which Utilitarianism holds that rules that political action must ensure *to each individual*, as well as promoting for society as a whole, happiness, absence of pain, or any other benefit. The 'happiness' or 'good' which Utilitarianism seeks to promote is in any case undesirably vague, but even were that not the case, the lack of guarantee that the good is to be secured for each individual is a serious deficiency.

Human rights theory, on the other hand, proposes that there are certain rights which everyone has simply by virtue of being a human being. Human rights theory thus defends the claims of the individual against being sacrificed to some general social good. What these human rights are, of course, is a subject much debated by social philosophers. 'Life, liberty and the pursuit of happiness' is a familiar formulation, and the important point about it, in contrast to Utilitarianism, is that it provides for individuals to follow their own goals, rather than having governments deliver happiness to them. Individual freedom of action, as well as inviolateness of the person, is therefore the goal of human rights theory. As Cavadino and Dignan (1992: 53) put it, this theory sees human rights as 'a right – belonging equally to each human individual – to maximum "positive freedom", by which we mean the ability of people to make effective choices about their lives'.

Punishment is an obvious interference with this right, and therefore, as Cavadino and Dignan insist, needs special justification. The only justification can be that to allow unfettered exercise of an offender's right to positive freedom violates the positive freedom of another: the victim. This rationale is unashamedly forward-looking and crime-reductionist. Since the first interference with positive freedom has already happened, punishment is an unwarranted additional violation if it achieves no freedom-promoting purpose – it must, therefore, be orientated towards preventing further incursions by the offender into the rights of potential victims. Cavadino and Dignan then suggest that the distribution of punishment should be along the lines of Morris's desert maximum. Their reasons for adopting this retributive maximum are somewhat vague, but the Rawlsian arguments of the retributivists that were introduced in Chapter 3, to the effect that a desert system is the one which the offender would rationally choose because it is the system under which s/he could most surely avoid punishment by his/her own actions, would seem consistent with this notion of positive freedom.

Rights theorists do make one provision for departure from desert being an inviolate distributive principle because of its regard for the rights of offenders, and that is when the rights of offenders to freedom from more-than-commensurate punishments are overridden by rights of victims and potential victims to protection. This consideration was used by Bottoms and Brownsword in relation to sentences more than proportionate to the current offence for dangerous offenders. The main difference between rights theory and utilitarianism, it has been said, is that while the latter allows for disregarding of the individual's rights for the social good, the former only allows one individual's rights to be set aside or curtailed if not to do so would threaten the rights of another individual. The political and legal philosopher Dworkin applied this general principle to the compulsory detention of the mentally ill, and said that a person should only be detained against her/his will if s/he presents a 'vivid' danger to others (Dworkin 1977: 11). Applying this to dangerous criminals, Bottoms and Brownsword (1983) suggest they should only be given public-protection sentences if the danger they present is vivid. In place of the clinical 'vivid' danger, criminal law usually prefers the term 'clear and present danger'. Morris allows a similar exception to the desert limit in the normal case. This is, of course, vague, but is widely taken to mean that the offender in question has already committed a dangerous offence. Circumstances such as repeatedly targeting a certain kind of victim would increase both the presumption of dangerousness and the specificity of potential victims, so would certainly satisfy the requirement that the rights of an actual individual (the victim) should be threatened for another individual's (the offender's) rights to be overridden.

Human rights theory is claimed to be especially fruitful with regard to the question that proves so difficult for deserts theorists, that of the overall severity of penalty scales and, in particular, of disallowing certain kinds of punishment, notably capital punishment. If everyone, including offenders, has a right to life, then capital punishment is obviously a violation of this human right, however widely it may be held as the only commensurate punishment for some crimes, or however effective it may be as a deterrent. The right to protection from 'cruel', 'inhuman' or 'degrading' punishments rules out torture and punishments of public humiliation, and is used to argue against prison conditions such as overcrowding and lack of proper sanitation. Indeterminate sentences have also been held by some rights advocates to be 'cruel and unusual', and thus a link between rights and commensurate amounts of punishment is established (American Friends Service Committee 1972). This right is being drawn on, by lawyers in countries where human rights are constitutionally enshrined, to demand penal reform and, as we saw in the section on new rehabilitation, it is the foundation for *rights-based rehabilitation*.

Indeed, Rotman's version of new rehabilitation could as well be included in this section since he does see that rehabilitation can only be guaranteed, and has the best chance of effectiveness, if it is linked to human rights. It is the order of his argument – that he starts with rehabilitation and asks under what conditions it can be required and can be effective, rather than starting with human rights and asking what kinds of sanction would then be desirable and permissible – that leads me to place him with the new rehabilitationists rather than the human rights penologists. Rehabilitation along the lines proposed by Rotman could, however, well be the answer to the question of what kinds of punishment would be compatible with human rights theory, for this is the only rationale which aims to increase the offender's positive freedom by increasing her/his capacity for refraining from crime. Carlen's version of state-obligated rehabilitation may well conflict with human rights theory, since rights-derived rehabilitation would have to be consistent not just with whatever civil liberties were recognized by a society, but also with 'positive freedom'. Treatments such as psycho-surgery, mind-altering drugs and aversion therapy, which were objected to by civil rights critics of 1960s rehabilitation, would be proscribed by rights rehabilitation.

These limits on rehabilitation or any other penal goal are established because human rights theory holds that

1 there are some forms or degrees of severity which are so 'cruel' or 'inhuman' or 'degrading' that people have a right never to be subjected to them;
2 that they have this right regardless of what utility or desert seems to dictate.

(Walker 1991: 133)

Human rights theory thus establishes, first, that the general justification of punishment is indeed crime reduction, that punishment for its own sake is unjustified; and second, that some limits to punishment are guaranteed by human rights, and that these limits cannot be set aside for any crime reduction or talionic purpose. It is, therefore, an extremely helpful advance towards a secure and principled synthesis of reductivism in justification and retributivism in distribution.

A theory that has many similarities with the human rights perspective is Braithwaite and Pettit's (1990) agenda for *republican* criminal justice. They, too, see that the different purposes and principles can only be reconciled by reference to a general political theory. Like the human rights theorists, they too reject Utilitarianism as being insufficiently careful of the rights of offenders. Their preferred political perspective is republicanism, which, they claim, offers a conception of human rights and liberties which is preferable to that of rival traditions, such as social contract liberalism, in that it sees the values that must be promoted and protected as those that arise for the individual in society. The liberal perspective on rights sees the individual as free if s/he is protected from encroachment by other individuals; the republican ideal sees the individual as free if s/he is participating on a full, equal basis with others. The republican ideal, then, is full citizenship in a free society (Braithwaite and Pettit 1990: 57), the enjoyment of which they call *dominion*. Dominion, they argue, is preferable to apparently similar terms such as autonomy, because it carries the connotation of participating alongside others, whereas autonomy connotes a separateness of the individual from others.

Punishment interferes with freedom in its negative and positive, liberal and republican senses, and so for Braithwaite and Pettit, as for the human rights theorists, punishment can only be justified if it promotes desired consequences – that is, if it enhances dominion overall. Like rights theorists, and in contrast to the Utilitarians, republican theorists also insist that the threat to dominion posed by an offender must be a threat to another individual, and like rights theorists and deserts theorists, they argue that the reduction in dominion to an offender resulting from punishment must be balanced by increased dominion to another individual: what all these approaches have in common is that rights – or dominion – are due to each individual, including offenders, and individual dominion cannot be curtailed in the name of some unspecified general threat or general good.

Republican theory, like rights theory, is thus different from Utilitarianism because of republicanism's upholding of the claims of individuals against society. It is different from desert in recognizing that principles of distribution should not be allowed to override general – consequentialist – purposes, and therefore no principle of distribution, including desert, can be inviolable.

The egalitarianism of Braithwaite and Pettit's republican political theory means that treating offenders equally has a strong claim on them, as it has on deserts theorists. They see the demands of equality and the necessity of limits on pursuit of crime reduction – key tenets of deserts theories – as values which are implied by ideas of republicanism and its operational concept, the promotion of dominion, and so put them forward as *restraints* on the pursuit of *goals* through criminal justice. Like most of the theorists discussed in this chapter (Robinson being the exception), they therefore give desert the role of setter of upper limits to punishment, but, like Morris, they advocate parsimony as preferable to proportionality in sentencing decisions in actual cases. Parsimony is for them the 'master principle' (Braithwaite and Pettit 1990: 87) because even though punishment may be being inflicted purposively, the increases to dominion are speculative and distant, whereas the damage to the offender's dominion is certain and immediate. Their preference for parsimony is not, therefore, reliant on their argument, cited above, that it is more consistent with equality than is proportionality. They are even more thoroughgoing adherents of parsimony than Morris, however, because they do not allow a desert minimum of punishment: any punishment that does not serve dominion-promoting purposes, they see as unjustified.

Braithwaite and Pettit elaborate their theory of republican justice after explaining that any penological theory must adopt a goal which is capable of being uncontroversially accepted within the relevant moral community (a condition similar to Rawls's reflective equilibrium); that it should be stabilizing of a fair allocation of rights, and that it should be satiable. Crime prevention, they suggest, may be uncontroversially accepted by most members of society, but it generates huge inequalities in rights, as for example in incapacitative strategies when the greater the respect for rights of potential victims, the greater the diminution of rights of offenders. If the criterion for granting parole, for instance, was that there should be no risk of future crime, then almost no one would be paroled; it is only if pursuit of crime prevention is limited by some other consideration that there is any balance between offenders' rights and potential victims' rights. On the other hand, concern with rehabilitation may be (and is often said to be) unduly insensitive to victims, for example if convicted sex offenders are allowed to live near victims for the sake of the offenders' reintegration into society and maintenance of existing ties. It is only, according to Braithwaite and Pettit, a concept such as dominion that allows for an equilibrium of safeguarding of both victims' and offenders' interests. Goals promoted through criminal justice must also, they insist, be satiable. Crime prevention is inherently insatiable, as can be seen in the USA and in England and Wales where demands for tough action on crime have led to more and more punishment, yet where crime rates go on rising and crime becomes more and more violent. Dominion, they claim, is satiable, as long as it is recognized that the loss in dominion involved in punishment is balanced by promotion of dominion through crime prevention efforts.

Braithwaite and Pettit argue that the import of their theory is that punishment should be employed much less than is usual, especially in England and Wales, the USA and Australia in the 1990s. If punishment does not prevent crime, then it should not be inflicted, if the purpose of criminal justice is to promote dominion. They urge, first, that levels of punishment made available by penal legislation should be reduced until there are significant, and demonstrably linked, rises in crime rates. Second, they urge the development, and use in more and more cases, of non-punitive responses to crime. In this they share a preference of many penal progressives, especially those whose orientation is to human rights, for *restorative* rather than punitive responses to crime (de Haan 1990).

The restorative approach stresses that punishment is an ineffective means of securing the goods that are claimed as the justification for penal sanctions. Not only, as the new rehabilitationists argue, can reductions in crime rates be achieved more effectively through social and economic policies than through punishment, but restoring the rights (or dominion, or advantages) of victims can be more effectively secured by compensation or reparation. Victims whose property is stolen or damaged lose the right to, or advantage of, its use: compensation gives them the wherewithal to replace the property. Compensation could be by the offender, or if s/he does not have the means, by the state. In the case of crimes of physical violence, the victim loses the right to move about without fear, and this can best be restored by mediation between victim and offender. If the criminal can be brought to realize the impact of the crime on the victim; if s/he demonstrates contrition through some sort of reparative action, then the victim's fear may be lessened. If the offender is punished, then the fear of the victim, or of similarly placed potential victims, may be increased, because the offender may have added resentment at the punishment to whatever impulses led to the crime in the first place.

Braithwaite and Pettit, like Cavadino and Dignan and others writing from the same general perspective, urge that in most cases the first choice of response to crime should be voluntary restitution or compensation by the offender to the victim, and where this is not feasible (the offender does not have the money to replace property) the victim should receive state compensation and there should be some act of reparation by the offender. Imprisonment or hospital detention should only be used where there is demonstrable need for public protection, and non-custodial penalties such as probation or community service should only be imposed where the offender is unwilling to make reparation.

Other penologists are engaged in similar attempts to reformulate the goals which punishment should serve so as to include the values defended by deserts theorists as limitations on consequentialist approaches. The 'good' which is identified as being the goal which should be followed by all legal, social and political action is variously termed *communitarianism* (Lacey 1988), *social justice* (Hudson 1993) as well as human rights and republicanism, but whatever the term selected, there is a shared belief that rights are due to all individuals, and individual rights should not be sacrificed to the general good; that punishment which is not facilitative of some future good is unjustified; and that the 'good' to be promoted and protected by criminal justice must be consistent with a general obligation of social policies and institutions to promote people's participation in society as free and equal citizens.

Conclusion

This chapter has looked at some ideas for reconciling the conflicts between consequentialist and retributivist principles in practice, and for incorporating the strengths and remedying the deficiencies of these different theories of punishment. After the apparent triumph of retributivism in the 1980s, the 1990s appear to be witnessing a re-emergence of consequentialist approaches, to the extent that even deserts writers such as von Hirsch (1993) are making it clearer than in their earlier works that they are retributivists only in distribution, not in general justification. Whether this is a compromise with consequentialism or 'a quiet conversion to it', as Walker (1991: 119) judges it to be, is debatable, but certainly retributivists are more comfortable in acknowledging consequentialist purposes than they previously seemed to be. At the same time, the latest formulations of rehabilitationism, such as Rotman's, incorporate the values of deserts theories much more firmly than did the first reaffirmations of rehabilitation appearing after the just-deserts and get-tough movements had between them appeared to destroy the credibility of rehabilitation so thoroughly (Cullen and Gilbert 1982).

Whether another general political theory will replace Utilitarianism as the source of penal purposes remains to be seen, but in the mid-1990s human rights appeared the most promising candidate. Political developments such as the end of the cold war and the need to find a basis for the legitimacy of international action by organizations such as the United Nations and the European Union gave impetus to the development of theorizing about human rights. As concern for human rights generally develops, it would scarcely be surprising if it became a generally accepted standard for evaluating the practices of criminal justice in different countries. Furthermore, as criminal justice becomes more international, with more transnational crime such as terrorism and drug-trafficking, and with the establishment of bodies such as the European Court of Human Rights, such a standard seems bound to grow in influence.

chapter five

Restorative justice: diversion, compromise or replacement discourse?

Introduction
Definitions, principles and models
The range and limits of restorative justice
Retribution, rights and restorative justice
Conclusion

Introduction

During the 1990s, and continuing in the 2000s, restorative justice has been one of the most rapidly proliferating criminal justice innovations. At the start of the 1990s, restorative justice was confined to the margins of criminal justice policy and practice, and although its principles were enthusiastically promoted by its advocates, restorative justice was more of a movement than a theorized approach to punishment. By the end of the decade, it had emerged as a full-blown model of justice, with its principles clarified; with a sounder theoretical base; and with evaluations, critiques and debates appearing in the penological literature. In the 2000s, although its principles are well understood, its range of applications and its pro- cedural standards and safeguards continue to be unresolved issues. The two sets of questions are closely connected, since if it is to be used as a diversion from justice for offenders who would otherwise be cautioned or expect a sentence of the lowest severity, the safeguards necessary will be different from those that would be necessary if it is to become a major form of criminal justice, a 'replacement discourse' dealing with the full range of offenders and offences (Hudson 2002a).

Restorative justice has been advocated from several different directions (Daly and Immarigeon 1998). Firstly, there were the penal abolitionists, who wanted to replace traditional notions of crime and punishment with principles of *harm* and *redress*, and who had been prompted to move away from the abolitionists' stance of not proposing alternative forms of penality because of the increasing punitiveness of penal policy and practice (Mathiesen 1974; de Haan 1990; Hudson 1998). Secondly, there were those who were concerned to make criminal justice more responsive to the needs and the suffering of victims, who took as their starting point the argument that formal criminal justice disempowered and often excluded victims by not allowing them to describe their suffering in their own words, only having a part in the process if and insofar as they were asked to give evidence that the court decided was relevant (Christie 1977). Restorative justice developed as a way of making victims central to criminal justice without becoming more punitive and repressive to offenders. Although victims are at the heart of restorative justice concerns, it is not simply a part of the victim movement; it is proposed as a way of avoiding the zero–sum thinking that what helps victims must hurt offenders (Zimring 2001; Hudson 2002b). Another direction from which restorative justice has been advocated is from 'first nation' groups and people working with them, who wish to retain the values and traditions of their justice processes. These groups also wanted to challenge the prosecution and sentencing processes of white justice which have continually resulted in over-representation of minority groups in prosecution and imprisonment rates. The Maori tradition in New Zealand and 'first nation' traditions in Canada have been particularly influential, as have the traditions of some religious groups, such as the Canadian Mennonites.

As restorative justice programmes have proliferated, there has been more attention to agreeing definitions and principles, and to elaborating underpinning theories. As it has come to be more widespread and to be coming in from the criminal justice margins, more attention has been given to views about the appropriate range of applications, and questions of its relationship to more established forms of criminal justice. Should it apply only to juvenile offenders or also to adults? Should it apply only to offences up to specified levels of seriousness or to all kinds of offences? Is it an alternative to retributive justice, or is retribution an element of restorativeness or at least compatible with restorativeness? What concern should restorative justice programmes have with values such as proportionality and due process? These matters are receiving increasing attention in theory and in policy.

A sign of the importance being accorded to restorative justice and its widespread and increasing use in a range of settings is the adoption in April 2000, by the 10th United Nations Congress on Crime Prevention and Criminal Justice in Vienna, of a resolution calling upon member states to incorporate the principle of restoration in their criminal justice systems. In preparation for the Congress, the UN Alliance of Nongovernmental Organizations developed a set of basic principles for restorative justice programmes which were accepted by the Congress (United Nations 2000; van Ness 2002).

This chapter will present an overview of the principles of restorative justice and of the issues of theory and principle that have been the subject of debate between proponents of restorative justice and critics and commentators from other penological perspectives. Important and comprehensive overviews of restorative justice theory, policy and effectiveness are provided by Braithwaite (1999) and Kurki (2000). As well as evaluating restorative justice as a general penological perspective and restorative justice programmes in practice, Braithwaite is concerned to defend his own theoretical model of restorative justice. Kurki provides a more general, non-partisan review, which includes information on North American programmes, in addition to the Australian and New Zealand schemes which are rather better known in the UK. Important reviews of restorative justice in Australia and in New Zealand are provided by Daly (2002a) and Morris (2002), respectively.

Definition, principles and models

The proponents and programmes of restorative justice are too diverse for there to be an agreed definition, but the essence is that it signifies a process in which offenders, victims, their representatives and representatives of the community come together to agree a response to a crime (see the special issue on 'Defining Restorative Justice' in vol. 3 of *Contemporary Justice Review*, 2000). Braithwaite cites the working party of non-governmental organizations in preparation for the UN Congress on Crime Prevention and Criminal Justice, which found the most acceptable definition to be:

> Restorative justice is a process whereby all the parties with a stake in a particular offense come together to resolve collectively how to deal with the aftermath of the offense and its implications for the future.
>
> (Braithwaite 1999: 5)

A definition which states the aims very clearly, as well as describing the process by which they are to be achieved, is van Ness's explanation that the purpose of restorative justice is

> the restoration into safe communities of victims and offenders who have resolved their conflicts.
>
> (van Ness 1993: 258)

The important strands common to these two definitions are the emphasis on process as much as outcome; the equal emphasis on victims, offenders and communities; the emphasis on relationships; and the forward-looking consequentialism of the approach.

Restorative justice processes include victim–offender mediation; family–group conferences; meetings of offenders, victims and community representatives; sentencing circles; and restorative cautioning schemes. On some definitions, state-imposed punishments such as community service or compensation would be included because the penalties include some element of restitution to victim and/or community, but on many definitions they would not because they are generally imposed as part of a traditional sentencing procedure, rather than agreed in a restorative conference or meeting. Some programmes are police-led; some programmes are led by specially trained facilitators, often representing non-profit 'alternative' criminal justice organizations, and some are led by community organizations, especially in areas of semi-autonomous indigenous or minority peoples. Restorative processes are sometimes an adjunct to, or part of established criminal justice systems, such as restorative cautioning in England and Wales. Elsewhere they may be introduced in places where traditional criminal justice is thought to lack legitimacy, or is associated with oppressive and discredited regimes. Examples include the introduction of restorative justice projects to replace paramilitary punishments of members of their communities in Northern Ireland, and of their introduction to deal with youth crime in South Africa, providing an alternative to the 'white man's justice' of the apartheid era (McEvoy and Mika 2002); (Skelton 2002).

The principles proposed for adoption by the UN cover aims, scope and standards for operation (van Ness 2002). They are inclusive in the sense that they cover most of the outcomes and most of the processes that have at any time been described as restorative. The first principle states that a 'restorative justice programme' is any programme that uses restorative processes or aims to achieve restorative outcomes. A 'restorative outcome' is defined as any programme or response designed to accomplish reparation to the victim and community and reintegration of the victim and offender, while 'restorative process' is defined as any process in which victim, offender, and any individuals or community members affected by the crime participate together in a process to resolve matters arising from the crime, usually with the help of a fair and impartial third party. Having defined the meaning of restorative outcomes and restorative processes, further principles provide that participation should be with the free and voluntary consent of the parties; that participants should be able to withdraw at any time; that agreements should contain only reasonable and proportionate obligations; that the basic facts of the case should be acknowledged by all parties; that power imbalances on the basis of age or intellectual capacity should be addressed; that participants should have access to legal counsel and be advised of their rights; that undue pressure should not be brought on any party to agree to participate or to agree outcomes; that discussions should be confidential; that failure to reach agreement may result in referral back to formal judicial processes but should not be used as justification for a more severe sentence in subsequent legal proceedings; that facilitators should be recruited from all sections of the community and should be impartial, ensuring that parties act with respect towards each other, and that facilitators should provide a safe and comfortable environment (van Ness 2002).

These basic principles are agreed by most people involved as advocates or as practitioners of restorative justice programmes. They are general enough to accommodate a wide variety of projects: for example, the section on the 'facilitator' would support police-led, professional facilitator-led, or community representative-led schemes. Similarly, the principles say nothing about the range of restorative justice, whether it should be a state or an informal proceedings, and they make fairly vague references to due process issues. While there is nothing in the principles with which most restorative justice theorists and practitioners would disagree, many would want to augment them – for example, by adding avoidance of power imbalances linked to race or gender to the possibilities of oppression in proceedings which facilitators should guard against. The principles also support a wide variety of restorative justice process models.

The two most influential models are those in operation in New Zealand and in Australia. Family Group Conferences, on the New Zealand model, emphasize participation by family members of the offender. As well as the family, conference participants include the victim, a police representative, a youth advocate (if one has been appointed) and anyone else whom the family wishes to have present. The conference is arranged by a Youth Justice Co-ordinator, who acts as facilitator and mediator. Usually, the police representative outlines the offence, and if the offender agrees the basic facts and admits involvement, then the victim outlines the impact of the offence, and views are put forward as to how the offence should be dealt with. The family then holds further discussions in private, after which the conference reconvenes to see if recommendations and plans for reparation and controls to reduce the likelihood of reoffending, proposed by the family, can be agreed. The Australian Wagga model involves meetings of the family, friends and other supporters of the victim and the offender and any other community members who may be affected by the offence, who hold their discussions together. Like the New Zealand model, the offence must be admitted and the basic details agreed before a conference can be held as an alternative to criminal justice proceedings. In the Wagga model, the facilitator/co-ordinator is a police officer or someone appointed by the police, and the discussions follow a prescribed script. This model has been adopted in Canberra (Australian Capital Territory), where conferences can proceed without victims or with community representatives standing in for victims, if the victim does not want to be involved.

The English model of 'restorative cautioning' introduced by the Thames Valley Police approximates most closely to this Canberra model, in that it is police-led, although there is some debate as to whether this really is restorative justice or whether it is 'cautioning plus'. This is because the process is used for offenders who would otherwise be cautioned (a formal warning administered by a police officer, as an alternative to prosecution), and who are given some reparative imposition (which may be anything from an apology to some work for the victim or community) to 'make amends' for the offence. Although there is some evidence that the existence of this option is encouraging more use of cautioning as an alternative to prosecution than would otherwise be the case, fears of 'net-widening' – using the scheme for young people who would otherwise have no formal, recorded action taken against them – and 'net strengthening' – some form of reparative imposition accompanying the caution, for those who would have been cautioned in any event – remain (see Young 2001, for an evaluation of the Thames Valley scheme and an overview of police-led schemes more generally).

Outside the Australian Capital Territory, other Australian states have introduced schemes more or less closely resembling the New Zealand or Wagga models, with South Australia following the New Zealand model most closely. Programmes in Europe, the USA and elsewhere have also been influenced by the New Zealand and Wagga initiatives.

Variety in restorative justice practice reflects variety in its theoretical underpinnings, but there are some general, fundamental strands. Christie's idea that formal criminal justice 'steals' conflicts from their rightful owners – victims and offenders – by redefining them as crimes against the state has come together with more recent theories of community justice (Clear and Karp 1999). Community justice has been described as a philosophy of justice, a strategy of justice, and a series of justice programmes:

> As a philosophy, community justice is based on its pursuit of a vision of justice recognizing that crime and the problems of crime are a central impediment to community quality of life. Thus the community justice approach seeks not only to respond to criminal events, but also to set as a goal the improvement of quality of community life, especially for communities afflicted by high levels of crime. Strategically, the community justice approach combines three contemporary justice innovations: community policing, environmental crime prevention, and restorative justice.
>
> (Clear and Cadora 2001: 60–1)

This fits the extension of restorative justice in England and Wales, where it has moved from being an experiment introduced by an individual enthusiast (the then Chief Constable of Thames Valley Police) to something much more widely adopted as part of the development of a community safety strategy. The Crime and Disorder Act 1998 and the Youth Justice and Criminal Evidence Act 1999 both called for use of restorative justice processes (Dignan 1999; Holdaway *et al.* 2001; Crawford and Newburn 2002). The reforms to youth justice announced in the 1999 Act were specifically presented as a move away from 'exclusionary punitive justice and towards an inclusionary restorative justice' (Muncie 2000: 14). All forms of restorative justice involve some transfer of process responsibility and punitive power from state to community, and in important ways displace the state as victim by the community as well as by the actual individual victim. Recognition of the community as one of the parties with an interest in the crime and consequent measures is introduced: in restorative justice the community, as distinct from the state, has rights. The community also becomes a resource for ensuring the future safety of the victims and reintegration of the offender, as Braithwaite suggests graphically when he talks of the 'Uncle Harrys' who can be enlisted to be with offenders in circumstances where they may be tempted to reoffend – stopping them driving home after a session in the pub, for example (Braithwaite 1999: 67).

Another important theoretical strand is the emphasis on relationships (Burnside and Baker 1994). Restorative justice emphasizes 'right relationships' rather than 'right rules' (Zehr 1990). The important task of justice is to restore the balance to relationships that have been damaged by crime (victim–offender; victim–offender–community; offender–community; offender–family) rather than making sure that the correct legal rule is followed, and that it is interpreted and applied correctly. What might be called relational morality is an important element of much of feminist jurisprudence (see Chapter 10). It is also a significant element in critiques of liberal theories of justice that have come from critical legal theorists, from communitarians and from feminist political and legal theorists (Minow 1990; Young 1990; Fraser and Lacey 1993). Such critics charge that liberal theories are based on the idea of individualist, atomized selves, 'unencumbered' by the context of relationships and the values of the community in which they live their lives. Relational theories point out that status differences between people – black/white, male/female, offender/victim – arise in the context of social relationships. So, for example, a child learns that it is black through the way in which it is treated by its school companions and others it comes into contact with; males and females develop gender identity through experience of same-sex and different-sex relationships. The crux of restorative justice is that offenders will come to think of themselves as having done wrong and will want to change their behaviour through recognizing the real harm they have done to an actual victim. Taking responsibility for their behaviour, which is the primary aim of restorative justice, depends first and foremost on recognizing a relationship with the victim, a relationship in which they have harmed and the other party has been harmed, and then being willing to undertake reparative work to restore an equilibrium in the relationship so that it is no longer one of harming and being harmed.

These theoretical strands are just that: strands rather than a full-blown theory. A social-criminological theory for restorative justice is provided by John Braithwaite's idea of *reintegrative shaming* (Braithwaite 1989). Reintegrative shaming theory suggests that crime will be reduced if society is structured so that people feel ashamed of bad behaviour, and if people who do things of which they are ashamed are not made to feel permanently excluded from society. The first principle is that societies should have clear moral standards, and that would-be offenders are aware that the contemplated behaviour would be disapproved of by those they care about, as well as by the wider society. The second principle requires that reactions to bad behaviour should concentrate on the wrongness and harmfulness of the behaviour, and should not make wrongdoers feel that they are totally worthless. The paradigm is that of the good parent, who makes it very clear that bad behaviour is wrong and cannot be ignored, but who nevertheless continues to love the child and brings some closure to the incident: normal relationships resume after an apology or some other form of atonement has been made. Braithwaite explains that in restorative justice processes,

> discussion of the consequences of the crime for victims (or consequences for the offender's family) structures shame into the conference; the support of those who enjoy the strongest relationships of love or respect with the offender structures reintegration into the ritual.
>
> (1999: 39)

Discussion of the offence and its consequences in restorative justice proceedings means that there cannot be any denial by the offender of the hurt, and the standard victim-blaming justifications (she was asking for it; he started it) by which offenders characteristically avoid acknowledging the wrongness of the act cannot be allowed to stand. Reintegrative shaming aims to inculcate a sense of shame for the behaviour rather than annoyance at being caught, and to bring about a desire to make amends rather than the resentment of being punished which is the more likely outcome with standard criminal justice. Braithwaite summarizes the core claim of reintegrative shaming as being that more crime is likely to result from tolerance of crime, and from disrespectful shaming which treats the offender as an outcast; reintegrative shaming expresses clear, unambiguous disapproval of the offence by people whose opinions matter, but offers the offender a way of being reaccepted as an equal member of the community.

Braithwaite's theory has been extremely influential, although, as he says himself, restorative justice practices have been carried out throughout history: the processes of aboriginal peoples, the religious traditions of 'hating the sin and loving the sinner', experiments in 'alternative conflict resolution' in the USA and elsewhere in the 1970s, and the experiments with family conferencing in New Zealand and other jurisdictions proceeded before or without reference to his publication of the theory. While some projects (the Canberra programme) are very consciously based on reintegrative shaming and designed to test effects (the Reintegrative Shaming Experiments (RISE) project randomly assigns appropriate offenders to court or to the Canberra programme), other restorative justice theorists and practitioners do not see 'shaming' as a proper aim for justice processes of any kind (Walgrave and Aertsen 1996). Admitting responsibility and wanting to make amends, on this view, is not exactly the same as the more internal, psychological state of 'shame'. Whatever the nuances of shame or responsibility, admitting the harmfulness of the offence, listening to the victim, reparation and measures to reduce the likelihood of reoffending, arrived at in an atmosphere that is respectful of both victim and offender and which offers possibilities of reintegration to the offender, are general and agreed elements of restorative justice.

The range and limits of restorative justice

Restorative justice is being adopted and advocated as a response to minor offending by young offenders; to all offending (except murder and manslaughter) by young offenders; to minor offending by adult as well as young offenders; and to all but the most serious offences by all offenders. It is seen as a diversion from formal criminal justice; as a useful additional criminal justice option; or as a 'replacement discourse' , entirely displacing the values and practices of established criminal justice. Those who see it as a total replacement discourse are perhaps more properly classed as abolitionists, in that they want to dismantle the criminal justice system as it has been since the rise of modern industrial societies (abolitionism is discussed in Chapter 10). In this section I want to look at the arguments used by those who debate its range and limitations in the context of a continuing criminal justice system. The main points of contention are whether restorative justice is appropriate for adult offenders as well as young offenders, and whether it is appropriate for serious as well as minor offences. Arguments about the levels of seriousness for which restorative justice is appropriate and feasible which have considered its potential for responding to sexual offences have been the most revealing in terms of the assumptions they demonstrate about the nature of restorative justice and the place they see it occupying within criminal justice.

The least controversial use of restorative justice is as an alternative to court proceedings for young offenders convicted of offences of minor and medium-range seriousness. This puts restorative justice firmly in the tradition of diversionary innovations, of which cautioning has been the most widespread and lasting. It also fits with the tradition in many jurisdictions of dealing with young offenders by a panel, conducted in less formal language than that used in courts, and considering welfare and educational matters as well as the offence itself, such as the Scottish children's hearing system. The aims are to do something constructive that encourages young offenders to recognize the wrongness of their actions and to accept responsibility for changing their future behaviour, and providing victims with an apology and some sort of reparation, while at the same time avoiding the stigmatizing effects and possible reduction in non-criminal life chances resulting from possession of a criminal record.

Restorative justice is used for a wider range of offences in some jurisdictions than in others. South Australia, New Zealand, and Bethlehem, in the US state of Pennsylvania, are among the programmes reviewed by Young (2001), and he reports conferences and panels dealing with more serious offences than in the Thames Valley scheme. In such programmes, the rationale is even more strongly diversionary than in the English example. If restorative justice is being used in place of cautioning, it is arguably diverting young people into the system, in that it is involving them in a hearing rather than a warning delivered by one officer, and it is imposing some form of reparation rather than the warning standing alone; but where it is being used as an alternative to court proceedings for more serious offences, it is more unambiguously diversionary.

Maxwell and Morris (2001) report on two New Zealand projects dealing with adult offenders, mainly convicted of property offences. These authors endorse the diversionary aim of restorative justice as valid for adults as well as juveniles, but they also claim that restorative justice can be more effective in reducing repeat offending than court proceedings and the sentences resulting from them. They present some evidence of success, but are not able to distinguish whether this success was due to the nature of the restorative proceedings – inducing a sense of responsibility and remorse – or to the lack of the damaging effects of deeper penetration into the criminal justice system. In any case, the point here is that the reason for using restorative justice continues to incorporate the idea of diversion from normal criminal justice procedures.

It is this idea of restorative justice as diversion that is at the root of arguments against its use for very serious offences, and the arguments have been most clearly pursued in relation to gendered and sexualized offending. The argument is that sexual assault and domestic violence have been tolerated for too long, and that although these crimes are now more generally condemned, they remain underpenalized. Feminists and others who campaign for these behaviours to be taken more seriously want the most robust forms of justice available; they want forms of justice that will combine strong censure with effective incapacitative action. What they most emphatically do not want is diversion, and so they will be opposed to the use of restorative justice if they understand it as diversion, if it is assumed that: 'Conferencing represents the most recent entrant into a long list of previous attempts to "divert" violence against women and into the hands of others' (Lewis *et al.* 2001: 123). As long as restorative justice is advocated as diversion, then it will be seen to have a quite narrow range of applications, and will remain on the margins of criminal justice.

Those who do advocate use of restorative justice for sexual and domestic violence, and for other serious offences, are not doing so because they wish these types of behaviour to be diverted from criminal justice processing. Daly (2002b), in reviewing the effectiveness of restorative justice in South Australia, gives careful consideration to the appropriateness of its use in cases of sexual assault. Although the incidents she reports concern young offenders, she is clear that the objective in such cases is not diversion, but to make the offenders appreciate the behaviour as wrong and as harmful, and to help the victim feel that their hurt matters, and that the family of the victim and other members of the community will be actively involved in trying to ensure that the offender does not repeat the harm.

   Proponents of restorative justice in serious cases, then, are arguing for it not as diversion, but as effective justice (Hudson 2002a). A starting point is often the failure of criminal justice to prosecute and convict in more than a small proportion of sexual assault and domestic violence cases (Snider 1998). The frequent lack of corroborative evidence, the ordeal of cross-examination, the fear of provoking more attacks if the offender is angry with the victim for calling the police and then going through with prosecution – there are many reasons why conventional criminal justice, even when society in general feels that these crimes should be taken more seriously, finds it difficult to provide effective remedies. Even if convictions are obtained, offenders may not be challenged about the attitudes which prompted the crime; indeed, they may have these attitudes reinforced through a combination of resentment at conviction and being punished in ways which reinforce sexist and aggressive values (Hudson 1998). Restorative justice's principles of condemnation of the behaviour, acknowledging harm and putting measures in place to prevent reoffending, it is argued, offer a prospect of more effective justice than has been secured until now.

   Another misconception about restorative justice which leads to its being seen as inappropriate for these kinds of offences is that it is the same as mediation. Critics charge that restorative justice is based on a 'logic of mediation', and that this logic not only fails to offer condemnation and protection, but also dissolves the distinctiveness of victim and offender, and casts the behaviour not as a crime, but as a relationship difficulty, a distorted communication, or a failure to grasp reciprocal perspectives (Cobb 1997). While there is undoubtedly a relational basis to restorative justice, there is no necessary dilution of the criminality of the behaviour, or the identities of offender and victim.

   This argument about the logic of mediation is at odds with the conditions for the operation of restorative justice put forward by most of those who advocate its use in sexual and domestic violence cases. Rather than expecting a coming together of views of the offence, it is recognized that in most cases there are two distinct perspectives, his and hers (Finstad 1990). In such circumstances, the victim's perspective is to be primary, and it is part of the advantages claimed for restorative justice that the conference process means that the offender will hear the victim's account vindicated and supported by people they themselves respect (Morris and Gelsthorpe 2000). Most supporters of restorative justice for such cases stipulate that the conference or meeting cannot go ahead unless the offender at least admits guilt and a minimal willingness to apologize, and also that the offender cannot include as supporters anyone with pronounced sexist views. In her evaluation of the South Australia programme Daly (2002a) writes that movement towards awareness and acceptance of the other's perspective is involved in the concept of restorativeness, but that does not imply a merging of perspectives or some sort of meeting in the middle.

   The depiction of restorative justice contained in those critical works which oppose its extension to sexualized and domestic violence and/or other serious forms of crime, is very different from the account of restorative justice given by Braithwaite (1999) or the other proponents and sympathetic reviewers cited here. Objecting to the extension of restorative justice on the grounds that it is 'merely' diversion or mediation fails to recognize that conferences result in measures – sometimes quite demanding – to secure the safety of victims in the future. One difficulty is that restorative justice writers tend to avoid the word 'punishment', and there is some of the euphemism of old-style rehabilitation, which talked about 'treatment' when what was imposed in the name of treatment was experienced as punishment by the offenders (Hudson 2002b). Another is that evaluations of effectiveness in preventing reoffending talk about process – conference or court – and usually do not compare results on the basis of the 'measures' or sentence imposed. There is often no indication whether the combination of reparative impositions and treatment/education oriented to the circumstances producing the crime (addictions, unemployment, etc.) is being compared with cases which resulted in short prison sentences, fines, or community penalties involving similar treatment or re-educative components. More careful evaluation research needs to be conducted to ascertain the balance of conference, reparation and treatment that is more effective than, or as effective as, conventional court proceedings plus different kinds of sentence.

Another way in which restorative justice might do well to limit itself is in the claims it makes for itself. Daly and Immarigeon (1998) argue persuasively that the modest but significant gains that can properly be claimed for restorative justice might be overlooked or undermined because of very grandiose claims that could not be tested, still less validated. One claim that seems to be supported by all studies of restorative justice in practice is that offenders and their families find the process fairer than conventional criminal justice, and feel that they are allowed to put their point of view. Victims also confirm that they feel enabled to give their accounts of the crime in a way they find satisfactory; they usually report the proceedings as being less intimidating than they had feared, and say that they felt comfortable and supported. Even fears that police-led conferences would mean that police dominated proceedings, with police facilitators treating offenders disrespectfully, pushing them to admit crimes they had not committed and to give information on others they were involved with but had not been charged with, and not allowing offenders' families to say what they wanted to say, have receded as restorative justice has become more established (Braithwaite 1999; Young 2001). Offenders, especially young offenders, gaining respect for criminal justice processes is an extremely worthwhile outcome.

Daly (2002a) challenges the more excessive claims that are occasionally made for restorative justice: she has not seen, she states, road-to-Damascus-style total attitude change in any of the conferences she has observed. Similarly, Braithwaite comments that his observations led him to conclude that restorative justice ideals of forming a 'community of care' for both victims and offenders, putting in place measures to meet the needs of both, remain as 'empty ideals in all the restorative justice programs of which I have experience' (Braithwaite 1999: 69).

Another sense in which the range and limits of restorative justice remain undecided is that of whether it is to be avilable on a one-off basis, as a first rung on a punitive ladder, or whether it is to be the principle philosophy throughout the punitive ladder. Braithwaite (1997; Ayres and Braithwaite 1992; Braithwaite and Daly 1994) has outlined the idea of an 'enforcement pyramid'. This would see an escalation of punitive response if an offender repeated the crime, or did not carry out the reparative and safety measures agreed at the conference. Ultimately, a repeat offender or a non-complying offender could be diverted back to conventional court processes and could face imprisonment. The relationship between restorative justice and court processes suggested here is that of formal criminal justice as a 'big stick', which would be wielded less frequently than presently, but which would remain in the shadows, ready for use when needed.

In a further elaboration of the idea of the enforcement pyramid, Braithwaite (1999: 61) describes three punitive stages. The first stage, the base of the pyramid, is restorative justice, which is reserved for virtuous or well-intended actors who are genuinely willing to enter into restorative justice negotiations. Then comes a deterrent stage, which is for rational calculating actors who are not responsive to moral appeals about the harmfulness of their conduct but may be prudentially persuaded by the threat of punishment; this stage looks very much like the criminal justice system envisaged by contemporary retributivists such as von Hirsch (1993) and Duff (1986). The final stage is incapacitation, which is for those who are either incapable of refraining from further offending or unwilling to do so. Braithwaite explains that his strategy is one of 'active deterrence' in that the existence of threats of punishment in the background will encourage people to make genuine efforts to make amends and refrain from reoffending, but it will maintain the image of the power of criminal justice for those who do not respond to the moral appeal of restorative justice or the rational appeal of deterrence. He distinguishes the enforcement pyramid from selective incapacitation, the actuarial approach to the risk of reoffending which is so much in evidence today, by his model's treating everyone equally at the base of the pyramid: 'Restorative justice is not about picking good apples for reconciliation and bad apples for deterrence; it is about treating everyone as a good apple as the preferred first approach' (Braithwaite 1999: 64).

Critics of Braithwaite's enforcement pyramid point out that it limits restorative responses to the bottom of the pyramid, and thus cannot serve the ideal of restorative justice as a replacement penological discourse. For such an objective, restorative responses would have to be available at all stages and, moreover, to be the standard sanctions at all stages (Dignan 2002). Dignan suggests that the essential difference between retributivism and full-blown restorative justice is that, in the latter, 'censure' of the offence is clearly and thoroughly separated from the imposition of 'hard treatment'. Where offenders were dealt with by formal courts (and this would usually be because they had not admitted the offence), the outcome would still be measures of reparation necessary to reflect the harm, rather than hard treatment for its own sake. Courts normally would only be able to impose penalties with restorative aims and restorative efficacy. The only exceptions would be a (small number of) very dangerous offenders where needs of public protection might outweigh restorative considerations.

Retribution, rights and restorative justice

Most proponents of restorative justice have seen it as an alternative to retributive punishment (Zehr 1990, *inter alia*). While restorative justice may be compatible with some goals of punishment – censure, rehabilitation, public protection – retribution has usually been cast as its antithesis. Critical debate with desert theorists, however, has prompted rethinking of the relationship between retribution and restorative justice in two important respects: first, the role of proportionality in restorative justice; and second, whether there is a place for retribution in restorative justice. There is no consensus between restorative justice writers on these questions, but an active 'standards' debate has emerged which has clarified thinking on both issues (Ashworth 1993, 2002; von Hirsch *et al.* 2002; Braithwaite 1999, 2002; van Ness 1993).

The issue of proportionality has come to the fore gradually, as restorative justice has developed from being a marginal form of justice proposed, debated and practised by a movement of dedicated adherents, to an increasingly important and officially encouraged criminal justice option in the jurisdictions in which the most prominent desert theorists live and work, and where proportionate retribution is a central principle of established justice. It becomes the more pressing, the more restorative justice moves away from being merely a diversionary process dealing with offenders who would otherwise be cautioned. In these diversionary cases, where no due process criminal hearing has taken place, reparative measures would not be expected to be onerous. There is a clear understanding of what is reasonable, and offenders have the option of having a court hearing instead if they feel that unreasonable demands may be made upon them. Restorative justice theorists have agreed that offenders should have access to legal advice, and some have conceded that legal advisers should be present throughout the proceedings, not just becoming available if the offender decides to withdraw from the conference.

The issue of proportionate demands becomes more urgent if restorative justice is extended to more serious offences, for which the demands of reparation and safety-promoting measures would be greater. Braithwaite

(1999) reviews the possibilities of victims exaggerating the harm suffered, or of making demands that are disproportionate to the harm done, and concludes that the same discursive pressures which act upon the offender to admit responsibility and agree to make amends, act upon the victim to give a true account of the harm and to accept proportionate measures by way of both reparation and forward-looking guarantees. It is reasonable to hold that, since restorative justice was not formulated in terms of proportionality, lack of proportionality is not a valid criticism; nevertheless proportionality in penalties is generally regarded as, if not a basic human right, then something approaching rights status. As we have seen, the basic principles for restorative justice proposed by the UN mention proportionality, and there does seem to be some general agreement among restorative justice supporters emerging from experience of schemes in practice and from the debates with desert theorists, that proportionality is an important value, even if for them it does not hold quite the same status as a basic principle as it does for deserts theorists.

Interestingly, Braithwaite (1999) concedes that there has not been the same consideration given to what would count as just outcomes for offenders as has been given to questions of justice for victims. So far, the credentials of restorative justice theorists and practitioners have allayed fears of excessive impositions: restorative justice has developed among those who wish to see penal deflation rather than penal inflation, and who wish to provide remedies for victims without further deprivations of offenders. As restorative justice spreads, however, stronger safeguards become necessary. In England and Wales, for example, restorative justice was encouraged by legislation introduced by Jack Straw when he was Home Secretary, one who was no opponent of tougher penalties and increased incarceration. The fact that proportionate impositions are contingent on the goodwill and reasonableness of those responsible for conferences and hearings, rather than guaranteed by theory and procedures, is unsatisfactory for desert theorists (Hudson 2002b).

Concern is increased not just by the spread of restorative justice in practice, but by the expansion of its claims to effectiveness by its proponents. Ashworth (2002) and Dignan (2002) are both anxious that the enforcement pyramid allows incapacitive sentencing of recalcitrant offenders who are somehow deemed 'beyond restoration', and that it offers no adequately specified guide as to how offenders should be assigned to the restorative justice track or the deterrence/incapacitation track, nor any principled statement as to what kinds of limits to punitiveness should regulate the non-restorative track. I have also expressed concern that restorative justice's attempts to promote itself as effective in reducing crime rates lead into a forward-looking consequentialist framework which could not provide adequate reassurance that measures will be proportionate (Hudson 2002b).

There is some divergence between the paths being taken by restorative justice supporters such as Dignan (2002), who sees justice as being essentially backward-looking and who is critical of any move which builds future-oriented incapacitation in as a normal penal consideration, and Braithwaite, who wants to argue for restorative justice because it 'incapacitates crime better than criminal justice practices grounded in selective incapacitation' (1999: 65–7). This last statement is worrying, and makes the invocation of 'Uncle Harry' take on a more sinister guise than the cosy nomenclature suggests. Concern about the failure to articulate normative limits to restorative/safety measures is raised by other defences of restorative justice which suggest that because of its constructive purpose and nature it does not stand in need of justification in the same way that other punitive rationales do (Walgrave 1999).

The second aspect of the relationship between restorative justice and retributive justice is whether they are as dichotomous as often seen, or whether in fact they are compatible, whether in fact some measure of retribution is part of the restorative process (Cavadino and Dignan 1997; Daly and Immarigeon 1998; Zedner 1994). To some extent, the differences are linguistic rather than anything else: restorative justice and retributive justice are articulated in different discursive formations. There are obvious parallels between the principle of censure in contemporary retributivism and the principle of acknowledging the wrongness of the act in restorative justice. The communicative retributivism developed by Duff (1986; 1996) is not so far removed from the aims of inducing shame or at least acknowledgement of responsibility; while the centrality of harm done in both perspectives is another link.

While censuring the act and attaching blame and responsibility to the offender are parts of both retributive and restorative theories and processes, the parallels cannot be pushed too far. Retributivism is clearly tied to the culpability of the victim, and harm to the offender is standardized (von Hirsch and Jareborg 1992). Offenders can only be expected to anticipate standard harm to a standard victim, so except in cases where a particular type of victim is persistently targeted, the fact that an actual, individual victim felt specially harmed by the offence is not relevant to the culpability of the offender. For restorative justice, actual harm suffered by the individual victim is at the very heart of the matter.

Daly (2002a) suggests that a retributive element is essential to restorative justice to retain the element of 'wrongness' as well as harmfulness of crimes. It is this wrongness which distinguishes crimes from other sorts of injury, and marking this wrongness is part of the interest that communities have in criminal justice. Although reparative measures imposed might make amends to the individual victim, there still remains the right of communities to have their rules and moral standards affirmed. It is obvious that this symbolic element of criminal justice is important in both restorative and retributive (or established) justice; it is less obvious that both processes achieve this function in the same way. Although communicative retributivism might make theoretical distinctions between the moral message and the prudential deterrence of hard treatment, in practice and also in standard retributivism the moral message is conveyed through the proportionality of the hard treatment. Restorative justice, especially on the model of theorists such as Dignan, seeks much more separation between the iterative dimension (the naming of the harm as crime and the acceptance of responsibility), which is concerned with the wrongness as well as the harmfulness of the act, and the active reparative dimension (the impositions and obligations resulting from the process). There is a real division between those who see restorative justice as a replacement discourse, in which case its difference from retributive justice is its very point, and Daly and also Braithwaite (1999) who are tending towards presenting it as a more effective means of achieving traditional criminal justice objectives.

Restorative justice has become prominent in an era of rights. In the UK, all criminal justice agencies must have their practices approved as 'Human Rights Act compatible'; other countries, for example Canada, have reviewed their penal codes in the light of a charter of rights and freedoms. Although restorative justice tends towards a language of ideals and aspirations rather than rights, it is nevertheless pertinent to ask to what extent its procedures meet the standards of rights that are enshrined in the European Convention on Human Rights and similar charters.

As far as victims' rights are concerned, most restorative justice projects do fairly well. In most schemes, victims have rights to participate or not; to withdraw at any time; to choose their representatives, and in some programmes to veto any supporters chosen by the offender whom they do not wish to have present; to have a significant influence on any measures decided upon; to give their account of the offence in a manner of their own chosing. The only stipulation, which is a stipulation on all participants, is the rather vague direction that they should act 'respectfully' towards others involved.

Offenders' rights are not nearly so well defined and protected. Proportionality has already been mentioned: proportionality of measures is often said by restorative justice advocates to be necessary for the process to provoke a constructive rather than resentful response on the part of the offender; but it is merely desirable on grounds of utility, rather than a right. Offenders can refuse to participate or can withdraw at various stages in the proceedings, but the alternative is formal court. Although it appears that offenders are not unduly pressured into admitting the offence and being referred to restorative processes and although most diversionary schemes stipulate that the conference or panel should only consider acts for which there is sufficient evidence for a good prospect of conviction and which are admitted by the offender, it is doubtful whether all young offenders fully appreciate the defences and mitigations they may have available in a court of law. Due process protections given by rules of evidence are not secured, and Ashworth (2002), like other desert theorists, argues that restorative justice violates the right to have a hearing before an impartial arbiter. Although the conference facilitator is trained to be respectful to all parties, the victim's view of events is firmly entrenched as central and more or less unassailable, so the process as a whole is not impartial. Letting everyone have their say is not the same as being impartial.

In his lengthy and comprehensive review of 'optimistic' and 'pessimistic' accounts of restorative justice, Braithwaite (1999: 104) concludes that 'our Pessimistic Account is correct that rights can be trampled because of the inferior procedural safeguards in restorative justice processes compared to courts'. Restorative justice provides a good illustration of the relational nature of rights; the difficulty is not that of believing that victims and offenders both have rights, but of achieving a balance of rights. At the moment, victims' rights are better articulated and therefore better protected than offenders' rights in restorative justice, which many would say is the reverse case to that of conventional criminal justice. What needs to happen, and indeed what seems to be vigorously under way, is further work on better articulation of offenders' rights – regarding process *and* outcomes – while taking care not to diminish the rights of victims that are embedded at the heart of restorative justice.

Conclusion

Restorative justice is an innovative criminal justice development which has much to commend it. Its strongest appeal is that it offers a way of taking crime seriously and providing redress and some improved prospect of safety for victims and communities, without adding to the penal burdens on offenders, or to their stigmatization and exclusion. What remains to be seen is the place that it carves for itself, whether it settles into a role as one alternative among several ways of responding to crime, or whether it becomes an important penal principle, either replacing or supplementing penal objectives such as retribution, rehabilitation and incapacitation. In other words, restorative justice may continue to be used as the preferred option for some kinds of offenders and offences; it may come to be used as an option under certain circumstances for a much wider range of offences and offenders (for example, if pre-court appearance reports show that the offender is already showing signs of remorse and wanting to make amends), or it may be that as well as these applications, all sentences become expected to incorporate restorative elements.

The wider the range of applications, the more important issues of procedural safeguards and just outcomes become. Constructive engagement between restorative justice proponents and their critics from other penal perspectives is therefore much to be welcomed. This chapter has been concerned with issues of theory and principle, since these are the concerns of the book, rather than issues of practice. Descriptions of different programmes; evaluations of effectiveness and other issues of practice and application are available, and several have been mentioned during the chapter. Restorative justice is very much a growth area in practice and in penological literature, and one that holds much interest and promise for the future.

part two

Punishment and modernity: the sociological perspective

Punishment and progress:
the Durkheimian tradition

Introduction
Durkheim: punishment and solidarity
Durkheim's sociology of law: critical evaluation
Weber: bureaucracy and rationality
Durkheimian and Weberian themes: some contemporary applications
Punishment and culture: contemporary formulations
Conclusion

Introduction

The chapters in Part One described various principles of punishment which have been advocated by philosophers and other social and legal theorists. Often, these penal philosophies imply a penal strategy: punishments of graduated severity are concomitants of deterrence and proportionality; rehabilitation as a penal rationale leads to therapeutic and/or educative penalties; protection leads to lengthy imprisonment for those considered dangerous. What the philosophers do not, in the main, concern themselves with is why, in different places or at different times, societies use different kinds of penal strategy. Why, for example, did punishments such as ducking stools and stocks go out of fashion? Why have so many industrial democracies given up capital punishment? Why has imprisonment become such an important form of punishment? These questions – the kinds of punishment favoured by particular societies, the changes in penal strategy that have taken place – are the central concerns of sociologists who have taken punishment as a topic of enquiry.

Almost all sociologists who have engaged with these questions have concluded that changes in the types of punishment in use come about not just because of the persuasiveness of philosophers' arguments. As was shown in Part One, ideas such as retribution, deterrence, protection from dangerousness and rehabilitation have had their advocates throughout history. What changes is the relative influence they exert – at some times, retribution seems to fit the mood of the day, at other times there is a swing in favour of rehabilitation or some other consequentialist aim. As with the aims of punishment, so with the kinds of penalty with which the aims are pursued – sometimes, the prison seems to be the place where the offender has the best chance of reform, away from the influences which drove her/him to crime; at other times, prisons are thought of as places which make people more rather than less criminally inclined. At some times, there are climates of tolerance and optimism that most criminals can be successfully reintegrated; at other times the prevailing social temper seems harsh and vengeful. At some times the rights of offenders are considered as of great importance, the way society deals with those who transgress its rule is considered the index of its civilization; at other times, such views are considered soft-headed, and the right of victims to have their feelings assuaged by harsh penalties is projected as more important. Sociological studies of punishment have shown that the penal temper of a society, and thus its preferred penal goals and strategies, is related not so much to the weight of penal ideas but to their congruence with other areas of social life, such as the economic base of society and the form of government.

Sociological writing on punishment has been focused on penal *change* and *development*; on the relationship between punishment and other aspects of social life; on the functions punishment performs for various sections of society, and on the ideas and expectations people have of punishment. As Garland (1990a: 10) summarizes, the sociology of punishment is 'that body of thought which explores the relations between punishment and society, its purpose being to understand punishment as a social phenomenon and thus trace its role in social life'.

The sociology of punishment has developed as part of a more general question: how are order and authority to be maintained in modern society? Sociology, like the steam engine, is very much an invention of the industrial revolution. At the core of the discipline are questions to do with social order, with how the rules of society are transmitted from one generation to the next, and how people are induced to behave – most people, most of the time – socially rather than anti-socially. In particular, sociology has homed in on the question of how modern industrial society, which is characterized by the demise of traditional sources of order and authority such as religion and absolute monarchy, and where parents do not generally have economic power over their adult children, manages to maintain order and, indeed, to maintain any sense of being 'a society'. How, in other words, do societies change, but still continue to exist? Pre-sociological political philosophers, such as Herbert Spencer, thought that people act socially because it is in their own interests to do so; sociological thinkers such as Durkheim and Marx questioned this identity between self-interest and social interest, and analysed the ways in which people are conditioned to take the social interest to be their own interest.

Durkheim: punishment and solidarity

Émile Durkheim (1858–1917) is often said to be the 'father of sociology', in that he was one of the first scholars consciously to differentiate sociology from other branches of social and political philosophy. He observed that society has a reality apart from the individuals who comprise it, in that social rules and social relationships influence the behaviour and thoughts of members of society. People behave in accordance with social rules even when no one is watching; therefore, according to Durkheim, the existence of social rules, of customs and traditions, forms a culture which gives each society its distinctive character, and which is formative of the character of its members.

As well as distinguishing 'society' as an objective reality, external to the individual, Durkheim's sociology took the form that has come to be known as *functionalism*. This means that whatever aspect of social life is being studied, it is approached with a view to discovering what functions it performs for the society as a whole. This is an approach which is now generally regarded as conservative – since it assumes that any social institution or custom that survives is in some way useful for society, and thus worth maintaining – but in Durkheim's day it was an innovatory perspective which arose in anthropology. Functionalism encouraged anthropologists not merely to look at unfamiliar social practices as quaint or misguided, but to assume that people would not engage in them if they did not serve some useful purpose. Rain-making ceremonies in arid countries, for example, to a Western eye at first encounter look nonsensical, since Western science tells us that stamping one's feet on the ground can never produce rain, but if looked at from a functionalist perspective, it becomes apparent that they may be useful in keeping the society together, making members stay in one place until rain comes rather than dispersing to look for water. As will be evident in the following chapters, although Durkheim's delineation of the functions of punishment may have fallen from favour, the functionalist perspective persists in the study of punishment.

Durkheim's engagement with punishment, as with any other social phenomenon, is twofold. First, he asks what it reveals about the nature of society. Since society, although it has a reality and an externality, is not visible, it cannot be studied directly. The character of a society can only be deduced by reading its expressions, by apprehending what he calls a 'visible index', and one of the important indices of a society's culture is what it chooses to punish, and how. The second strand of his sociology of punishment is the functions punishment fulfils for the maintenance of social order and for the reinforcement and transmission of culture. By following these two strands, he develops a theory of the relation between the nature of punishment and the nature of society, and the importance of punishment for social solidarity.

Durkheim's theory of punishment is part of his more general theory of law, and appears first in probably his most famous work *The Division of Labour in Society* (1960, first published in 1893), and is then elaborated, and changed somewhat, in his article 'Two Laws of Penal Evolution' (1984, first published in 1901). In *The Division of Labour in Society*, Durkheim analyses the difference between modern industrial society and forms of society which went before it, and his main concern is to locate the sources and type of social solidarity – the common feelings, customs and traditions that make people recognize themselves as part of the same society – in the modern industrial state. He takes the specialization, or division, of labour to be the most important difference between industrial and pre-industrial societies, and takes other aspects of a society's culture, including its form of law, to be contingent upon whether a society specializes its labour or not.

In a pre-industrial society, most people carry out the same range of tasks. In a subsistence, pre-industrial economy, all are engaged in providing food, clothing and shelter for themselves and their families; there will be very few members of the society whose daily routines are different (priests and rulers, for example), and the majority will also share the tasks involved in providing for these exceptional members. Shared life experiences will make for shared beliefs, shared understandings, shared traditions. There will be a solidarity based on similarity. Durkheim calls this *mechanical* solidarity; perhaps someone writing today might call it homeopathic solidarity. The society's rules and customs will be functional to the survival of the society – for instance, the rules about marriage and kinship that arise in accordance with different societies' needs to keep the group tightly together or to recruit members of nearby societies. In such societies where people's experiences of life are similar, there will be, Durkheim tells us, a general belief in the rules and customs as essential; rules will in a very real sense be the rules of the whole society.

In contrast, once specialization of tasks develops, people's experiences of the society they live in and its relation to the outside world will differ, and instead of a solidarity based on sameness, there must be a solidarity based on interdependence with fellow-members whose lives, and therefore attitudes and beliefs, may be very dissimilar to one's own. In such a society, shared beliefs, shared commitment to rules and traditions, cannot be assumed, but mechanisms must be found whereby the relationships necessary for the maintenance of the society and the satisfaction of the needs of its members can be sustained. Durkheim calls this kind of solidarity, a solidarity based on interdependence rather than sameness, *organic* solidarity.

In mechanical solidarity societies, beliefs and rules are so strongly shared that they come to be embodied as religion, or as quasi-religious attributes of society; they make up what Durkheim calls the *conscience collective* of the society. This term denotes the 'totality of beliefs and sentiments' which are held by all ordinary members of society. The task of rule enforcement in such a society is to provide procedures not whereby differences can be reconciled, but whereby the occasional transgressor can be shown the offence s/he has caused to the other members of society, and whereby rule-keeping members can be assured that the rules violated are still important. Durkheim says that the form of law that develops in such societies will be repressive: anyone who departs from the conscience collective is, by definition, mad or bad and thus needs to be repressed. Furthermore, offences are against the conscience of the whole society; they therefore have a quality of sacrilegiousness that calls for repressive punishment.

In a specialized, organic solidarity society, beliefs and sentiments are not shared. This has two consequences for the form of law. First, law needs to provide procedures for the reconciling of differences, and a framework in which people with different sentiments, engaged in different tasks, can do business together. Second, since sentiments are not shared, crimes cannot be said to be offending against the whole society, but are offences of one individual against another, and law needs to provide procedures for remedies and reparation rather than for expiation of wrongs against the collective conscience. Such procedures therefore take the form of modern civil law, more concerned with contractual relationships and with restitution than with repression.

By the time of 'Two Laws of Penal Evolution', Durkheim, while still maintaining the distinction between societies based on sameness and societies based on interdependence, had come to think that shared values were necessary in specialized societies as well as in traditional societies. He still held that the 'conscience collective' (although he stopped using this term) he had described for traditional societies could not exist in the same form, and derive from the same sources, in modern industrial societies, but suggested that because lack of identity of experience brings about the decline of shared sentiments and thus of religious beliefs and authority, the necessity of solidarity for the persistence of society means that another source of rules and authority must be found. This task he allocates to law in modern societies; law comes to have the authority formerly vested in kings or priests – what he proposes is, in effect, a doctrine of the rule of law.

He allows, therefore, that there are rule transgressions in modern societies which are still *crimes*, in that they are offences against collective values as constituted and expressed in law, rather than merely *torts*, wrongs against another individual, and that therefore punishment for crimes rather than restitution for wrongs will have a part to play in the legal provisions of modern societies. His two laws of penal evolution, however, continue to maintain that punishments will be less repressive, less retributive, in modern than in traditional societies.

Durkheim's (1984: 102) first law of penal evolution is that '[t]he intensity of punishment is the greater the more closely societies approximate to a less developed type – and the more the central power assumes an absolute character'. In developed (industrial) societies, although there are collective sentiments, these are constituted by law rather than being enshrined in religion, so that even if the values violated by crimes are strongly and generally held, the fact that law is recognized as a human rather than divine construction means that crimes are seen as transgressions against fellow humans rather than as transgressions against the gods, and, as Durkheim (1984: 125) says, '[t]he offence of man against man cannot arouse the same indignation as an offence of man against God'. There is also, in crimes against fellow-humans, more similarity between victim and offender than there is in crimes against the divinity; the human sympathy which the crime arouses towards the victim is also present towards the offender, and pity for the offender is not overwhelmed by the need to appease the gods. Retribution, therefore, in more developed societies, will be tempered by mercy.

Durkheim cites the transitions in penalties from ancient societies to the France of his time as evidence for his 'first law'. He relies heavily on the disappearance of 'aggravated death' penalties – death accompanied by torture and mutilation. The use of particularly slow and painful forms of death, the accompaniment of death by mutilation, the preceding of death by torture, Durkheim tells us, was much reduced in the Athenian city-state compared to recorded societies such as ancient Egypt and pre-biblical Israel which went before it, was even further reduced in republican Rome, and gradually went out of use in Europe with the establishment of republican and constitutional forms of government.

The second part of his first law, predicting severity of punishments under absolutist governments, is necessary to account for the interruptions to this progressive cessation of aggravated death, torture and mutilation. He contrasts imperial Rome with the Roman republic, absolutist monarchies in pre-Enlightenment Europe with post-Enlightenment constitutional government, and draws attention to the barbarity of punishments in pre-Revolutionary France, the France of the absolutist *ancien régime*. Absolute rulers, he explains, take on quasi-religious status, through such doctrines as divine right. Even where this kind of claim is absent, they tend to eliminate, or take over the functions of, other sources of power and authority such as the Church. Punishments in absolutist societies will, therefore, resemble those in simple, traditional societies, because in absolutist societies crime also comes to seem sacrilegious as well as anti-social.

Durkheim's (1984: 114) second law of penal evolution makes more specific the notion of 'lesser intensity' which he says punishments acquire as societies develop. He says that imprisonment will become the main sanction, replacing death and torture: 'Deprivations of liberty, and of liberty alone, varying in time according to the seriousness of the crime, tend to become more and more the normal means of social control.' Again, he cites as evidence the absence of prisons in primitive societies, their slight use in Athens, and their development first in religious institutions in Christian societies, with their later transfer to secular society as legal punishments.

He cites the penal law of 1791 following the French Revolution, which made imprisonment the main punishment, and the refinement in the Penal Code of 1810 (the famous Code Napoléon which was the basis for much of the penal law of continental Europe in the nineteenth and into the twentieth centuries) which abolished accompaniments to imprisonment such as meagre diets and the wearing of chains. Durkheim associates the use of imprisonment as punishment with the developing moderation in punishment, but in his explanation of the second law he says more about why imprisonment took so long to be established as a punishment, rather than accounting positively for why it did become so established. In his account, he to some extent prefigures the explanations linking the rise of the prison to the rise of other forms of 'total institutions' in capitalist industrial societies, which will be examined in the following chapters.

Durkheim makes clear throughout his work on punishment that he sees its function in promoting social solidarity as being achieved through the affirmation of values, not through control or prevention of crime. He allows that punishment is an ineffective way of preventing crime, but sees its importance as allowing expression of sentiments of outrage consequent upon the commission of a crime. Punishment is, he says, a 'passionate reaction' to crime. His expressive view of punishment thus emphasizes the censure that is highlighted in the most recent variants of retributionism: the pronouncement of a punishment affirms that the rule violated is important, and that people are right to feel outraged by the crime. The target of punishment is, for Durkheim, the whole society, rather than just the offender actual or potential.

It is worth remembering that Durkheim was writing at the time that consequentialist theorists such as Bentham were influential, and when in France the penal strategy known as 'social defence' (Ancel 1987) was being elaborated. Development of the human sciences was facilitating the growth of positivist criminology and its correlate, correctional penology, with reformist penalties for the 'corrigible' and preventive detention for the 'incorrigible'. It is unlikely that Durkheim was unaware of these developments in a realm in which he was so interested. It is plausible, then, to imagine that Durkheim is suggesting that even if punishment in general, or any form of punishment in particular, such as imprisonment, is ineffective in the control of crime, it will (and should) persist because of its functionality for social solidarity through the expression of outrage and thus the affirmation of values, rather than to attribute to him actual repudiation of correctional or preventive aspiration on the part of those who legislate or administer punishments. Again, the analogy of the rain ceremony is helpful. Here, the stated function of the ceremony is not fulfilled, yet the ceremony persists and, so the functionalists argue, there must be some other function which is served. The same approach seems to fit Durkheim's arguments about punishment, that if penal practices seem to be ineffective in achieving the stated goals of penal policy, they may be accomplishing some other social function. This distinction between stated goals and 'real' functions is, as we shall see in the following chapters, a theme that recurs throughout the sociology of punishment.

Critics of Durkheim, however, have sometimes appeared to suggest that he is claiming that these expressive functions are all there is to punishment (Garland 1983; 1990a). Garland and other critics are undoubtedly correct when they say that expression and reinforcement of collective sentiments are represented as the core functions of punishment, that they are depicted as its essential features, and that in Durkheim's account the aspect of punishment that is a strategy for the control of crime is downplayed. The critical case is overstated, however, if it is claimed that Durkheim *reduces* punishment to the expression of collective sentiments (Garland 1983; 1990a; Lukes and Scull 1984).

Durkheim's sociology of law: critical evaluation

Two major strands of criticism of Durkheim's writings on punishment concern his evidence for change and development, and his understanding of the nature of modern society. His evidence for progression from repressive to restitutive law as society developed was challenged by Sheleff (1975), who said that as strong a case could be made for progression in the opposite direction, from restitutive to repressive law, as for Durkheim's model. By the time of 'Two Laws of Penal Evolution', however, Durkheim seems to have acknowledged that he had previously underestimated the continuing importance of repressive law in modern society, and this is reflected in his changing theory of solidarity. He continued, however, to insist that generally, punishments become milder as societies develop. Spitzer reviews the evidence for this proposition, which he calls the *organic differentiation thesis*, and concludes that it 'seems to be built upon a foundation of facts and assumptions for which contemporary investigators can find little support' (Spitzer 1979: 214).

Spitzer also reviews the opposite hypothesis, that societies have moved from restitutive forms of law to repressive forms. This theory, which he terms the *political centralization hypothesis*, rests on the argument that less advanced societies have lesser capacity for repressive control, and so 'less complex societies placed more emphasis on reconciliation through a *dispute-settling process*, while advanced societies are more likely to have the capacity and inclination to implement coercive rule enforcement' (ibid. emphasis in original).

Spitzer finds this hypothesis more persuasive than Durkheim's organic differentiation hypothesis, but says that by simply inverting the original, the political centralization thesis repeats the oversimplifications in Durkheim's model. In spite of the empirical evidence, however, the idea of progressive humanization of punishment continued to be generally shared by liberal penal thinkers until the so-called 'revisionist' histories of punishment began to appear in the 1970s (in particular, the work of Michel Foucault, discussed in Chapter 8, and the histories derived from Marxist analyses, discussed in Chapter 7).

One aspect of Durkheim's work which Spitzer does endorse, and which has not been substantially refuted, is the connection he makes between the severity of punishment and the symbolic representation of victims. The quality of sacredness of the victim, the anti-religious quality of crime Durkheim attributes to traditional societies, is indeed, allows Spitzer, a correlate of severe punishment. However, rather than, as Durkheim sees it, crimes in advanced societies being against individuals, as political power becomes centralized in the modern state, the state itself becomes the victim, and so crime retains the aspect of being against the whole society. This is made obvious by the convention of law which describes the parties in criminal cases in England and Wales as *Regina* versus the defendant, and in the USA as 'the people' versus the defendant. The 'sacrilegiousness' of crime, therefore, persists.

Before his ideas about the nature of change in penalties were challenged, however, sociologists had pointed out the deficiencies in his ideas of social evolution. He describes two kinds of society, with two legal forms, but reveals nothing of the stages between those societies. Durkheim does not posit any kind of dynamic theory of social development which explains the transition from one form of society to another. This is, of course, most apparent in his discussion of absolutism, which seems to float free of any historical or material forces (Spitzer 1975; Garland 1983; 1990a; Lukes and Scull 1984; Cavadino and Dignan 1992). Although it is true that Durkheim lacks a dynamic theory of change, it is well to remember that such a dynamic theory of a progression from one state to another, powered by some discoverable effective cause, is a version of social theory elaborated in Hegelian concepts of history, and associated in particular with Marxist dialectical sociology. Another historical tradition, exemplified recently and influentially by Foucault, does not analyse the process of transition, but looks at discrete societies and describes their differences, as though in a series of snapshots (see Chapter 8). Durkheim's writing reads as though he were influenced both by the evolutionary theorists of his time (Spencer and Darwin) and by this predominantly Gallic view of history as a series of discontinuities, and his resultant work is a somewhat uneasy compromise between the two.

The second defect highlighted by almost all his critics is that he ignores the power relationships in societies. Although his ideas about the construction of solidarity in modern industrial society are predicated on the absence of shared experience and therefore of any naturally arising common values, he sees law as a solution to this problem with its potential for social conflict, instead of seeing law itself as a site of conflict. Laws as often express the interests of the victors in power struggles as they express any consensus or compromise – much more often, according to the theorists in Chapter 7. Moreover, conflicts, for Durkheim, are between individuals, and differences in interest are between the individual and the social: Durkheim appears to lack any perception of individuals as members of groups which may have opposed interests (Garland 1983; 1990a). This neglect of power and of the conflict between interest groups means that his view of the state is altogether too benign; he also omits any reference to the state as enjoying a monopoly of legitimate violence (Lukes and Scull 1984).

Durkheim's view of punishment is entirely positive, but many people have pointed out that it can be dysfunctional. The most famous statement of the dysfunctions of punishment probably remains that of the social psychologist George Herbert Mead. Mead (1918) shows that the very passion that Durkheim identifies can prevent dispassionate attention to the causes of crime, and can lead to society's energies being directed towards denouncing individuals rather than doing anything to ameliorate the social conditions which give rise to crime. This is, of course, an argument which continues unabated to this day!

What Durkheim achieved in his writings on punishment was, first and foremost, the establishment of the connection between forms of society and forms of punishment, a connection which has remained at the heart of the sociology of punishment. Second, his direction of attention to its expressive functions is important in understanding why there is still a public/political demand for punishment even if it is widely recognized as failing in its correctional/preventive aims. His contribution is elegantly summarized by Garland (1990a: 80):

> The sense he gives of the sacred, of the emotions which are stirred by crime and punishment, of the collective involvement of onlookers, of the role of penal rituals in organizing this, and, finally, of the social and moral significance of penal practices – all these interpretative insights have been shown to be important and also relevant to an understanding of punishment today.
>
> Above all, his claim that punishment can be at once politically necessary – for the maintenance of a particular form of authority – and penologically limited in its capacity to control crime, seems to touch upon a crucial characteristic of punishment which goes unnoticed elsewhere. This sense of being simultaneously necessary and also destined to a degree of futility I will term the *tragic* quality of punishment.

Weber: bureaucracy and rationality

Max Weber (1864–1920) was another of the great founding fathers of sociology. Although he did not engage directly with punishment, many of his ideas about the character of authority in modern society and about the forms of social institutions – including law – found in modern societies are relevant to an understanding of some of the contemporary developments in, and debates about, penality.

Weber, like Durkheim, saw constitutive connections between economic forms and cultural forms. In contrast to Marx, who, as we shall see in Chapter 7, saw the economic system of a society as determining other cultural subsystems, Weber looked at the connection between culture and economy the other way round, and in his famous work, *The Protestant Ethic and the Spirit of Capitalism* (1930, originally published in 1905), he explored the reasons why capitalism had arisen in the societies of northern Europe rather than elsewhere. He found his answer in the religious beliefs of the capitalist countries: Protestantism, he said, had a positive attitude to the accumulation of wealth by individuals and their families, and it encouraged individual achievement rather than sacrifice on behalf of the wider community. Weber sees, as do Durkheim and Marx, that once an economic system has developed, it then influences other social formations. In his other major work, *Economy and Society* (1978, originally published in 1920), he looks at the types of social institution that will best serve a modern capitalist state. It is his descriptions of modern forms of authority and rationality that have been most fruitful for the sociology of punishment.

Having differentiated *authority* rule by consent) from *power* (rule by coercion), Weber distinguishes three types of authority. These are *traditional* authority, where rules are obeyed because those making them have been accorded the right to do so through tradition (for example, hereditary monarchs); *charismatic* authority, where a ruler or group of rulers is regarded by the populace as having some special qualities which give them the right to rule; and *legal* authority, where rules are made by a person or persons who are given the right to rule through following some special procedure, such as being elected to office. Legal authority is promoted by Weber as being the most appropriate form of rule for modern industrial societies, because other forms of authority are more likely to be resistant to change, or are more likely to rule in the interests of the rulers rather than of the society as a whole.

Under legal authority, those granted the right to rule must themselves obey the laws. It follows that if procedural rules are the source of legal authority, then these procedural rules will have some special status in the society, akin to the aura of monarchy or religion in traditional societies. The status of the Constitution in the USA is a good example of rules having almost 'sacred' status. Like Durkheim, then, Weber seems to be suggesting that in modern societies law itself becomes the ultimate source of authority: Weber's conception of legal domination has been drawn on extensively in the elaboration of the doctrine of the 'rule of law' by modern legal theorists (Cotterrell 1984).

Weber extends his analysis to uncover the characteristics of legal authority, the forms of behaviour that best suit the maintenance and enhancement of legal authority. Systems of laws, he says, may be rational or irrational, formal or substantive. In a rational system, decisions are made by following rules and procedures for classes of cases rather than seeing each case as unique and establishing *ad hoc* rules of judgment for every new case. Systems are substantive if they appeal to rules or beliefs outside the system of law itself (for example, religion); they are formal to the extent that the definitions and beliefs involved in making judgments are defined by law itself (Cotterrell 1984). A formally rational system of criminal law, then, would have a set of definitions of crimes and a set of rules of adjudication, and a formally rational penal code would complement this with a prescribed set of penalties. Weber sees formal rationality as the best principle for the formulation and operation of law (and other subsystems of authority and government) in modern capitalist societies. The characteristics of formally rational systems, of proceeding according to rules, of authority being vested in roles rather than persons *qua* persons he calls *bureaucratic rationality*, and he sees this as an essential feature of an efficient, legitimately governed, modern state.

If we look at punishment in modern industrial societies, we can see many of the characteristics of Weber's bureaucratic rationality. Judgments must be made according to rules; authority is vested in position-holders rather than in people themselves (judges can only impose punishments while they are sitting in court; they lose their right to punish when they retire). To the extent that criminal justice systems do not conform to the ideal of bureaucratic rationality, there is public criticism. Much of the impetus for sentencing reform in the USA, in England and Wales, and elsewhere in the 1980s was because of inconsistencies in sentencing, and perceptions that judges were sentencing according to their own prejudices rather than according to the facts of the case and the rules of due process (Frankel 1973; Hudson 1987). These criticisms of criminal justice systems in the 1980s can be seen as pointing to inadequacies in relation to bureaucratic rationality: critics of criminal justice in this period used decidedly Weberian language when they posited a 'crisis of legitimacy' (Cavadino and Dignan 1992: 74).

Weber uses the notion of the *ideal type* to help him with the problem of transitional phases and intermediate societies. An ideal type is a set of correlated characteristics – such as a capitalist economy, an elected government, a secular society – which will be approached rather than fully realized in any actual society. Modern society and traditional society are thus divided by a continuum, not a dichotomy. Contemporary England and Wales, for example, has a capitalist economy, an elected government, a secular majority, but retains a traditional monarchy, vestiges of religious authority and vestiges of substantive law. Other societies, such as the USA, may be further along the continuum towards modernity on some characteristics (for example, not having a monarchy), and Weber certainly viewed the English system of justice, especially in its reliance on precedent rather than the codes of continental Europe, and its reliance on a lay magistracy, as not having gone so far along the continuum towards formal legal rationality. He is consequently much challenged by England's success as a capitalist, imperial nation in the nineteenth century, and concludes that 'England achieved capitalist supremacy among the nations not because but rather in spite of its judicial system' (Weber 1978: 814).

Many of the developments in punishment systems in the 1980s took societies such as England and Wales further along the continuum towards Weber's ideal type of a modern, bureaucratic society. Changes in the granting of parole, the dissemination of sentencing guidelines, and the move to make sentencing more predictably correlated with the seriousness of the offence (Ashworth 1989) all pointed in this direction of making criminal justice more rational in the bureaucratic sense: more firmly tied to the following of rules and precedents, less open to individual assessment of circumstances of cases.

These reforms continue the *rationalization* of punishment that is a prominent theme in sociological-historical studies of social control appearing from the 1970s onwards (Spitzer 1983). On this reading, developments such as regular paid police forces, a professional judiciary, rules of evidence and due process, penal codes with graduated punishments, the move from torture, mutilation and death to imprisonment and fines, are not so much progress in humanitarianism as progress in bureaucratized rationalism, necessary to meet the social control needs and legitimacy conditions of modern societies.

Some historians and sociologists of punishment have, on the other hand, rather like the functionalist anthropologists, challenged the idea that simple societies have irrational means of social control and modern societies have rational means. They have argued that control systems may well be rational for the societies in which they exist (Philips 1983); different types of society pose different problems of social order and generation of solidarity (as Durkheim saw) and may call forth different models of rationality (as Weber demonstrates).

As well as his analysis of authority and rationality, Weber's great contribution to sociology was his argument that the logic of social science is interpretative, not predictive. Unlike Durkheim, he did not view society as something extra and external to individuals, but saw that society consists of the actions of its members. Human beings carry on their lives through interpreting each other's actions, and from this build up patterns of identity, behaviour and meaning which become generalized within their own lives and within a society. These stable patterns become the customs, social roles, laws and institutions that we call culture, and for Weber and the sociologists who have followed his *Verstehen* (understanding) methodology, cultures must be studied by observation of the actions of individuals. Sociological understanding will take the form of interpretation of these patterned actions, and sociological theory can only be in the form of correlations and generalizations: because human behaviour is always contingent on interpersonal interactions, outcomes can only ever be probable; there cannot be predictive 'laws' as in the physical sciences. In relation to penal justice, Weberian methodology has given rise to a vast literature on observational studies of behaviour in courtrooms and prisons, of interactions between police and suspects, and between social workers and probation officers and their 'clients' (Rubington and Weinberg 1968).

Durkheimian and Weberian themes: some contemporary applications

Weber's ideas about the appropriate methodology for the social sciences are drawn from the branch of philosophy known as *phenomenology*. At its simplest, this urges observation and description of things themselves, rather than trying through abstract reasoning to arrive at some kind of 'essence' of phenomena under study. A well-known study which combines this phenomenological methodological approach with a Durkheimian emphasis on the symbolic, ritual aspects of the pronouncement of punishment by courts, addressing a wider audience, and in which the enactment of the ritual has significance over and above any deterrent or correctional effects of the punishment, is Garfinkel's 'Conditions of Successful Degradation Ceremonies' (1956). Garfinkel describes courtroom procedures as having as their prime outcome the construction of a new status for the offender, to which all present can agree. The offender may be variously agreed to be wicked, sick or unfortunate, but s/he will have acquired a label such as 'thief' or 'assailant', and the coupling of the pejorative adjective with the labelling of the action reinforces the sentiment that such acts are indeed wicked or mad or misguided. Garfinkel stresses, in Weberian style, that the ceremony will be more successful the more the different participants conform to the expectations of their role. Garland (1990a) is right to point out that, contrary to the assumptions of some commentators on his paper, Garfinkel does not show that the enactment of the ritual is constitutive of solidarity through promotion of the importance of the sentiments violated by the offence, but that, on the contrary, the degree of success of the ceremony will in large measure depend on the degree of social consensus about the importance of the sentiments that already exists.

Garfinkel's study has much in common with the so-called 'labelling' perspective on deviance. Labelling theory proposes that being the recipient of a label as a criminal or other deviant has consequences for the labellee's future behaviour and self-perception, but the extent and direction of such consequences will depend on the degree to which the offender or deviant him/herself, and others who are significant (such as close relatives and friends) or powerful (such as judges able to commit the person to prison, or psychiatrists to an institution, or potential employers), as well as the general population, share the values implied by the label (see, for example, Matza 1964; Lemert 1967; Cicourel 1968; Rock 1973).

The emphasis on roles and ceremonies in the enactment of penal rituals prompted the popularity, especially in the 1970s, of a 'dramaturgical metaphor', in which the various participants such as judges, advocates, defendants, social workers and witnesses were seen as actors in a drama, except that, unlike in a theatrical performance, these courtroom actors could determine the outcome by their performance. Each had a script – the law, the facts of the case, their professional guidelines, their desire to be judged innocent – but their skill in delivering the lines, as well as pleasing appearance and demeanour, could change the ending.

One of the most cogent uses of the drama metaphor is Carlen's (1976) study of proceedings in a London magistrates court. Like Garfinkel, Carlen follows a phenomenological, observational method, and for much of the book appears to be giving a straightforward Durkheimian account of the symbolic meaning of the event and its significance for the constitution and reinforcement of social rules. She then, however, highlights the deficiency which phenomenological perspectives share with Durkheim's theories in so far as they neglect the factor of power. Carlen points out that the way in which the judge's seat is raised above everyone else, the way the defendant is the furthest away from the judge, the clothes and wigs, the rising and bowing, all serve to emphasize the power relationships in the courtroom, which are, of course, reflections of power relations throughout society.

In fact, observations of interaction are uninterpretable without knowledge of the power relationships of the participants, so that while observational sociology (ethnography) may give us valuable insights into the ways in which members of societies conduct their lives, it can supply little real understanding outside an interpretative framework which contains a theory of the distribution of power and authority.

Punishment and culture: contemporary formulations

The legacy of Durkheim and Weber's establishing the connections between particular forms of society and the general criticism of the lack of attention to power in society in their work, reorientated the sociology and history of punishment in the directions described in Chapters 7 and 8. Concentration on the repressive justice aspects of punishment neglected by Durkheim and Weber, and on the power differentials between individuals and, even more importantly, between different groups in society, has meant that for two decades the links between punishment and non-material aspects of culture, as well as the symbolic aspects of punishment, have been overlooked. Two recent works have redirected attention to these neglected aspects of the social role and meaning of punishment, so that it may be that a new phase in sociology's engagement with penality is emerging.

First, John Braithwaite's *Crime, Shame and Reintegration* (1989), although focusing on the possibilities of reducing crime, rather than on social order in a wider sense, invokes Durkheim's view of punishment as an important statement of social values. Braithwaite argues that the ceremonies of criminal justice should be such as to encourage offenders to feel shame at their actions, but, echoing Mead and subsequent labelling theorists, he insists that actual punishments should be such as to help the offender feel reinforced in his/her membership of society. Braithwaite also argues that the shamefulness of anti-social action must be promoted through all of society's institutions, and says that punishment can only be effective in reducing crime in a society that generally views wrongdoing as something of which to be ashamed.

Another work which has exerted some influence on current sociological approaches to penality is Spierenburg's historical analysis of the decline of public executions, *The Spectacle of Suffering* (1984). Spierenburg's work integrates Durkheim's concern with the symbolic meaning of punishment and its function for social solidarity, with Weber's insights on rationality, and attempts to explain the changes that have come about in penality in Europe from the twelfth to the nineteenth centuries. He considers changes such as the movement of suffering from a public to a private space, the reduction in torments associated with execution, and the decline of execution itself. Unlike other theorists, he does not present readers with depictions of two distinct forms of society, but shows gradual changes in social formations, which he provides as the context for understanding changes in penality. He gives us a history of the *longue durée* of punishment, so that what emerges are evolutionary developments rather than sudden ruptures.

Spierenburg's work reverts to a language of progress and increased humanity in punishment, a language which had become unfashionable. He revives evaluative language reminiscent of Durkheim's 'lesser intensity', which had been challenged by more recently fashionable accounts which minimized the association between penal change and heightened humanitarianism, instead seeing changes in the techniques of punishment as being the outcome of changed control needs and more sophisticated possibilities of control with modern technology, psychiatry and pharmacology. Rather than returning to Durkheimian notions such as the conscience collective, however, Spierenburg draws on the work of Norbert Elias (1978; 1982) and his analysis of 'the civilizing process'. This process of civilization of behaviour and 'mentalities' among the populace of Europe, according to Elias, consists in a gradual refinement of 'sensibilities', as evidenced, for example, in more delicacy in eating manners, performing bodily functions only in private, and gentlemanly behaviour in the presence of females: generally, the enhancement of self-control and restraint in physical self-expression. Elias connects this development of 'conscience' to wider processes of civilization which came about with the formation of the European nation-states, and with the greater personal safety that came with the more settled state. Spierenburg applies this self-restraint, this lessening of physical expression, this general refinement of sensibility, to public executions, and shows that public punishment declined as the spectacle of suffering became less entertaining and more repellent to public sensitivity.

As Garland (1986) says, this is a welcome reintroduction of neglected themes, for any account of punishment must include the dimension of the audience: punishment will not be perceived as justice if it accords only with the social control needs of governments, the crime prevention expectations of the public and the principles of the philosophers. To be accepted as legitimate, to strengthen respect for law and abhorrence of crime, punishment must also accord with prevailing sentiments about what is barbaric and what is reasonable.

Conclusion

What is problematic with accounts such as Spierenburg's is the almost inevitable circularity of argument – decline in public executions is too easily taken as evidence of more gentle sensibilities. We cannot securely know, in the twentieth century, whether in earlier centuries the clamour of protest against public mutilation and execution grew to such an extent that it could not be ignored, or whether rulers began to listen to the voices protesting against the spectacle because to do so suited other circumstances. The idea of 'progress' in sensibilities is, after all, hard to sustain in an era which has witnessed the barbarities of the Holocaust, the Khmer Rouge, and massacres in Rwanda. Less sensationally, a future historian of punishment, noting the abolition of capital punishment in England and Wales, would be wrong to assume that this was because the tide of public sensibility had turned against it. The dimension of punishment that is expressive of culture, and sustaining of social solidarity, is important, and its renewed recognition is thus welcome, but it needs to be fitted together with the perspectives which connect forms of punishment with economic and political power, and which recognize its instrumental as well as its expressive functions (Garland, 1990b).

chapter seven

The political economy of punishment: Marxist approaches

Introduction
Key concepts in Marxist sociology
Punishment and the labour market
Why prison?
Ideology and the control of surplus populations
The challenge of feminism
Conclusion: the legacy of Marxism

Introduction

Durkheimian sociology of punishment is centred on a link between forms of society and forms of punishment; Spierenburg, Garland and others focus on the 'consistency' between 'the methods of treatment of criminals' and other aspects of culture (Sutherland 1939: 348); Durkheim, moreover, in his second law of penal evolution stated that imprisonment would become the dominant form of punishment in advanced societies. Marxist traditions of the sociology of punishment and law also affirm the link between forms of society and forms of punishment, and much penological research in the Marxist tradition is concerned with the question 'why prison?' (Melossi and Pavarini 1981: 1). Yet the two approaches differ radically. This chapter will first of all outline the concepts that are common to all Marxist social theory and which distinguish Marxism from other approaches to understanding modern society; it will summarize some of the most important penological works and ideas written from a Marxist perspective, and it will offer some critique and assessment of the value and limitations of Marxist explanations of punishment and justice.

Key concepts in Marxist sociology

Like Durkheim and Weber, Marx was concerned to identify the key features which characterize modern industrial society, and which differentiate it from primitive societies, feudal societies and other previous social formations. Like Weber, but unlike Durkheim, he sees modern Western industrial society first and foremost as *capitalist*: division of labour may exist in other forms of society, but what distinguishes the social forms that arose in western Europe and North America during the eighteenth century, and other societies somewhat later, is that capital is accumulated by some individuals, who then use that capital to invest in machinery and other productive equipment, and to buy the labour of members of society who do not have capital. This ownership of the means of production by a few, and the selling of labour by the many – the *relations of production* – Marx regarded as the crucial social arrangement that distinguishes capitalist from non-capitalist societies. The relations of production are, Marxists believe, reflected in all other social relationships.

For Marxists, then, the 'cultural consistency' found across social institutions, described by Sutherland, by Garland (1990a) and by other penologists, is derived from the relations of production: institutions such as law, education, social stratification and kinship systems are as they are because they mirror the relations of production and because they are functional to maintaining the relations of production. This derivation of social institutions from the economic form of society is known as the *base–superstructure metaphor*. The economy is the base upon which other institutions arise. All strands of Marxist theory incorporate this notion of base and superstructure, but in some variants (particularly the work of Louis Althusser), it is more significant than in others.

A second concept that is crucial to Marxists' understanding of society, and that is particularly important for theories of punishment and justice, is the *labour theory of value*. The capitalist (the owner of the means of production) invests in capital, raw materials, factory buildings and so on, but these are of no value until the workers, by their labour, turn them into goods which can be bought and sold. If an industrialist buys a roll of fabric, s/he cannot sell it for any more than s/he paid for it unless someone turns it into something else, dresses or tablecloths for example; it gains value by being transformed by work. A corollary of the labour theory of value is the theory of *surplus value*, which explains that the worker cannot receive from the capitalist the full value of her/his labour – the full difference between the raw material and the product which it becomes – because the capitalist has to keep something for running costs, reinvestment and profits. Exploitation is, then, not so much a matter of wicked capitalists withholding from workers their due rewards (although some may well do so!) as a fundamental requisite of the capitalist mode of production.

Surplus value, exploitation in this sense of workers having to produce more value than they are paid, makes for two groups of people who have common within-group interests but conflicting between-group interests. The capitalists and the workers, the owners of the means of production and the sellers of labour, the bourgeoisie and the proletariat as Marx identified them, coexist as opposed classes. Marxists see capitalist society not as an assembly of individuals, separate from each other but all with the same relationship to society – as in Durkheim's conception of society – but as a class society. The concept of class is applicable only to capitalist societies, because it describes the division of society into groups defined by their relationship to the means of production. The castes or estates in feudal society, for example, are not classes because membership is defined by birth: people continue to be members of the same caste regardless of what happens during their lives, but a capitalist/bourgeois who loses ownership of the means of production is no longer a capitalist/bourgeois, while a worker who becomes a millionaire and buys a factory and starts hiring labour and paying wages moves out of the working class and into the capitalist/bourgeois class. Within the factory, the capitalist maximizes his/her gains by paying the workers as little as possible, while the workers minimize their exploitation by inducing the capitalist to pay the workers as much as possible; more generally, because one class is the exploiter and one the exploited, the capitalist class has interests in maintaining the system whereas the workers have interests in overthrowing it.

Marxists argue that these relations of buying and selling labour, of exploiting and being exploited, of having interests in the maintenance of the system or in its overthrow, condition social institutions such as law, education, the family and the political system. The relationship between religion and the capitalist economy was explored by Weber as well as by Marx, as was shown in the previous chapter; but whereas Weber saw some religions as being more facilitative of the development of capital than others, Marxists would argue that the development of capitalism has influenced the form of religion in modern societies. A Weberian would point to the fact that Christianity preceded capitalism, and capitalism developed in Western Christian societies rather than in Eastern Buddhist, Hindu or Islamic societies, and that, moreover, capitalism did not flourish until the traditional authority of the medieval Roman Catholic church had been breached; Marxists would doubtless argue that capitalism has led to much modification in the religion of the West, while the non-capitalistic societies continued to follow their religious traditions, and it is only as the non-capitalistic societies, too, have become capitalized that religion has become modified and has lost authority.

All social institutions, according to Marxists, have as their prime function the maintenance of the capitalist system. Laws will protect rights to property necessary for capital accumulation; families reproduce workers, and give workers motivation to work for wages; education gives potential workers the skills that are needed in the workforce, and instils attitudes of respect for authority, for doing things because of future gain rather than immediate entertainment – in other words, the 'work ethic'. The various functions that social institutions serve are characterized by Marxists as regulatory (mechanisms to keep the system working), repressive (penalties for workers who do not accept the rules of capitalist production) and ideological (making workers believe that social arrangements which in fact serve the interests of capitalists, are in the interests of all). As we shall see, punishment, and law more generally, have been shown by different Marxist traditions to serve all three of these kinds of function.

One of the points made in relation to Durkheim was that he does not offer any explanation of how societies change from the simple to the complex. His theory is static – it gives accounts of two different forms of societies, but gives no account of forces or processes which lead one form to give way to another. Marxism, on the other hand, is a dynamic theory, a theory of change. Marx identified points of contradiction or crisis in each of the social formations he described, and it is the resolution of these contradictions or crises which leads to the transition to another social-economic form. In the feudal and mercantilist societies which preceded capitalism, rising populations strained the production systems, especially the capacity of the land to produce enough food, and a more efficient economic form thus developed.

In capitalism, the contradiction is surplus value – if no one is paid the full value produced by their labour, then the aggregate of people will not be able to purchase the full value of goods produced. While the crisis of previous economic forms was underproduction, then, the crisis of capitalist economies is identified as overproduction (hence the main task of government in advanced capitalist societies becomes that of trying to balance production and consumption, and the science of economics becomes the 'dismal science' of supply and demand). This progress-through-contradiction view of history is known as dialectical progression; because the forces producing social institutions and bringing about contradictions and crises are material, it is termed *dialectical materialism*.

Punishment and the labour market

Law generally has important regulatory functions. Laws surrounding the ownership of property, the performance of contracts, investment and finance, as well as laws enforcing education and maintaining the family and its gender roles, are important for carrying on business, and for reproducing workers with the requisite skills and attitudes. Anti-trust laws, rules about insider dealing, health and safety regulations and employment rights might appear to be operating in the interests of workers and curbing the interests of capitalists, but a Marxist case can easily be made that these regulatory systems are necessary to stop individual capitalists damaging the system as a whole. Marxist ideas about class, and about the importance of the system as against individual interests, direct attention to the way in which law in capitalist society will regulate in the interests of the economic system – of capital – rather than in the interests of any individual member of the capitalist class.

Punishment, however, has been associated with repressive functions, acting to curb dissent and any potential threat to the system. What Marxist penologists have suggested that it regulates is the supply of labour. The 'foundational text' of Marxist penology is Rusche and Kirchheimer's *Punishment and Social Structure* (1968). This book, first published in 1939, but only becoming influential on its republication in 1968, proposes the labour market as the key determinant of both the amount and the nature of punishment in society.

The first half of the book, written by Rusche, analyses changes in punishment systems in use in Europe from the thirteenth century until the flowering of capitalism. Like Durkheim, he records changes in the severity of punishments, but unlike Durkheim, he does not see these changes as forming a unidirectional progression from greater to lesser severity. Rusche finds that the severity of punishment is related to the value of labour: when labour is scarce, and therefore its value high, punishments become relatively lenient; when labour is abundant, punishments become more severe. He distinguishes three epochs, the first of which is the medieval period, around the thirteenth century. During this era, the labouring population was small in relation to the land that had to be worked, and the punishments most frequently used were fines and penances. By the fifteenth century, an emergent urban, impoverished population provided an excess supply of labour, and there was a corresponding increase in the use of mutilations and executions. Finally, from the seventeenth century, first mercantilism and then capitalism stimulated demand for labour, increasing wages and decreasing the use of punishments, such as death and mutilation, which remove offenders from the labour market. Offenders became a source of labour directly – providing cheap labour in workhouses and houses of correction, as well as for the new colonies through transportation. With the development of capitalism, imprisonment became the main form of punishment, and the prison regimes that developed during the eighteenth and nineteenth centuries not only provided labour directly but also aimed to increase the labour force by instilling the work ethic into inmates. The relationship between demand for labour and modes of punishment is that when labour is scarce and valuable, 'exploitation is preferred to capital punishment, and forced labour is the corresponding mode of punishment' (Rusche 1978: 7).

As well as the labour market, Rusche's key principle for understanding punishment was that of *lesser eligibility*. This states that in order to deter the 'reserve army of labour' from crime, conditions in prisons must be worse than anything the offender is likely to encounter outside the prison. Lesser eligibility is a principle that is applicable to workhouses as well as prisons: conditions should be such that people will take pains to avoid such institutions. According to Rusche, this principle limits any penal reform possibilities: reducing the severity of punishments or improving prison conditions will not go beyond the point at which the life of the offender comes close to the standard of life of the least advantaged non-offender.

Kirchheimer's part of the book extends the historical analysis into more modern times, and dilutes the economic grounding considerably. Nevertheless, the book as a whole is associated with the labour market hypothesis. It has been criticized for reductionism and for functionalism. That there is a demonstrable link between the labour market and penal strategies does not necessarily mean that this is the only, or the basic, explanation, that developments in punishment can be 'reduced to' shifts in the demand for labour. Similarly, if the kinds of punishment in common use (the penal strategy) do have an effect in increasing or decreasing the labour force, such effect is not necessarily the cause of changes in punishment systems. Critics who acknowledge the 'fit' between the economy and systems of punishment, object to overreliance on what Rusche (1978: 4) himself called 'a few simple economic axioms'. Such critics do not deny the relationship between labour markets and punishment, in other words, but suggest that Rusche oversimplified the connection (see, for example, Spitzer 1979).

Several penologists have, however, accepted the basic analytic framework established in *Punishment and Social Structure*, and have both tested and elaborated the labour market hypothesis. One well-known study by Jankovic (1977) tested the correlation between punishment and the labour market by studying US data on imprisonment and unemployment between 1926 and 1974. Jankovic broke the Rusche–Kirchheimer hypothesis into two propositions: a severity proposition, that punishments become more severe when there is an over-supply of labour; and a utility proposition, that punishments function to remove part of the surplus labour supply for the market. He found support for the first proposition but not for the second, but suggested that though this might weaken the hypothesis, his findings overall supported it. (Jankovic and other analysts have taken 'imprisonment' as an index of severity of punishment, which is of course quite different from Durkheim, for example, for whom rising use of imprisonment is an index of decreased severity. In contemporary penology, however, imprisonment is linked to severity because it is the most severe penalty for most crime in Western capitalist countries. Even in the USA, and in European countries before abolition of capital punishment, the death penalty is reserved for a small number of kinds of crime; for the most common crime categories, imprisonment is seen as severe, in contrast to penalties such as fines, probation or community service. Recent tests of the labour market hypothesis, then, generally test the association between imprisonment and unemployment.)

Other tests of the labour market hypothesis in this form have confirmed the association between imprisonment rates and unemployment rates:

Greenberg (1977) tested Canadian data, and Box and Hale (1982) conducted similar analyses in England. Such studies find that the association is *independent* of any changes in crime rates. Rusche and Kirchheimer and subsequent Marxist penologists have all insisted that punishment cannot be understood simply as a response to crime; rises in the use of imprisonment or other forms of increased severity cannot simply be explained as reactions to rising crime rates. These sociologies which see punishment as varying independently of crime, breach the link between crime and punishment that is, as we have seen, such a key feature of Durkheim's approach, and which is also the basis of the legal philosophies studied in the earlier chapters. Reviewing the labour market studies, Melossi (1989: 311) comments:

> What all these contributions had in common was their refusal to be content with what I like to call the 'legal syllogism', i.e. the commonsensical idea, originating in the classical school of criminal law, that punishment is simply the consequence of crime and that, therefore, if there is a need for sociological explanation, such explanation concerns criminal behaviour and not the punishment of this behaviour. In this view, in fact, the latter was not conceivable independently of crime: social structure explains crime and crime explains punishment. This is the way lawyers and judges and most of those who are in contact with the criminal justice system, tend to think. This is the way the general public tends to think too.

From Rusche and Kirchheimer onwards, sociologists have taken punishment as an object of study in its own right. Punishment is more than Durkheim's 'passionate reaction' to crime; it is more than the Utilitarians' crime prevention strategy; it is more than the retributivists' just apportionment of harm for harm done – it is a strategy for control of those on the downside of class relations (for the Marxists), or of power relations conceived outside of Marxist class terms.

Why prison?

Probably the most-quoted sentence in *Punishment and Social Structure* is the following: 'Every system of production tends to discover punishments which correspond to its productive relationships' (Rusche and Kirchheimer 1968: 5). In the modern industrial state, this corresponding punishment is imprisonment. Durkheim stated this in his second law of penal evolution, and 'why imprisonment' is a question which has preoccupied contemporary sociologists of punishment. Before the industrial revolution, prisons were places where people were held while awaiting trial, transportation or execution, or until they had fulfilled some court order. These uses of prison still exist (people are remanded in custody while on or awaiting trial or sentence; immigrants or asylum seekers may be remanded in custody prior to deportation; people are imprisoned for contempt of court), but imprisonment of itself, without accompanying punishment such as torture, was not imposed *as punishment* before the mode of production became capitalist. So, the question is posed: '*Why prison?* Why is it that in every industrial society, this institution has become the dominant punitive instrument to such an extent that prison and punishment are commonly regarded as almost synonymous?' (Melossi and Pavarini 1981: 1). For Rusche and Kirchheimer, the answer was simple: prison was a source of labour. Convict labour was an addition to the labour supply, which is why, according to them, prison became a dominant mode of punishment at a time when industrialization produced an almost insatiable demand for labour. Similar reasoning has been applied to the convict labour of the 'chain gangs' in North America: convict labour was a substitute for slave labour after the abolition of slavery (Hawkins 1986). Melossi and Pavarini, however, ask why imprisonment persists when there is no need to supplement the labour supply of free citizens with that of convicts, a question given added relevance by the studies mentioned above which find an association in recent years between imprisonment and over-supply of labour.

Melossi and Pavarini draw on the work of Pashukanis to provide an answer to their question. He suggested that the prerequisite for the development of imprisonment as punishment was the development of wage labour, which puts a price on time. Workers receive a wage per hour, contracts of employment specify hours of work (rather than, for example, the worker working until a job is finished, as people tend to do when working for themselves, either professionally or domestically), and there is, Pashukanis (1978: 181) points out, a correspondence between receiving reward for labour by the hour, and paying for crime by 'doing time':

> for it to be possible for the idea to emerge that one could make recompense for an offence with a piece of abstract freedom determined in advance, it was necessary for all concrete forms of social wealth to be reduced to the most abstract and simple form, to human labour measured in time.

This equivalence between labour measured in time and imprisonment has been incorporated into most Marxist thinking on the development of new forms of punishment in capitalist society (see, for example, Spitzer 1983). Its incorporation moves the argument away from a simple economic reductionism, to a more sophisticated appreciation that the form of the relations of production will be mirrored in other kinds of social relationships. Marxists argue that the principle behind social relationships in capitalist society is that of 'exchange of equivalents' (an amount of money for an amount of work). This fixing of exchange values, this exchanging of equivalents, spreads beyond the factory and is reflected throughout social life. Importantly, as Melossi and Pavarini highlight, the notion of ranking crimes in terms of seriousness, and responding with punishments graduated in terms of severity, involved in the deterrence calculus of Beccaria and in the proportionality of contemporary deserts theorists, is the juridical expression of this exchange of equivalents (Melossi and Pavarini 1981: 184).

In *The Prison and the Factory*, Melossi and Pavarini argue that imprisonment is the paradigmatic mode of punishment in capitalist society not only because of the time–price exchange relationship, but also because imprisonment as punishment and factory production share a parallel concept and requirement of *discipline*. The exchange form of social relationships presumes dealings between people who are free and equal; the *contract* is the ideal expression of such relationships. Under a contract of exchange, both parties are free to accept or reject the terms of exchange, and the contract places obligations to comply equally on both parties. The labour contract under capitalism, however, is made between people who do not have equal power. In accepting the labour contract, then, the worker is accepting a position of subordination. As Melossi (1979: 91) puts it, relationships and institutions in capitalist society are 'based on the fundamental contradiction between political liberty and social slavery'.

In order for the factory system to operate, workers must accept the discipline of time and space – that they are in the factory when the employer wants them to be – and the discipline of subordination to the authority of the capitalist – while in the factory they will do what the capitalist wants them to do. This disciplined existence, argues Melossi (1979: 91), comes about because of the needs of the factory, and is reinforced by being paralleled in other institutions, such as schools and prisons:

> The totality of these conditions finds its real basis in the factory situation but contemporaneously is reproduced in a whole series of other institutions which are born or receive new life with the advent of bourgeois society. These institutions have, by various instruments and methods, the function of forming and controlling the factory proletariat, of guaranteeing the adaptability of labour-power to be used and handled as one commodity among many.

As we shall see in the next chapter, writers on imprisonment from the 1970s onwards shared this recognition of discipline as the leitmotiv of punishment in capitalist society. Prisons that were built or reformed after the advent of capitalism had disciplinary regimes, rather than the unstructured, unoccupied confinement of earlier phases of imprisonment.

Melossi and Pavarini reinforce the Ruschean principle of lesser eligibility, agreeing that prison conditions will always be worse than those of the non-convicted worker, but point out that this excepted, the situation of the factory worker and that of the prisoner are similar: 'Finally: "for the worker the factory is like a prison" (loss of liberty and subordination); "for the inmate the prison is like a factory" (work and discipline)' (Melossi and Pavarini 1981: 188).

Melossi's reformulation and elaboration of Rusche and Kirchheimer's thesis, making central the important contribution of Pashukanis, has given substance to the fundamental claim of the Marxist approach, that punishment systems are appropriate to the economic base of the societies in which they exist, but has moved away from the most reductionist and mechanistic versions of the labour market hypothesis. While increased demand for labour, and therefore the rise in the value of labour, may have been the initial impetus for the shift away from physical punishments which remove offenders from the labour market (execution, mutilation) towards the use of imprisonment as punishment, imprisonment fits the form of social relations in capitalism so exactly that it gains a centrality which is independent of fluctuations in demand for labour.

Marxist theorists now place much emphasis on this equivalence of factory production and imprisonment, with discipline as the category which connects the two. Imprisonment is thus seen as the pre-eminent punishment in capitalist societies, regardless of rises or falls in the value of labour. The tests of the labour market hypothesis done in recent years have been tests not so much of the link between capitalism and imprisonment, as between imprisonment and various stages of the business cycle, within a capitalist economy (Greenberg 1977; Jankovic 1977; Box and Hale 1982; Melossi 1985; Barlow *et al.* 1993). They have supported the 'severity' correlation – that in times of over-supply of labour, punishments become more severe. In countries where imprisonment is the most severe penalty available for all or most offences, then, imprisonment would be expected to increase in times of depression or overpopulation, and this has been confirmed by the studies quoted above.

Prison conditions themselves, moreover, become harsher in such times. The combined effects of lesser eligibility and the lack of economic impetus to reform offenders into workers mean that prison regimes become less constructive, with fewer opportunities for education and training, less emphasis on rehabilitation, early release and parole. As Melossi (1985: 181) summarizes in his study of the association between punishment and business cycles: 'there is no doubt that times of depression are times for punishment'. Prison persists, but its rationale moves away from reform and towards retribution; the rehabilitative ethos of the expansionary 1960s giving way to the retributive ethos during the fiscal crises of the 1970s and 1980s provides clear support for this association.

Ideology and the control of surplus populations

Although the Marxist analysis may seem well supported by the history of punishment, problems remain in seeing this apparent 'fit' as causal explanation. While elaborations of the labour market hypothesis may resolve some of the dilemmas about ebbs and flows in the use of imprisonment or other severe penalties, the difficulty that remains is that of mechanism: just *how* do punishment strategies come to fulfil the requirements of the economy? Sympathetic critics such as Greenberg (1977), Spitzer (1979), Box and Hale (1982) as well as Melossi have pointed out that states, economies, do not build prisons or pass sentences in courts: these are the decisions and actions of human beings. If penality does follow a trajectory which is determined, at base, by the relations of production, then there must be some intervening process by which people in positions of power come to make the decisions that sustain the economic form, and the people who are affected by them accept them. This is the role of *ideology* in Marxist thinking.

Ideology, in Marxist theory, is a set of ideas which govern people's perceptions of the world. In capitalist society, it is argued, ideas which support or facilitate the relations of production come to be seen as ideas which are essential to the continuance of society itself, rather than merely society in its capitalist mode, and the ideas of the capitalist class are taken as being the ideas of society as a whole. Two important aspects of the Marxist theory of ideology have been drawn on by theorists of law and punishment. The first is *fetishism*, and the second is *hegemony*. Fetishism means the representation of relations between people – the representation of arrangements or institutions which, because they are human constructions, could be changed – as extra-human, as if they were somehow natural and universal. 'Market forces', for example, are often referred to as if they existed outside of human decision-making: 'the markets must decide' and 'you can't buck the markets' are phrases which show the fetishized nature of the concept, as if market forces were anything other than arrangements designed and perpetuated by human agents. Hegemony refers to the way in which the ideas of the ruling class – the capitalists – are accepted by the rest of society as their own.

The Marxist theorist who has been most influential in developing the idea of hegemony is Antonio Gramsci, an Italian communist who was imprisoned by the fascists from 1926 until his death in 1937. His most important work is contained in his *Prison Notebooks* (1971). The ideas of the ruling class are hegemonic, Gramsci explains, because not only does the working class submit to the discipline of factory production, but also it comes to share the moral, political and cultural values of the ruling class. Property ownership is respected, people enlist in armies to fight the working class of other countries, strikers and political dissenters are criticized, and – importantly – definitions of crime and justice are shared by those whom they disadvantage as well as by those whom they benefit.

Law, and the modes of punishment, are important institutions for the creation of hegemonic cultures. First and foremost, they must seem to express values of equality and solidarity which give credibility to the state's claims to be ruling in the interests of all, rather than of one particular class. Impartiality, equality before the law, the highest in the land being subject to law, are important for the exercise of law to be accepted as legitimate authority, rather than despotic power. 'Justice must be seen to be done', above all so that the exercise of punitive power will be accepted as the exercise of legitimate authority. Marxist historians of punishment such as Hay (1975) have accordingly stressed the importance of, for example, themes such as equality and mercy in securing popular assent to punishment in the eighteenth century; in analysing changes in punishments in capitalist societies, Spitzer (1979) and others have emphasized the ideological shifts as well as the more narrowly economic-determinist explanations.

Law and the institutions of punishment are part of a series of ideological subsystems which produce in the non-capitalist class the necessary attitudes for acceptance of the discipline of the factory and of the legitimacy of ruling-class power. Law is what Althusser (1971) calls an *ideological state apparatus*. These apparatuses, which include the education system, the family and the mass media, produce the categories of thought necessary to capitalism: the work ethic, the acceptance of property and capital accumulation, and the 'rightness' of obedience to law. When hegemony breaks down, when industrial or political dissent, or 'crime', occurs, then law invokes the punitive sanctions to reinforce its authority. The penal system is therefore what Althusser describes as a 'repressive state apparatus', since it enforces assent by coercion when consent by persuasion has failed to be secured.

Most Marxist sociologists see law and punishment functioning in both repressive and ideological spheres, and point out, for example, that the big prisons that were constructed as capitalism developed were situated in working-class areas. As well as punishing actual criminals, prisons are a reminder to all of what will befall them if they disobey the laws (see, for example, Reiman 1979); if workers reject the discipline of the factory, they will become subject to the even more austere discipline of the prison. Again, all Marxist theorists of punishment subscribe to these ideas about the repressive and ideological role of punishment; the differences among Marxist penologists are in the relative emphasis they place on the repressive and ideological functions, and in the degree of abstraction with which they describe the working of these state apparatuses.

Althusser (1969) is associated with a stance of 'theoretical anti-humanism', in which human agents appear as bearers of structures, rather than as active creators of social meaning and social institutions. The social institutions he describes are 'semi-autonomous' in their relationship to the base economic structure, and also in their relationship to each other. Althusser is a structuralist in the sense that he sees societies as social structures made up of interdependent parts which function together, and together give identity to the whole (Piaget 1971). Just as a bicycle is only a bicycle if its parts are arranged in a certain relationship to each other, so, for structuralist sociologists, social institutions only make sense in relation to each other and to the whole of which they are part.

For Althusserian Marxists, any change in one semi-autonomous institution will be accompanied by corresponding changes in others. For example, as the authority of the Church declines, the authority of the political body increases. The subsystems of society are constituent of each other and of the economic base: their 'reciprocal action' (Althusser 1971: 135) means that each will take on something of the form of the other; for instance, many commentators have shown how legal forms have penetrated social institutions which would appear to be untouched by law (Hunt 1987). Subsystems of society – institutions such as politics, law and the family – are, however, semi- rather than fully autonomous; they are part of the superstructure, and are overdetermined by the economy in the 'last instance' (Althusser 1969).

Although Althusser's work is abstract and theoretical, more concrete analyses have drawn on these ideas. Juliet Mitchell, for example, in her attempts to synthesize Marxism, feminism and psychoanalytic theory to understand the continued subordination of women, shows how the loosening of laws about women's employment and political participation could not be reversed when the need for their labour declined in the post-war period, and in compensation, ideological controls strengthened (Mitchell 1966). As Betty Friedan describes, in the post-war years women expelled themselves from the labour force, under the influence of the mass media retailing images of the happy housewife, the guilt and strain of working mothers, and, of course, the linking of delinquency with maternal deprivation (Friedan 1963). The subsystems accommodate each other, preserving the gender role division of capitalism.

Althusserian and other structuralist explanations, however, still do not contribute all that is needed to reach an understanding of how these shifts in control strategies, in making sure that the economy is served in 'the last instance', are achieved, and so contemporary studies of the legitimating function of law and punishment have drawn more on Gramsci's 'humanist' Marxism. As Greenberg (1977) and Box and Hale (1982) describe, the effects of repression of dissent, of regulation of the labour market, of the association between imprisonment and unemployment, are produced through the decisions of individual participants in criminal justice systems. Judges' beliefs about the risk of reoffending by unemployed offenders, about the undesirability of imprisoning an employed offender with the result that s/he will lose the possibility of a non-criminal livelihood, that children of lone-parent families are prone to delinquency, for example, will produce correlations between unemployment and imprisonment, single-parent families and young offenders in institutional care, and so on.

The connection between punishment practices and prevailing ideologies has been a focus of Marxist sociologies of punishment and social control since the mid- to late 1970s. What sociologists and penologists have been concerned to explain is the rise of 'law and order ideology', which has seen the rate of imprisonment rise in England and Wales, the USA and elsewhere; social welfare institutions and social policy being cut back and penal policy and penal institutions expanding; the demise of rehabilitative penal strategies and the rise of 'get-tough' retributive and incapacitative penal strategies. This law and order climate, it is argued, has arisen to meet the requirements of control in periods of economic down-turn: recession and consequent high unemployment rates mean that social compliance cannot be so easily secured by the hope of socio-economic rewards, and must therefore be secured through repression and coercion. For this repressive coercion to be seen as legitimate, the mass of people must be induced to blame subgroups of their own sections of society, rather than blaming capitalism itself. The main strategy for securing compliance has been the ideological creation of 'enemies within': illegal immigrants, welfare scroungers, one-parent families, and, of course, criminals.

Law and order ideology displaces fear of recession with fear of crime as the most urgent public problem; strong political action is thus demanded, sympathy for offenders disappears, and 'public opinion' consequently demands the sort of penal austerity and penal harshness that the labour market theorists have found to be correlated with periods of downturn within the business cycle.

Law and order ideology is

a complex if naive set of attitudes, including the beliefs that human beings have free will, that they must be strictly disciplined by restrictive rules, and that they should be harshly punished if they break the rules or fail to respect authority.

(Cavadino and Dignan 1992: 26)

Law and order ideology and its repressive and divisive strategies accompany loss of belief in the possibility of full or near-full employment. Current understanding of the impact of technology, the limits to the expansion of world trade, make it appear that the unemployed are no longer a 'reserve army' but a surplus population, a permanent 'underclass'. There is no economic impetus to deploy the reformative/rehabilitative penal policies of the constructive prison or the development of non-custodial penalties, and it is feared that the marginalization of whole sections of the community will give them no incentive to be law-abiding, and every incentive to turn to crime.

Whether or not times of depression really do lead to increased crime is debatable (Melossi 1985; Box 1987; Chiricos 1987; Hudson 1993), but what is not debatable is that in times of recession the vocabulary of justice becomes harsher. Blame is attached to individuals, and social responsibility for crime is denied; lack of investment in areas of high unemployment is blamed on crime rates rather than on the flight of capital; the unemployed are said to be happy to depend on welfare payments, to have a different (pro-crime) set of values from those of the rest of society.

Theories of justice in such times inevitably emphasize punishment rather than help or treatment, and the economic downturn has indeed seen the demise of the rehabilitative orthodoxy and the rise of deterrence, retribution and incapacitative strategies (Hudson 1987; 1993). In England and Wales and the USA, as the recession of the 1980s deepened, deterrence and retribution (in its contemporary form of 'just deserts') gave way to incapacitation. Deterrence, after all, can only be effective if people do have choices; retribution depends on concern for the rights of offenders – as economic choices narrowed, and as the legitimation crisis grew and so the scapegoating of 'suitable enemies' became more voracious, the right of offenders to be protected from excessive punishment became of less and less concern. The policies, advocated by Wilson (1975/1983), of containment of those judged to be persistent offenders have, during the 1990s, become the most influential penal theories, reaching their apogee in the 'three strikes' law passed in California, whereby a third offence (not necessarily a third serious or violent offence) can lead to imprisonment of 25 years or life, with no possibility of parole.

Analysts have linked the changing vocabularies of crime and punishment, and the hardening penal practices – the law and order ideology – to the so-called 'double-sided nature' of the radical right conservatism that developed during the era of Thatcher and Reagan in the UK and USA (Jefferson and Shapland 1994: 267). Described by Hall (1988: 123–49) as 'authoritarian populism', radical right politics centralized power by emasculating local government and the institutions of civil society, but legitimated their aggregation of power by appealing directly to 'the people', over the heads of intermediate levels of government. New rightism combined economic libertarianism with social authoritarianism (Scraton 1987): the deregulation of finance and commerce was accompanied by progressive tightening of the rules covering welfare benefits, immigration controls and the like, as well as increased hostility and punitiveness towards sexual diversity and 'alternative lifestyles'.

As well as the need to contain dissent, the law and order ideology is prompted by the ideology of conservatism itself. As Gamble (1988) encapsulates in his phrase 'the free economy and the strong state', new right politics is faced with the dilemma of its own economic beliefs ruling out interventionness in the sphere of life with which governments are most concerned, the economy. New right monetarism prescribes 'hands-off' economic management. Governments must not intervene, the markets must rule, is the dogma of neo-conservative economics, and this poses a problem for governments which wish to project themselves as strong. An aspect of social life must be highlighted as an area where strong, interventionist government policy is required, and crime has been the chosen area.

Much of this new Marxist sociology has been concerned with criminalization rather than punishment, with the study of the rise of 'mugging' as a new category of crime, and the associated moral panic, being one of the most celebrated contributions (Hall *et al.* 1978). Other writers (for example, Lea and Young 1984; Box 1987) have continued in this vein, and have looked at the spiral of criminalization and penalization, with hardening of penal politics accompanying rising crime rates and rising fear of crime.

These investigations of the trajectories of penality during times of economic recession have been concerned with the issue of legitimation of the power of the ruling class; they have, in one way or another, been concerned with the response to the fracturing of or challenges to ruling-class hegemonic ideology. An important ingredient of capitalist ideology is the authority of law, and the exposure of law as ideology has been undertaken by legal scholars in the newly emerged critical legal studies tradition (Fitzpatrick and Hunt 1987; Kerruish 1991). A sustained critique has been made of the fetishization in capitalist legal ideology of two ideas in particular: that of rights and that of equality. The liberal ideology of rights, it is argued, maintains that all people, regardless of their social-economic circumstances, share the obligation to obey the law, and consequently liability to punishment if they disobey, because the law protects the rights of all. The liberal theory of rights emphasizes, in Melossi's words, capitalism's political freedom, but neglects its social slavery. Critical legal theorists argue that the formal ascription of rights in law in modern societies 'has no meaning for people who do not have the wealth or power either to define which rights should be guaranteed by law, to secure for themselves rights which are specified, or to secure redress against violations of rights' (Hudson 1993: 197). Political obligation is anchored not in distribution of rights in practice, but in notional rights in theory, and the equal distribution of rights, and therefore of obligations and liabilities, is described by the 'procedural equality' which legal theory substitutes for the material inequalities of the social world. Rights are fetishized in modern legal theory, as Kerruish (1991) explains, by being projected as universal, natural and self-evident, equally possessed by all citizens of a society where all are equal before the law, rather than being seen as contingent, gained or lost by struggle, and emerging from power-structured social relationships. The impact of these fetishized concepts of rights and equality is that they enforce the ideas of crime as proceeding from freely-willed people who have equal chances of choosing to remain within the law, and who, whatever their material circumstances and social status, share in the benefits of a society which is protective of rights which are held by all.

All the accounts of the control of 'surplus' populations in times of economic downturn confirm the association between recession, penal severity, and a justice of individual culpability and individual threat; what does vary between the various authors is the degree to which this association is seen as mediated through an increase in crime. The so-called 'left realists' explain that marginalization of many of the unemployed, especially young black people, not surprisingly leads to an increase in crime rates among these groups, which in turn gives rise to increased penalization (Lea and Young 1984). Others concentrate on the increased criminalization of those (again, young black people) who are perceived – rightly or wrongly – as posing a threat of disorder (Gilroy 1987). In other words, the association between economic recession and penal severity is not in doubt; what does vary between various accounts is the extent to which the link between crime and punishment, the 'legal syllogism' rejected by Melossi, is fractured or restored.

The challenge of feminism

As well as showing the association between penal modes and forms of society, Marxist sociologies of punishment and law have directed attention to a very important aspect of penality: that it is targeted at a particular section of the population. The abstraction of legal philosophy, the commonality of Durkheim's individuals, is replaced by the depiction of human beings as occupying different positions in social structures. Marxist perspectives establish that punishment is directed at the working classes or the underclass. The penal system is seen as a 'penal-penalizing circuit' which represses and stigmatizes certain sections of society, but filters out others (Laffargue and Godefroy 1989). The regulation of capital is achieved mostly by the civil law and by administrative regulation; the repressive criminal law is directed predominantly at the kinds of wrongdoing that are most common among the poor: 'the criminal law is designed primarily for the non-affluent; the affluent are kept in line, for the most part, by tort law' (Posner 1985: 1204–5). Criminal justice deals most harshly with the most disadvantaged, acting as a 'homogenizing filter', by which at each stage (passing of criminal laws; law enforcement; proceeding with prosecution; sentencing; parole) those who are not filtered out become more alike in sharing the characteristics of disadvantage – the poor, the undereducated, members of minority ethnic groups (Shelden 1982; Hudson 1993).

One might expect that this appreciation that penality is directed by some sections of society against others, would have led to recognition of the significance of gender for the sociology of punishment. Although there is much feminist work which is concerned with the penal treatment of women, this work has largely remained on the margins of penology and criminology, and has not been incorporated into broader theoretical understandings of punishment and control as social institutions (Howe 1994). There are at least two points at which gender differences in punishment and control pose important challenges to any general theory of punishment: the labour market hypothesis; and the relations between punishment and other institutions of social control.

Women have traditionally been seen very much as a 'reserve army of labour'. As mentioned above in connection with the semi-autonomy of institutions, ideological, legal and political controls on women's participation in the labour market have tightened and loosened according to fluctuations in the demand for and supply of (male) labour. Women have made gains towards equality in times of war when their labour is more than usually needed; in times of recession, ideological controls focusing on the importance of mothers' presence in the home tend to become more pronounced. It would be expected, then, that trends in the imprisonment of women would demonstrate at least as much correlation with the labour market as those of men. Few labour market studies have differentiated their data by gender, although some do acknowledge that the unemployment–imprisonment correlation is strongest for certain groups, particularly young black males (Howe 1994). One criminologist who has analysed the correlations between the business cycle and the imprisonment of women is Braithwaite, who looked at data for New South Wales and Victoria for the latter half of the nineteenth century and the early part of the twentieth. He found that women's imprisonment declined in New South Wales during periods of economic decline (Howe 1994: 42).

This association, Howe suggested, points to women's importance to capitalism not as workers, but as reproducers of workers, and as carriers of important ideological roles as the socializers and educators of men. Braithwaite assumed that women's reduced imprisonment during depressed economic periods was because they were more important than ever in keeping families together, and under control, in depressed times.

This conjecture is supported by the literature on the imprisonment of women, which consistently finds that having care of children is associated with penal leniency (see, for example, Farrington and Morris 1983; Eaton 1986). Such findings would generally support the Marxist view of the family as important for reproducing the bodies and the disciplined mentalities of workers (Melossi 1979). It also fits with support for findings in studies of the penal treatment of women that conventional gender and familial roles are upheld by law and criminal justice (Carlen 1983; Edwards 1984; Eaton 1986). Taxation regulations, civil laws as well as criminal law, reinforce the roles of man as breadwinner, woman as carer, and people who transgress these roles (the unemployed man, the woman who has relinquished care of her children) are, alike, recipients of penal severity.

More difficult to reconcile with orthodox Marxist perspectives are the ways in which men and women are distributed between the different institutions of control. Why women should be treated more readily as mad, and men more readily as bad, needs insights beyond those that Marxism has so far offered. If females are most usually controlled by non-penal processes and institutions, such as psychiatry and social work (which the evidence would suggest is the case) but men are more readily penalized (Allen 1987; Carlen 1992) – if, therefore, the implications of non-performance of the roles ascribed to the genders in capitalism are different for men and women – then it would appear that there is some principle other than that of the relations of production, the relationship to the labour market, that produces social control strategies. It would seem, in other words, that the gender division is as basic to the social formation as the class division.

Catherine MacKinnon summarizes the challenges which Marxism and feminism pose for each other. Both, she says, are theories of power and systematic injustice; both show how principles of inequality structure all social relationships; Marxism shows how value is socially created and socially relational, while feminism shows how sexuality is similarly socially constructed and socially relational; both show how their basic organizing concept, value or sexuality, leads to the commodification of the body. She quotes Engels's characterization of women as like children in being incompletely adult, defined by their biology, in need of special protection (a view of women which seems exactly to describe their treatment in law), and in being exceptions to every rule of social analysis developed by Marx, and asks of Marxism and feminism:

> What if the claims of each theory are taken equally seriously, each on its own terms? Can two social processes be basic at once? Can two groups be subordinated in conflicting ways, or do they merely cross-cut? Can two theories, each of which purports to account for the same thing – power as such – be reconciled? Confronted on equal terms, these theories at minimum pose fundamental questions for each other. Is male dominance a creation of capitalism, or is capitalism an expression of male dominance? What does it mean for class analysis if a social group is defined and exploited through means that seem largely independent of the organization of production, if in forms appropriate to it? What does it mean for a sex-based analysis if capitalism might not be materially altered if it were fully sex integrated or even controlled by women?
>
> (MacKinnon 1989: 5)

Conclusion: the legacy of Marxism

The political economy of punishment is undoubtedly a perspective that cannot be overlooked if a full appreciation of justice in modern societies is to be gained. The connection between imprisonment, and also between theories of justice, which, whatever their differences, all carry a notion of graduated penalties, and the exchange of equivalents which is the form of social relationships in capitalist societies, seems well established. That there is a connection between the value of labour and the severity of punishments also seems well established, and the emphasis in recent studies of punishment in times of economic recession on ideology and legitimation has moved this connection from being an over-functionalist portrayal of the rational fiscal strategies of 'states' to a richer portrayal of the material grounding of theories of justice and strategies of punishment.

Garland (1990a: 130) is of the opinion that these insights which the less abstract Marxists provide, though valuable, amount to little more than a general statement of the relationship between penality and the material and ideological conditions of societies, and are not tied to a Marxist framework. On the other hand, Marxism has demonstrated the specificity of social forms and the dependence of analytic tools themselves on the societies in which they are embedded. Pashukanis, Althusser and others all assert the non-comparability of capitalist and non-capitalist societies, and if we wish to understand the workings of institutions in capitalist society, we need to start with conceptions which derive from the analysis of capitalism itself.

While the Marxist theory of ideology – the works on legitimation cited above – does offer an understanding of the expressive aspects of punishment that Durkheim and the other cultural theorists have identified, as well as illuminating the control and functional aspects, and while it makes possible a reading of the philosophies of punishment which can step outside the closures of liberal ideology within which these philosophies are confined, two problems of Marxist social analysis remain. The first is that discussed by MacKinnon, that sexual divisions may be as basic as class divisions. The second is that Marxism itself is rooted in an ideology of modernism with its assumption of historical progression, an ideology whose time appears to be over.

The disciplined society: Foucault and the analysis of penality

Introduction
Foucault's disciplinary penality
Delinquency and normalization
Critique and controversy
   Periodicity
   Overgeneralization
   Partiality
   Functionalism
   Politics
Summary and conclusion: Foucault's legacy

Introduction

Almost ten years after the republication of *Punishment and Social Structure* (Rusche and Kirchheimer 1968) another book appeared which transformed the sociological understanding of punishment in modern industrial societies. Michel Foucault's *Discipline and Punish: The Birth of the Prison* (1977) offered a yet deeper analysis of the relationship between forms of punishment and the society in which they are found. *Discipline and Punish* incorporated Rusche and Kirchheimer's links between the rise of imprisonment and the capitalist economic form, as well as Durkheim's understanding of the forms of authority and solidarity in modern societies, but also encompassed the connection between forms of punishment and forms of knowledge, suggesting a symmetry between epistemology and penal practice. Foucault identified an emergent 'penal rationality' (Pasquino 1991); he described not a simple phenomenon of punishment but *penality*, a complex of theories, institutions, practices, laws and professional positions which have as their object the sanctioning of offenders.

Foucault's disciplinary penality

Like Melossi and Pavarini (Melossi 1979; Melossi and Pavarini 1981), he highlights 'discipline' as the key element in modern punishment, linking penal forms to the capitalist mode of production. But in Foucault's work, discipline appears not (merely) as the mechanism which links the superstructure of punishment to the economic base; in *Discipline and Punish*, discipline is foregrounded as the defining characteristic of social control in modern society, and, furthermore, as a key element of modern society itself.

Foucault's work is original, stimulating, but complex; *Discipline and Punish*, though standing alone as a fascinating and thought-provoking commentary on the development of imprisonment as the main modern form of punishment, forms part of a larger philosophical-sociological investigation of forms of thought and of the exercise of power in modern society. His work has generated a large secondary literature of exposition and critique, as well as having influenced subsequent analysts of penality and social control (among them Cohen 1979; 1985; Garland 1985; 1990a; Howe 1994). This chapter will examine the main themes of *Discipline and Punish*; refer to other works by Foucault where this is helpful to understanding his approach to punishment; mention some of the more recurrent criticisms of the work; and finally, introduce some texts, substantial and important in their own right, which have taken Foucault's text as a departure point, and one or two works which have attempted to trace the development to contemporary times of some of the trends identified by Foucault.

Like Durkheim, and Rusche and Kirchheimer, Foucault is concerned with the transition in modes of punishment from the harsh physical penalties of the pre-capitalist, pre-industrial eras to the graduated, rule-governed sanctions of the age of industrial capitalism. Like them, and like Melossi and Pavarini, he focuses on the question 'Why prison?'. The themes pursued in *Discipline and Punish*, then, are essentially the same as in all the social histories of punishment that have been considered in the preceding chapters: they are concerned with the relationship of modern punishments to the structure and character of modern society. Apart from the richer intellectual context in which Foucault places his account of penal forms, the main difference between *Discipline and Punish* and the other texts so far discussed lies in the methodological approach taken in the former.

Durkheim and the Marxist sociologists are structuralists following the deductive methods of positivist sociology. That is to say, their accounts are top-down: they look at societies in large-scale, abstract terms, with any references to actual penal institutions, policies or practices included as evidence for, or examples of, their hypotheses concerning the general nature and functions of punishment. Foucault, on the other hand, develops a bottom-up account, deriving generalizations and theoretical propositions from a detailed examination of penal practices. This is the phenomeno-logical method. Simply, phenomenology means to describe things – phenomena – themselves, and from such descriptions to gain a sense of their common characteristics and their differences, their relationships to each other and to the contexts in which they occur, building theory and explanation out of commonalities and patterns which emerge. Although he is by no means the first author to apply phenomenological method to punishment – Garfinkel (1956), for example, is a well-known phenomeno-logical study of courtroom proceedings, described in Chapter 6 – Foucault was certainly the first major scholar to connect (inseparably, seemingly, from the way in which his ideas have dominated subsequent sociology of punishment) the analysis of punishment to the mainly French tradition of phenomenological social and political philosophy, represented by writers such as Bachelard (1968), Merleau-Ponty (1962) and Sartre (1958; 1974). Indeed, Garland (1990a: 133) has expressed the opinion that it is not so much in the originality of his themes or his conclusions that the importance of Foucault's contribution lies, but in this deployment of the detail of phenomenological method to the day-to-day operation of penal policy and practice.

Foucault builds his characterization of modern penality, then, on descriptions of two punitive phenomena: a public execution and the timetabled regime of a 'modern' prison. The opening pages of *Discipline and Punish* quote an account in the *Gazette d'Amsterdam* of 1 April 1757 of the public torture, execution, drawing and quartering of Damiens, the regicide, in Paris, and then an extract from the rules for the 'house of young prisoners in Paris', drawn up 80 years later by Leon Faucher, which pre-scribe a strictly timetabled regime of eating, washing, praying, schooling and working. Foucault (1977: 7) claims that these two phenomena, the public execution and the timetabled regime, though they do not punish the same types of crime or the same types of offenders, 'each define a certain penal style'. He then proceeds to describe and differentiate these two penal styles, and shows how each is linked to certain fundamental characteristics of the societies – the *ancien régime* and the modern industrial-capitalist state – in which they occur. The passing of the *ancien régime* is also the passing of the public execution; the emergence of the factory society is also the emergence of the imprisoning society.

Foucault makes clear from the outset that in describing penality he is describing what he calls 'technologies of power'. His central topic is the way in which power is exercised in modern society; he is not primarily con-cerned with the constitution of moral authority, as is Durkheim, or with the logic of the capitalist economy, as are the Marxists. These perspectives he incorporates by taking them for granted, posing law as a kind of modern moral mythology, and treating the symmetry between economic relations and other elements of social structures as more or less self-evident; what Foucault is concerned with first and foremost are the inter-nal workings of the institutions brought forth by the structural imperatives of capitalism. In particular, he seeks to demonstrate the way in which power is exercised within these institutions.

The power that he is especially concerned with in *Discipline and Punish* is *bio-power*, power of and over the body. Power is manifest first and foremost in its relationship to the body: the most obvious and compelling power that one person can have over another is the power to interfere with his/her physical integrity. In the *ancien régime*, power over the bodies of subjects was expressed by the right to use the bodies of others for the pursuit of the goals of the powerful through military service and through serfdom, and to eliminate or mutilate the bodies of those who were perceived as enemies. The public execution is a demonstration as well as an exercise of this power – the horrific nature of the punishment reflects, as Durkheim would have it, the terrible, the sacrilegious nature of the crime, as well as, in Foucault's (1977: 55) terms, 'reaffirming the dissymmetry of forces' of the sovereign and the subject.

With the modern state, the sovereign no longer has power as of right, is no longer a representative of the divine, but has the delegated power of the people. As Durkheim and the Marxist theorists tell us, and as Foucault affirms, the modern state is, formally at least, an association of equal citizens, where the paradigm social relationship is the contract between legal equals. Foucault's analysis of bio-power draws, in its essentials, on reasoning very similar to that of Melossi, seeing that penal forms must balance the facts of legal equality and socio-economic inequality that characterize capitalist society. The power to punish in modern industrial society affirms asymmetries of power just as much as in the *ancien régime*, but it must be exercised in ways that recognize the legal equality and contract form that the modern state has instituted. Infliction of pain is thus rejected in favour of suspension of rights; emphasis thus shifts from what the sovereign can do to the subject to what the citizen may forfeit by illegal or anti-social actions. So, in modern society, 'from being an art of unbearable sensation punishment has become an economy of suspended rights' (Foucault 1977: 11).

Punishments come to take the form of deprivation of right to liberty and to control of one's own time and space, as well as to deprivation of property rights in financial penalties. Even where the right to life is removed, in capital punishment, it is the withdrawal of the right that is the penalty, not the infliction of pain, which is why jurisdictions which retain the death penalty are concerned with whether or not death is instantaneous and does not leave the condemned person in minutes of agony. (The story of the development of the electric chair in the USA is illustrative of this concern; proponents of the alternative AC and DC systems pressed their claims on the basis of producing the least burning of the flesh, the least chest pain, the quickest, cleanest and most painless death (Miller 1994).)

Rights, which are suspended by punishment, can be calibrated just as can the degree of pain in older penalities. For example, punishment for infraction of prison regulations typically takes the form of loss of privileges, loss of rights of association, of the right to wear one's own clothes, rather than the infliction of pain; similarly, rewards for conformity take the form of partial or progressive restoration of rights, through home leave, parole or remission.

Foucault also shares with the Marxists the appreciation that the modern industrial state is primarily interested in people for their labour. He argues that Rusche and Kirchheimer are right when they say that the severity of punishments is linked to the value of labour, and says that this means that punishment, like other social institutions, will be charged with the transformation of bodies into labour power. Punishments will therefore have as their objective the turning of rebellious bodies into productive and subjugated bodies (Foucault 1977: 24), bodies with both the capacity and the willingness to work under the conditions laid down by the industrial economy. Hence the prison has the mission of inducing in inmates a change of goal, from profiting from crime to earning by labour, as well as providing the skills necessary to achieve this. The timetable of the house of young prisoners, then, is readily understandable as the regime to accomplish this transformation.

Foucault gives us the nineteenth-century prison as the arena for personal change and social experimentation. He describes in detail the architecture, the regimes, the personnel, and the knowledge of offenders to which the project of reform through imprisonment gives rise. The nineteenth-century prison regime combines discipline with surveillance: the prisoner must follow a strict timetable of improving activities, and is under constant observation while doing so. Observation is for reasons of security and good order within the prison, but it is also to monitor the progress of the prisoner. For Foucault, the ideal type of the institution which combines the architecture and the regime where these twin elements of surveillance and disciplined activity can be combined and enforced to the maximum degree, is the *panopticon*. Concretely, the panopticon was a design for a prison formulated by the Utilitarian social philosopher, Jeremy Bentham, which combined the ideas of permanent surveillance and purposive activity that Foucault sees as central to modern penality. The panopticon prison as described by Bentham was never realized in full, but elements of his design were widely adopted, and are familiar to those of us who have ever visited any of the Victorian prisons in England such as Pentonville or Strangeways. What comes instantly to mind in association with the idea of the panopticon prison is the central control circle, with wings of cells radiating from it. A controller situated in the circle can look down the wings, and in the perfect panopticon a system of prisms would allow the controller to see inside the individual cells, without being seen by the prisoner. Thus the prisoner can never know whether s/he is being observed at any particular moment, but must therefore assume s/he is.

For Foucault, the panopticon is more than just an architectural drawing and a timetable, it is a principle of punitive power. The panopticon is the possibility for realizing the project of disciplinary confinement:

The perfect disciplinary apparatus would make it possible for a single gaze to see everything constantly. A central point would be both the source of light illuminating everything, and a locus of convergence for everything that must be known; a perfect eye that nothing would escape and a centre towards which all gazes would be turned.

(Foucault 1977: 173)

Consciousness of the possibility of surveillance makes the inmates discipline themselves; they are induced to behave at all times in accordance with the dictates of the regime, so that at the moment the gaze falls upon them, they will be approved and will avoid further punishment. Panopticism supplements regulation, then, with self-regulation:

the major effect of the Panopticon: to induce in the inmate a state of conscious and permanent visibility that assumes the automatic functioning of power. So to arrange things that . . . the inmates are caught up in a power situation of which they are themselves the bearers.

(ibid.: 201)

It is this suggestion of the disciplinary gaze, the all-seeing panopticon eye being at the heart of punitive power in the modern society, that gives Foucault's work something of the character of a Big Brother dystopia. This judgement is enhanced when he goes on to argue that panopticism is a characteristic not just of imprisonment in modern society, but of the exercise of a wider power which reaches outside the prison and brings more and more of the population, and more and more aspects of their lives, within its ambit. This 'dispersal of discipline' is one of the most distinctive and controversial of Foucault's arguments. It is central to his claim that the shift from corporal punishments to the penality of suspended rights was not necessarily a transition to more lenient and more humane punishment, and, as he claims in one of the most frequently quoted passages in the contemporary sociology of punishment, that the objective of the new strategy that developed in the eighteenth and nineteenth centuries was

to make of the punishment and repression of illegalities a regular function, coextensive with society; not to punish less, but to punish better; to punish with an attenuated severity perhaps, but in order to punish with more universality and necessity; to insert the power to punish more deeply into the social body.

(ibid.: 82)

Delinquency and normalization

Modern penality substitutes suspension of rights for infliction of pain; it substitutes disciplining of the body-persona for mutilation of the physical body – it also substitutes the professional gaze for the public spectacle.

Foucault emphasizes the significance of this move from punishment in public to discipline behind the closed walls of the prison, and the change from the public to the experts as participant-observers.

One of the things that this shift of audience means is that the offender changes from being a member of the public, who after punishment is either removed from society altogether (through death, transportation or exile) and is therefore no longer of public or professional interest, or else returns to his/her normal location within the society after the occasion of punishment; to being a member of a specially marked out subgroup of the population, a group of 'delinquents', specially constituted and differentiated from non-delinquents. Membership of this group of delinquents is enduring. Foucault compares this effect of modern punishments to the way in which society deals with lepers: offenders become the lepers of modern society, consigned to a space which is separated from 'clean' and 'healthy' citizens, but none the less connected to it in that the leper colony is serviced by 'healthy' society, and the healthy citizens are aware of the existence of the leper colony and in fear of it.

An underlying principle of modern penality, then, is exclusion combined with differentiation and classification:

> It is the peculiarity of the nineteenth century that it applied to the space of exclusion of which the leper was the symbolic inhabitant (beggars, vagabonds, madmen and the disorderly formed the real population) the technique of power proper to disciplinary partitioning.
>
> (Foucault 1977: 199)

Nineteenth-century imprisonment did not exclude criminals to make them invisible, however: the prison was not a dungeon, an *oubliette*. Foucault describes how the newly developing social sciences were enlisted to make the criminal into an object of knowledge – a delinquent. Disciplinary punishment was not aimed at punishing the crime, but at changing the offender, and change was dependent on knowing the offender. Hence the development of criminology (Pasquino 1991), the body of knowledge concerned with the diagnosis, classification and correction of the types of criminal and the causes of their criminality.

It is at this point that Foucault engages with the debate over whether the prison failed or succeeded. If, as he explains, the rationale of imprisonment is correctionalism, then it would seem to be a failure. Furthermore, as he acknowledges, its failure in reforming offenders has been recognized throughout the history of the use of imprisonment as the primary form of punishment. Foucault would not necessarily disagree with Mathiesen's (1990) charge that prison fails according to any penal rationale. Nevertheless, Foucault claims that the nineteenth-century prison succeeded in relation to a very important function, which is that of constituting 'delinquents' as a social category, and of transforming crime from 'popular illegalities' – acts such as poaching which were not disapproved by the general population because they were seen as ordinary acts necessary for material survival – into delinquencies which were seen not to be part of mainstream life but as threatening to mainstream life and values. Prison created, in other words, a criminal subculture, of whom the 'respectable' working class disapproved, and whose punishment was regarded as legitimate.

Modern prisons, says Foucault, cause recidivism: former inmates have a higher chance of committing crime than if they had remained out of custody; and imprisonment encourages the organization of delinquents into a subculture with loyalty to each other. If, he says, one takes at face value the idea that the function of punishment is to reduce offences, then prison must be admitted to fail. But, he suggests,

> perhaps one should reverse the problem and ask oneself what is served by the failure of the prison; what is the use of these different phenomena that are continually being criticized; the maintenance of delinquency, the encouragement of recidivism, the transformation of the occasional offender into a habitual delinquent, the organization of a closed milieu of delinquency. . . . Penality would then appear to be a way of handling illegalities, of laying down the limits of tolerance, of giving free rein to some, of putting pressure on others, of excluding a particular section, of making another useful, of neutralizing certain individuals and of profiting from others. In short, penality does not simply 'check' illegalities; it differentiates them, it provides them with a general economy.
>
> (Foucault 1977: 262)

Foucault is thus denying that the basic function of penal sanctions – and therefore of imprisonment – is to reduce crime, or even to exact retribution, rather than to manage crime in a way which enhances and bolsters the legitimacy of power. He is endorsing the Durkheimian function of giving expression to social values and the rules derived from them, but he is also highlighting the way that the actual use of imprisonment and other punitive sanctions serves to differentiate crimes from each other: specifically, the way in which it marks out the crimes of the poor as the crimes which are most threatening, and concentrates public concern on them, thus deflecting attention from the sorts of crime with which it either cannot or does not wish to deal, which are generally the crimes of the powerful. Prison is the punishment used mainly for the poor and the marginal (see, for example, Mathiesen 1974; Hudson 1993), and its transformation of occupants of these statuses into 'delinquents' – incorrigible, determinedly anti-social, dangerous predators from whom 'ordinary folk' as well as the state need protection – is its true utility. From this vantage point, '[s]o successful has the prison been that, after a century and a half of "failures", the prison still exists, producing the same results, and there is the greatest reluctance to dispense with it' (Foucault 1977: 277).

This 'disciplinary partitioning' that Foucault describes as the result of the fusion of legal specification of crimes with social science's production of 'delinquents', realized through punitive architecture and techniques that demonstrate and reproduce delinquency, connects his work on punishment with other aspects of his *oeuvre*. A continuing strand through his works is investigation of the categories through which human subjectivity came to be known, as first the Enlightenment and then the progressive development of the modernist age facilitated the emergence of new traditions of moral and political philosophy, as well as social and life sciences such as psychiatry, pedagogy, evolutionism and sociology. These new disciplines provide a vocabulary in which the human condition can be expressed, and gave rise to techniques with which human populations can be managed. In a series of works, he traces the 'dividing practices' which differentiated the sane from the insane, the delinquent from the respectable, the decent from the perverted (Foucault 1973; 1977; 1978).

Through his description of the creation of forms of knowledge about human beings, and the divisions around which these discourses are centred, Foucault's celebrated *power–knowledge* dyad emerges. As well as acknowledging that knowledge can bestow power, Foucault claims the reverse, that knowledge can be an emanation of power. One everyday experience of this is the status that is given to knowledge claims according to the position of the person making the claim: if, for example, a patient tells her/his doctor s/he has a particular disease, this may well be treated as hypochondria or guesswork; if, on the other hand, the doctor tells the patient s/he has the disease, this is a diagnosis. Again, this perception is not unique or original to Foucault, and was already well established in the sociology of social deviance and control. Goffman had written about the power relationships between psychiatrists and their patients, and the interactionist or 'labelling' school as a whole had directed attention to the way in which deviant identities are constructed not just from deviant behaviour but also from the pronouncements of judges, social workers and others who categorize and stigmatize (Goffman 1959; 1963; Becker 1963; Rubington and Weinberg 1968).

Foucault's significant contribution, however, was to locate these insights into a wider political economy of power, and to see them as part of the modernist project of 'normalization'. Penality, he has observed, in modern times is concerned not so much with actions as with actors, with creating the normal, properly socialized subject. In this, penality is continuous with other institutions of socialization which were established or became universalized during the nineteenth century – institutions such as schools, hospitals, mental asylums, and factories, with their roles and their knowledges organized around the production of the normal, properly functioning citizen-worker.

By seeing law and the human sciences as jointly engaged in the modernist project of normalization, Foucault explains how the reconciliation of legal equality and social inequality is achieved. Law establishes the characteristics according to which we are all equal, and prescribes the rules which we must all equally obey and the moral bounds within which we must all equally remain; the human sciences produce, describe and make both visible and legitimate the social divisions which define our identity, experience and social location. Foucault juxtaposes law and social science, the one with its mythology of sameness and the other with its reproduction of difference, sometimes posing social science as subversive of law (Hunt 1992), but depicting them as none the less interdependently entailed in the strategies of normalization. This mutual involvement of law and the human science disciplines in the task of normalization is, for Foucault, the defining characteristic of the exercise of power in the industrial age; it emerges as the governmental rationality of the nineteenth century; it is *governmentality*, which has taken over from the simple exercise of power by an absolute sovereign in the *ancien régime* (Foucault 1978; Burchell *et al.* 1991).

Foucault's insistence on penality as the production of the delinquent as an object of knowledge – the production of delinquency as a particular kind of illegality and delinquents as a particular social group – provides at least a partial answer to the question why the nineteenth century adopted a correctionalist penality rather than the alternative, classical strategy of graduated retribution. Why, in other words, did the theories of Bentham become more influential than the theories of Beccaria?

Classical penology, proportional punishment, does not construct a 'delinquent'. Rather, classical penology depends upon an image of the offender as no different from the non-offender; crime is seen as rational activity, arising out of the same sorts of calculation of costs and benefits as any other purposive human activity. There is no image of the offender as socially deprived, or psychologically disturbed, and its adoption would exempt punishment from participation in the normalization project which, according to Foucault, all social institutions shared in the modernist era. Law could not defend itself from the spread of human sciences, because the strategies of power were directed at normalization. Classical penology, with its dependency on categories of sameness rather than difference, would not serve the management of illegalities, the subjugation of populations, the production of docile bodies that Foucault sees as the essential functions of penality in the modern society.

Showing that punishment is one strategy within a wider project of normalization is the essential element of Foucault's argument that penality is continuous with other socializing institutions, that together they produce the 'disciplinary society'. Foucault goes further than saying that prisons, schools, mental asylums and factories all serve the same (capitalist-industrial) purposes, and that there are similarities in the regimes of them all. He goes further than Melossi and Pavarini's (1981) coupling of the prison and the factory as complementary disciplinary polarities. What Foucault claims is that the panopticon principle, the principle of disciplinary regulation, is the fundamental principle of social regulation in modern society. Because panopticism is essentially a principle of punitive segregation, society becomes a *carceral archipelago*, where all members of the population are subject to disciplinary regulation – are under surveillance and are liable to punitive suspension of rights – at all times and in all places, across all aspects of their lives. Where the gaze of the expert or the enforcer cannot penetrate, as in intimate relationships, self-discipline takes over (Foucault 1978; 1986).

The potentialities of disciplinary regulation can be most fully realized in the prison, the enclosed institution where surveillance and coercion of time and space can be total; disciplinary, segregative incarceration is thus the principal technology of power in modern society, and disciplinary regulation is thus present in all sites where people interact with each other. While not all discipline is punitive, the asymmetry of power which is a component of any human relationship, according to Foucault, means that elements of panopticism characterize the web of social relations. Punitive discipline is dispersed out from the prison, and becomes a component of modern 'non-custodial' punishments, but its essential characteristics spread to other forms of relationships. Foucault can claim as evidence the introduction of socializing-penalizing institutions such as the reformatory, the workhouse and the asylum at the same time as the prison; more recent inventions such as probation, supervision orders, community service, and now electronically monitored curfews, also contain these carceral fundamentals, the coercion of time and space, surveillance, the construction of stigmatized identity.

More controversial is his claim that these principles underlie all social relationships in the modern society, that prisons, factories, schools, families differ only in the degree to which they are permeated by disciplinary regulation. Foucault dissolves the difference between imprisonment and freedom, between punitive and non-punitive institutions and relationships, and shows us a mesh of disciplinary relationships, such that the citizens of modern industrial society are inhabitants of the *punitive city*, within the carceral archipelago.

Critique and controversy

The publication of *Discipline and Punish* seems to have set the seal on 'progressive' histories of penal change, and also effected a sociological surge of interest in penality as a part of a wider problematic of social control. This may have happened even without Foucault: the interactionist perspective had refocused the study of crime within a wider field of 'deviance', with deviance–control displacing crime–punishment as its subject. Foucault's siting of penality within a power–knowledge strategy of normalization could provide a counterpart to the sociology of deviance in a way that a narrower engagement with the punishment of crime could not. Whether the shift from a jurisprudence of punishment to a sociology of control would have happened without Foucault's intervention or not, *Discipline and Punish* was a text for its time, a book which provided a language to conceptualize and interrogate the phenomena which fell within the range of the 'new' sociology of deviancy and control. As Rusche and Kirchheimer (1968) decisively established the periodicity of the transition of penal forms, so Foucault established its essential analytic concerns: 'the role played by penality in the construction of social order, the furtherance of state control, and the constitution of individuals as social subjects' (Garland 1990b: 2).

The analytic field established by Foucault has, however, been subject to critique, both in general and in detail. Several of his strongest claims about the character of modern society, as revealed by its technologies of power, have also been contested. Some of the critique is idiosyncratic and has not been widely shared; some of the criticism and the controversies over his normative stance towards modernity are focused on works other than *Discipline and Punish*; I shall concentrate on criticisms that are widely shared among sociologists of penality, and that concern specifically the arguments presented in *Discipline and Punish*. Good critical summaries are contained in Garland (1990a; 1990b) and Howe (1994). I acknowledge most of their shared concerns, but will offer a partial defence of Foucault on some points, while, on the other hand, also raising one or two additional concerns that they do not mention.

The disputes most commonly raised by sociologists/criminologists, as opposed to those concerned with Foucault's wider political and philosophical arguments, are about periodicity, partiality and functionalism. Essentially, critics have disputed his account of when and where various penal changes occurred; the extent and direction of those changes; the neglect of aspects of penality other than those which are expressions of the will to power and the control of subjects; and his offering of 'deep' or 'covert' functions against accusations of the failure of prisons. These criticisms are, of course, inter-related.

Periodicity

Penal events, according to some critics, did not occur when and where Foucault says they did. The strongest argument along these lines is made by Spierenburg (1984), who shows the decline of physical punishment as more gradual and more patchy than Foucault allows. Specific points are the restoration of corporal punishment by the Napoleonic regime, and we could perhaps now add the restoration of physical punishment in the form of the chain gang in Arizona in 1994. Foucault's posing of imprisonment as the successor to public executions is also challenged, and it has to be admitted that this is a dubious claim in view of the retention of capital punishment by most advanced industrial states until well into the twentieth century, and its continued use in some of the most advanced states (especially the USA) to this day. The real shift is, then, not so much from physical punishment as from punishment in the public square to punishment behind the prison walls. Foucault himself, however, emphasizes the shift from visible to hidden punishment, and in *Discipline and Punish* the location of punishment, the vantage point of the overseer in the control tower, the change in the audience from the general populace to the expert practitioner and administrator, are given at least equal weight to the progressive abandonment of physical mutilation of bodies.

To some extent, criticisms of Foucault's periodization can be seen as a misunderstanding of, or disagreement with, his method of analysis. Foucault is not trying to show the process of transition of penal forms in the same way that Spierenburg is. Foucault does not offer an extensively documented history of changes in legislation, policy and practice. Instead, he builds his analysis from the two 'snapshots' of penality with which the book opens: the execution and the timetable of the institution for young prisoners. Instead of giving a longitudinal study of how the one came to displace the other, he gives a horizontal, a 'genealogical' as he calls it, analysis, showing us what ideas, practices, policies and technologies each is linked to. This is rather like viewing snapshots of social occasions or street scenes taken at different times: we cannot tell from the photographs exactly when fashions or manners changed, or when shops that are present in one street scene but not in another opened and closed, when modes of transport came into use, or when trees were cut down, but we can use the photographs to get an idea of the social life of the times depicted in them. Foucault, therefore, is not showing us how or when one thing changed into another, but is drawing our attention to the context in which the practices he describes take place, and the nature and meaning of the penalities of which they are part.

In his review of Spierenburg's book, Garland (1986) welcomes this *longue durée* account of the decline of public execution and torture, while acknowledging that Spierenburg's approach is very different from Foucault's. The difference is not just that Foucault is interested in discontinuities rather than continuities, or that he uses the very French tradition of engagement with 'ruptures' (Bachelard 1968) rather than the *longue durée* mode of historical analysis which is more familiar to British readers, and which shows institutions *evolving* gradually rather than changing abruptly; rather, it is this snapshot mode which is distinctive of Foucault's work.

Overgeneralization

One consequence of Foucault's method is that it can lead to overgeneralization from particular examples. Foucault gives as his example of disciplinary penality a young offender's institution, and it is with regard to young offenders that the correctionalism he describes has become most developed. There is an extensive literature demonstrating the way that young offenders have been subjected to a control regime in which crimes were said to be treated rather than punished; in which due process was disregarded and decisions were taken by special courts and tribunals modelled on social work case conferences, rather than courts of law; in which supervision and intervention were extensive and of indeterminate duration (see, for example, Pearson, 1977; Platt, 1977; Donzelot, 1980; Hudson, 1984a; 1987; Cohen, 1985; Pitts, 1988). Foucault's characterization of modern penality seems to provide a perceptive and accurate description of the development of reformatories, probation, supervision and care orders, assessment centres, detention centres and other institutions and orders which juvenile courts have at their disposal.

The analytic framework of the disciplinary mode seems to fit less well, however, when applied to adult offenders. Adult prisons – especially adult male prisons – are not noticeably correctionalist, at least not always; a labour market account, which suggests that prisons will be reformative when there is a high demand for labour but will revert to mere 'warehousing' when there is over-supply of labour, seems more plausible. Certainly the main protagonists in the debates about the reality and extent of the 'dispersal of discipline' quote selectively from adult or juvenile penalties depending upon which side of the argument they are urging. Cohen (1979; 1985), in particular, in his Foucauldian depictions of the continuing dispersal of discipline in the 1960s and 1970s, draws extensively on programmes and institutions developed for young offenders, while Bottoms (1983), who takes the view that the dispersal-of-discipline thesis is flawed, or at least greatly exaggerated, points to the fact that fines are the most common punishment and are not disciplinary in the sense that probation or community service orders are. The fine, of course, is the most used punishment for adult offenders.

Another way in which Foucault perhaps overgeneralizes from particular examples is geographical. His account of a penality in which the diagnoses of experts displaced the values of law seems to fit the continental European 'social defence' penal rationale (Ancel 1987; Pasquino 1991), rather better than the English situation where, juveniles apart, penality has always retained a strong commitment to retribution. Downes's (1988) description of the differences between Dutch and English penal traditions, for example, shows much lesser reliance on retributive imprisonment in the Netherlands than in England.

The group other than juveniles to whom ideas of normalization and disciplinary regulation seem to apply are, as Howe (1994) points out, women. At around the same time as the publication of *Discipline and Punish*, a burgeoning sociology of the regulation of women was demonstrating the continuity between punishment of crime, control of sexuality, and control of women's lives through psychiatric labelling (Hutter and Williams 1981).

Female offenders have been treated as pathological, as irrational, and their penal treatment has been such as to try to make them into 'normal' women. Criminal justice processes have often seemed to overlook the actual offence committed, and to judge female offenders according to whether they were good mothers or conventionally feminine women. Feminist criminologists have identified paternalism and chivalry as characteristic of the criminal justice response to 'nice' or 'feminine' women, who have been seen as needing help or treatment rather than punishment, but women who do not fit the stereotypes of conventional femininity are vulnerable to a double jeopardy, punishment both for the crime they have committed and for their failure to be 'proper' women (Carlen 1983; 1985, *inter alia*; Eaton 1986; Worrall 1990). Studies of the sentencing of women have revealed a 'familial' model of justice, whereby sentences correlate with circumstances such as whether women have care of their children or the children are in institutional care, rather than with factors such as their offences or their criminal records (Farrington and Morris 1983). Women's prisons and women probationers' groups have attempted to 'normalize' through hair-styling and make-up sessions as well as by offering therapy to help them overcome their 'unfeminine' criminality.

Although in the last few years awareness has grown that the most pressing problems for most criminal women are poverty, abuse and addictions rather than lipstick and access to hairdressers, the modern period investigated by Foucault and others working within the social control paradigm was a period when 'normalization' was an apt description of the objective of penal and non-penal control of women. Furthermore, during this period there was certainly a continuity between penal institutions and institutions within the health/welfare systems, so that women were frequently treated in psychiatric hospitals or given probation orders in response to crime, while, on the other hand, young women were committed for 'welfare' reasons to custodial institutions, the majority of whose male inmates were offenders.

To the usual and well-merited (feminist) protest that females are over-looked in the work of Foucault and others writing in the Foucauldian traditions, one could add that had he foregrounded the fact that it was with regard to juveniles and females that normalization most fully displaced retribution or deterrence, and that the balance between law and social science in dealing with their offences was most heavily tipped towards social science, Foucault might have enriched his development of his ideas of normalization and discipline. The ways in which its applicability to groups who differed in characteristics other than the nature of their 'illegalities' varied, is surely important to knowing just how far, and in what way, modern society is 'disciplinary'.

Partiality

Although it is a widely shared judgement, Garland (1990a; 1990b) argues forcefully the view that Foucault's analysis overemphasizes the instrumental aspects of punishment – its function for the transformation of unruly bodies into docile, productive bodies – and ignores its expressive aspects. Much of Foucault's argument about the differentiation of illegalities and the construction of delinquency does, however, touch on the expressive role of punishment, in fairly straightforwardly Durkheimian terms. He does point out that penality expresses the limits of society's tolerance; where he differs from Durkheim's account is that he takes the Marxist view that penality is not constitutive of a value consensus. Rather, Foucault argues, in dividing the working classes into the respectable and the delinquent, penality legitimates law's role in promoting and protecting the interests of the bourgeoisie, through criminalizing violation of property rights and creating a basic division between the dangerous delinquent class and the remainder of society, who are threatened whether working-class or bourgeois. The construction of the delinquent subgroup means that their punishment has, presumably, an expressive utility for the non-delinquent, and therefore the substance of the prison building, which the non-delinquent can see whose delinquent inmates s/he can imagine, as well as the reporting of sentencing in newspapers, become the object for satisfaction of punitive emotions.

Even if, however, it is conceded that Foucault's analysis is complementary to those of Durkheim and the Marxists rather than trying to supplant them (and there is strong reason from within the text itself to think that this is the case, as Garland also makes clear), *Discipline and Punish* certainly is far more concerned with the instrumental than the expressive roles of punishment. It presents an account of those aspects of penality which most clearly demonstrate its operation as a technology of power.

If Foucault's analysis is partial (rather than total) in the sense that it interrogates some of penality's roles but not others, some instances of punishment but not others, it is also partial (as opposed to impartial) in that it is an account from a particular standpoint: the standpoint of power. As Garland argues, the pre-eminence of *Discipline and Punish* among the various social histories of punishment that were produced in the 1970s and 1980s has meant that what is *an* account of penality has been treated as if it were *the* account, and so although its author's intent may have been to complement rather than to supplant other perspectives, it has in fact overshadowed if not totally supplanted them:

> We now think of punishment as power and not just *in terms of* power. A consequence of this may be to mistake a deliberately *partial* account (in both senses of 'partial') for a general one which cannot really stand on its own.
>
> (Garland 1990b: 5)

Penality is not, according to Garland, reducible to an expression of the will to power, even if the fact that punishment essentially involves the power of the state over the individual, of one individual over another, means that a sociology which neglects the power perspective will not be adequate. Penality is not 'merely' a technology of power, although it is a technology of power. Power reductivism would repeat all the faults of economic reductivism, and it raises the same questions of agency, questions as to on whose behalf power is being exercised; towards what goal power is being deployed; and whose interest is represented by 'modernity' (Gordon 1980).

Discipline and Punish is also partial in that the first term of the dyad of the title, 'discipline', is privileged over the second, 'punishment'. Foucault does not reveal much about penality as punishment. Modern penalties may not be painful in the physical sense as were torture and mutilation, but they do cause distress, deprivation, mental breakdown, and even suicide. Furthermore, it is of the essence of punishment that it is deliberately unpleasant. Because *Discipline and Punish* forms part of a larger project of understanding normalization and the constitution of subjectivity through the human sciences, punishment is neglected in favour of discipline, because it is discipline which fits this overarching theme of normalization and the formation of the human sciences. The analysis of discipline thus overwhelms the analysis of punishment (Pasquino 1991; Howe 1994).

Functionalism

Foucault has also been criticized for his functionalism, especially in relation to his argument for the 'success' of imprisonment. Ignatieff's (1983) refutation of the 'prison succeeds' line of reasoning is perhaps the best-known expression of this critique. He charges that most of the 'revisionist histories' of the rise of imprisonment as punishment, when they find that the prison has consistently been acknowledged to produce recidivism rather than reform, have argued that because, in spite of this failure, imprisonment continues to be used, there must be some other function which it performs for those in power. Dividing the working classes against themselves, and invoking fear of penalties in would-be criminals, are the usual suggestions for the 'real' function of punishment. Foucault's explanation of the production and management of delinquency certainly fits this functionalist mode. Ignatieff argues that although the prison may have some useful effects, it nevertheless fails according to the predominant penal rational of the modernist phase of society in which it developed, and persists only because nothing has been found which produces better results. Mathiesen (1990) echoes this to a great extent, arguing as he does that prison fails according to all penal rationales, and that this had better be admitted.

Foucault, say Ignatieff and others such as Garland who endorse this criticism, mistakes 'unintended consequences', which may well have utility for ruling élites, for intended purposes. This way of arguing is *sociological functionalism*, deriving from the assumption that all social institutions which persist must be functional, or else they would die out. This way of looking at institutions promotes a blindness to looking at aspects which really are dysfunctional, and it mistakes effects for purposes. If the effect of the prison produces a delinquent subgroup, this functionalist line of reasoning urges, then that must be its purpose. By his functionalism, Foucault undermines one of his own stated purposes in writing *Discipline and Punish*, which is to disturb the 'taken-for-grantedness', the 'self-evidence' of prisons. What Foucault achieves is to reinforce imprisonment's self-evident status, by showing that, regardless of the failure that critics have ascribed to it, it really is a socially useful – an indispensable – institution.

Politics

A criticism of Foucault's general interrogation of modernity, and one which certainly applies to his work on prisons, is political. His presentation of the panopticon society, with the gaze of power intruding into every aspect of the lives of citizen-subjects, overstates the subjugation of the citizens of modern societies. Although the 'progressive' account of the development of modern penality was complacent and over-optimistic in its assumption of the advance of humanitarianism, Foucault himself uses words and phrases which carry an evaluative charge, such as 'better', 'more sophisticated', 'penetrating deeper'. He thus produces a mirror image of the histories which he refutes, and gives a history of the march of unfreedom and the enslavement of the human personality as well as the human body (Geertz 1978). As another influential philosopher, Jürgen Habermas, has argued, Foucault ignores the guarantees provided by modern law and philosophies of rights that counterbalance the forces of discipline (Couzens Hoy 1986).

In the latter part of *Discipline and Punish*, when he discusses panopticism as a general principle of social organization in modernity, and when he presents his vision of the carceral archipelago, it is objected that Foucault ignores differences between prisons and other institutions (non-custodial penalties as well as non-penal institutions such as schools and factories), which, though they may only be differences of degree, are none the less important:

> it is Foucault's claim, and I think he is partly right, that the discipline of a prison, say, represents a continuation and intensification of what goes on in more ordinary places – and wouldn't be possible if it didn't. So we all have to live to a time schedule, get up to an alarm, work to a rigid routine, live in the eye of authority, are periodically subject to examination and inspection. No one is entirely free from these new forms of social control. It has to be added, however, that subjection to these new forms is not the *same thing* as being in prison: Foucault tends systematically to underestimate the difference, and this criticism . . . goes to the heart of his politics.
>
> (Walzer 1986: 58–9)

Walzer describes Foucault as being 'importantly wrong': he is wrong in denying the differences between imprisonment and life outside the prison, but his work is 'important' in drawing attention to one of the main dangers of the modernist project of producing the disciplined, productive populace, the 'normal' person. Law's limits on the exercise of power are indeed challenged by the social sciences, with their promise of painless reform, and this tension between law and science, the reduction of law's limits by correctionalist penal strategies, led to the critiques of rehabilitative punishments that emerged strongly in the 1970s and 1980s (von Hirsch 1976; Cohen 1985; Hudson 1987).

Nevertheless, to point out a danger is not the same as to claim that the technologies of discipline have penetrated the whole of society, that Bentham's panopticon blueprint has become the actual strategy and shape of modern penality (Garland 1990b). Foucault, it is said, makes no distinction between the society of the Gulag and the Western liberal welfare society, and gives law and adherence to concepts of rights no credit for maintaining the boundary between the penal apparatus of societies such as Britain and France, and the Gulag:

> he provides no principled distinction, so far as I can see, between the Gulag and the carceral archipelago. Nor does he provide a genealogy of the Gulag and, what is probably more important, his account of the carceral archipelago contains no hint of how or why our society stops short of the Gulag. For such an account would require what Foucault always resists: some positive evaluation of the liberal state.
>
> (Walzer 1986: 62)

Summary and conclusion: Foucault's legacy

Foucault's work provided powerful intellectual tools for analysing the development of penality in the modernist era and, further, for providing insights into the expansion of the social control net that seemed to be occurring in the 1970s and 1980s. Garland's *Punishment and Welfare* (1985) takes a Foucauldian framework – and like Foucault, incorporates much of the economic and class analysis of Marx – to analyse the development of 'criminological punishment' in England at the beginning of the twentieth century. He demonstrates how the new, psychologically orientated science of criminology was developed and enlisted in the state project of a correctionalist penal strategy.

Foucault's framework has also been used by critics to draw attention to the excesses of, and the repression involved in, contemporary penal policies and practices. Works on the ever-increasing interventionism of juvenile justice, on the abuses of rehabilitation, such as the use of psychotropic drugs in prison, indeterminate sentences and the regulation of young women, utilized his analytic framework. Donzelot (1980) uses Foucault's 'snapshot' method to show the way in which punishment and assistance were fused in the control of juveniles, a control which involved intervention into the lives of their families, and surveillance of their whole social milieu. Sim's (1990) account of the development and operation of medicine in prisons shows how, while presenting itself as benign and independent of the punitive apparatus of prisons, the medical presence in prisons is very much part of the technology of punishment and control. Sim's work is distinguished by his attention to generally neglected aspects of imprisonment: the punitive control of women, and deaths in custody.

There have been some, but not many, attempts to present a Foucauldian analysis of the punishment and control of women (Howe 1994). Dobash *et al.* (1986), for example, trace the emergence of modern penality as applied to women, showing the transition from the use of public, physical punishments such as the ducking stool, to the establishment of the view of women's crime as primarily calling for treatment rather than control.

More recently, this body of literature has been reinforced in a detailed historical analysis by Zedner (1991), whose focus is not, like that of Dobash *et al.*, confined to what befalls those women who are imprisoned, but also includes the issue of the numbers of women who were involved in criminal justice processes over the period studied by the male social histories discussed so far. Zedner finds that as the Victorian era progressed, the proportion of women involved in criminal justice processes decreased. She has attributed this decrease to the progressive decline of moralistic, religious theories of crime and punishment, based on understandings of the criminal as acting from free will, and the rise of the social scientific theories of crime and the correctionalist penality described by Foucault and his followers. She describes the contours of the emergence of the 'treatment' orientation which, as noted above, took hold most strongly in penal policies towards women, and provides a wider contextualization to the practices described by Dobash *et al.* and others who have studied the imprisonment of women (Carlen 1983). Zedner shows the emergence of the social construction of women as 'mad' rather than 'bad', a construction which is still prevalent today, although somewhat in decline. Although punishment has been more in vogue than treatment in recent years, women are still more likely than men to be redirected from the penal to the health/welfare system (Allen 1987).

Among Foucauldian analyses which look at the expansion of social control in the 1970s and 1980s, Stanley Cohen's *Visions of Social Control* (1985) provided a powerful account of the various transformations, deepenings and strengthenings that the social control net had undergone up to the time of his writing. Expressions such as 'net widening', 'blurring the boundaries' between freedom and control, prison and the community, were used in connection with juvenile justice programmes, with so-called therapeutic regimes in prisons, and with innovations such as electronic tagging. Cohen sketched out a scenario whereby the intentions of penal reformers, legislators and practitioners, whether benign or malign, always result in more control, less freedom, more persons under surveillance for greater portions of their lives – because of the inexorable forces of normalization.

This powerful work has had a corrective effect on many over-enthusiastic penal professionals, and has led to some groups, such as probation officers and juvenile justice social workers, endeavouring to roll back their own contributions to the disciplining network (Hudson 1987). It has, however, fed the mood of 'penal pessimism' which developed in the 1980s, and which led to a new enthusiasm for retributive punishment (see, for example, Hudson 1987; Carlen 1989). Sociologically, the reaction against the dystopian visions of Foucauldian works paved the way for the rise of 'left realism'. Works such as Cohen's were accused of 'impossibilism', of perpetrating the view that any attempts at more humane and constructive penal strategies were bound to lead to more discipline, more control, less freedom (Matthews 1989).

Of late, there have been attempts to recapture the sociology of punishment from the grasp of Foucault's framework, most notably Garland's wide-ranging *Punishment and Modern Society* (1990a), which argues that a full sociological understanding of penality needs the insights provided by all the perspectives – Durkheimian, Weberian, Marxist and Foucauldian – if all its facets are to be apprehended. All these traditions contribute some understanding, but none is sufficient of itself. Garland draws on the Marxist and Foucauldian appreciation of the relation between social institutions and the economic and power dynamics of the societies in which they occur; on Durkheim's appreciation of law and punishment as constitutive of the moral character of society; on Weber's thesis of the rationalization and bureaucratization of society; on Spierenburg's insistence on the importance of cultural sensibilities, of levels of tolerance for violence and for the removal of the right to violence from individuals to the state; as well as incorporating Foucault's power perspective. It is a powerful synthesis, showing penality as both constituted by and constitutive of social forms.

chapter nine

Understanding contemporary penality

Introduction: punishment and contemporary culture
Governmentality, risk and actuarialism
Penal policy as problem-solving
The mass imprisonment society
Summary and conclusions: punishment in the twenty-first century

Introduction: punishment and contemporary culture

The previous chapters in this second part of the book have been concerned with the development of systems of punishment which emerged during the era of industrial capitalism, the period from approximately 1750 to 1975. Although the writers considered in these chapters have emphasized different aspects of modern penal systems and have put forward different balances and configurations of factors which caused, or at least are correlated with, these developments, Durkheim, Marx, Rusche and Kirchheimer, Foucault, Melossi and Pavarini and the other theorists mentioned are essentially analysing the same phenomenon. The system they are describing and seeking to explain was a system of state punishment; a system in which imprisonment became the normal mode of punishment; a system which became less concerned with tormenting the body and more with disciplining the mind and character; a system which had a demonstrable relationship with the demand for labour; a system which maintained an interest in the offender after conviction and sentence; and a system in which, in most places, the use of the death penalty first diminished and then ended. All the writers describe a system in which a penalty of bodily degradations is replaced by a penalty of suspended rights; all describe a system where a variety of professionals – psychiatrists, social workers, educationalists – became involved with the management and treatment of offenders. Whether the aim of penality is identified as normalization, and its character as disciplinary, or whether the aim is thought of as a simple regulation of the labour supply, or whether the key characteristic is taken to be that it is increasingly secular and constitutional, we can readily perceive the contours of the penal system found in industrial democratic societies, and we can recognize that this modern penal system is different in important, defining ways from penal systems that preceded it. We can also see the similarities among Western industrial penal systems: the penal architecture; prison regimes; the range of non-custodial sanctions; penal professions; the use of imprisonment as routine punishment – are all found in the modern era in the UK, and also in North America, western Europe, Australia and New Zealand. Though there are differences – some countries use imprisonment more than others; non-custodial sanctions may differ – they are recognizably penal systems of the same type. This type of penal system has been replicated by other countries throughout the world as they have industrialized.

In the last quarter of the twentieth century, another major change in the nature of penality appeared to be under way. One of the first manifestations was a pronounced decline in the influence of the 'rehabilitative ideal'. In country after country, state after state, sentencing reforms were introduced which removed features of rehabilitative sanctions, and replaced them with features of modern retributivism. For example, indeterminate sentences, with release when good rehabilitative progress was deemed to have been made, were replaced by determinate sentences, fixed according to the seriousness of the offence (Hudson 1987). The 'justice model' of proportionate sentencing replaced the 'treatment model'. In some US states, the change was abrupt, delivered in one piece of legislation, the first of which was the California Determinate Sentencing Act 1976. This Act introduced a fixed schedule of presumptive sentences for each offence category, with very little variation allowed for in a small number of aggravating or mitigating circumstances, mainly linked to the offence rather than the offender. In England and Wales the transition was more gradual, but in a series of Acts from the 1982 Criminal Justice Act to the 1991 Criminal Justice Act the movement was all away from individualized, indeterminate sentencing which considered the offender's circumstances alongside the nature of the crime, towards standardized, tariff sentences. The new values were consistency, proportionality and predictability. This change from rehabilitation to straightforward proportionate punishment affected community penalties as well as imprisonment. Probation, for example, in the UK and elsewhere progressively incorporated elements of control and deprivation of liberty commensurate with the offence as well as elements of rehabilitation commensurate with the offender's needs. Probation changed from an alternative to punishment to an alternative form of punishment; its role changed from social work with offenders to community punishment.

In political terms, this move from rehabilitation to proportionality represented a shift from being 'soft' on offenders to swift and certain punishments; in terms of legal theory, it represented a recognition of the rights of offenders to limited, finite punishments linked to what they had done rather than what they might do in the future; in sociological terms, it represented further progress towards Weber's ideal-type of a rational, predictable system with the discretion of individual professionals (including judges and magistrates) reduced as sentencing guidelines, national standards for probation, and tighter rules for bail and parole took penal systems further in the direction of rational, bureaucratic character of modern regulation by rules rather than persons.

These changes affected criminal justice for juveniles, the penal sphere where the rehabilitative ideology, the disciplinary features of penality described by Foucault, had penetrated most deeply. In the UK and USA, and to some extent elsewhere in Europe, North America, and Australia and New Zealand, juveniles began to be detained in institutions oriented to containment and punishment rather than to treatment and education (in some countries, such as the UK, institutions for the confinement of young offenders have been transferred from local authority social services to Home Office penal establishment management; in other countries the administrative configuration remains unchanged but the same changes in regime ethos have, to a greater or lesser extent, taken place).

As the twentieth century drew to a close, the desert model in turn lost influence, but this time to incapacitation. States passed laws introducing harsher and harsher sentencing, with offenders incarcerated in increasingly austere prisons. The notorious California 'three strikes' law prescribed 25 years or life imprisonment, without parole, for anyone convicted of a third offence. Other states followed California's example, although most were more careful to stipulate a third serious or violent offence. As well as being socially embarrassed over the publicity given to a man who received a 25-year sentence for stealing a slice of pizza, California was soon financially embarrassed by the exponential rise in prison expenditure as the numbers of inmates convicted for very long terms began to rise. Under slogans such as 'truth in sentencing' and the more explicit 'war on crime', a mix of measures was introduced at state and federal levels in the USA, that together comprised a 'get tough' agenda, which incorporated retribution, deterrence and incapacitation (Wicharaya 1985). Even more disturbingly, a revival of the death penalty after 1976 marked this turn away from sanctions aimed at reintegration of the offender into society as a law-abiding, productive worker, towards incapacitative sanctions aimed at exclusion of offenders from lawful society in the most emphatic way possible.

Understanding one's own times is infinitely more difficult than understanding the past, and not surprisingly the range of analysis and explanation is much wider than we have seen in relation to the development of modern penal systems: there is disagreement about what these contemporary trends represent as well as about how they may be understood. We do not yet know how things turned out, and although penal innovations sometimes appear to be 'volatile and contradictory' (O'Malley 1999) rather than following a consistent pattern, we can observe that trends towards penalities of exclusion rather than inclusion, an emphasis on public protection rather than justice and fairness, and a general toughening of sanctions propelled by greater outrage and anger towards offenders are manifest across many countries. While the USA is far ahead in its punitiveness (no other Western country has reintroduced the death penalty, and indeed former Soviet bloc countries such as Hungary have repealed it as a condition of membership of the European Union), the UK is following trends towards longer periods of imprisonment in more austere prisons. Even states such as the Netherlands and the Scandinavian countries which have until recently had reputations for penal moderation and social tolerance had rising imprisonment rates in the 1990s, although their rates remain below those of the UK and are a very long way below those of the USA.

Though some writers argue that we are witnessing the end of penal modernism and the arrival of a postmodern penality (Pratt 2000), a more general view is that contemporary penality is the penality of late modernity rather than postmodernity. Late modernity has been defined as

> the social, economic and cultural configuration brought into being by the confluence of a number of interlinked developments. These include (i) the transformative dynamic of capitalist production and exchange (the emergence of mass consumerism, globalization, the restructuring of the labour market, the new insecurity of employment); (ii) the secular changes in the structure of families and households (the movement of women into the paid labour force, the increased rates of divorce and family breakdown, the decreasing size of the average household, the coming of the teenager as a separate and often unsupervised age grade); (iii) changes in social ecology and demography (the stretching of time and space brought about by cars, suburbs, commuting, information technology); (iv) the social impact of electronic mass media (the generalization of expectations and fears, the reduced importance of localized corporate cultures, changes in the conditions of political speech); and (v) the democratization of social and cultural life (the 'desubordination' of lower class and minority groups, shifts in power ratios between men and women, the questioning of authority, the rise of moral individualism).
>
> (Garland and Sparks 2000: 199)

Most sociological accounts of penal change locate its roots in the culture of late modernity. Factors which feature prominently in social analyses include the mutation of political liberalism (sometimes referred to as welfare capitalism) into contemporary neo-liberalism, and the emergence of a preoccupation with the containment of risk (Garland 1996; O'Malley 1999; Sullivan 2001, *inter alia*). This chapter will examine these accounts of contemporary penality that link its emergence and its forms to the culture of contemporary, late-modern society. This cultural analysis is synthesized powerfully by Garland in his important book, *The Culture of Control*

(2001a), which discusses some of the most important analytic themes that have been brought to bear on understanding contemporary penality, as well as presenting his own distinctive analysis of penal change as demonstrating problem-solving, using a culturally specific range of available resources.

Governmentality, risk and actuarialism

Punishment is, of course, one of the strategies of crime control that societies have at their disposal, but it is not the only one. From the mid-1980s onwards, under the influence of a political climate in which crime was prioritized as the social sphere marked out for government action and was very clearly differentiated from welfare needs and social policy more widely, and also under the academic influence of realist criminologies of right and left, control of crime was separated from other forms of deviance in analytic as well as in policy terms (Wilson 1975/1983; Young 1986; 1988). Moreover, the social histories of punishment, although causally situating the rise of modern penal systems in a context of social, economic and constitutional functionalism, had nevertheless separated the study of punishment from the study of other forms of control. Garland (1990a) argued that punishment should be viewed as a cultural phenomenon in its own right, rather than as in some way an epiphenomenon of social control.

In the late 1990s, however, the cultural analysis of punishment became reconnected with cultural analysis of the more general response to crime, if not with social control in its wider sense. This reconnection is clearly signposted by Garland's (2001a) title, *The Culture of Control*, after being signalled in the first, widely quoted article in the project culminating in this work, the article published in the *British Journal of Criminology* entitled 'The Limits of the Sovereign State: Strategies of Crime Control in Contemporary Society' (Garland 1996).

Reconnected to the wider problematic of crime control, the new contemporary penality looked to some like part of the new strategy of governance described and investigated by theorists writing in the g*overnmentality* perspective (O'Malley 1992; Stenson 1996; Crawford 1997). Governmentality theorists are interested in the ways in which governmental power is deployed in late-modern societies (Miller and Rose 1990; Burchell *et al.* 1991; Rose 1996a). Foucault's later works, his lectures and essays on governmentality, have provided the starting point for these analyses (Foucault 1991; Gordon 1991).

In this work Foucault looks at the project of modern government, which is, above all, to provide security for governed populations. Security, in the modern era, means not only security from foreign invasion, but also security from disease, starvation and other public ills. The obligation to protect the currency thus becomes as important as the obligation to protect external borders, and modern governments have undertaken a wide range of previously unknown functions in relation to public health, education and social security – what today we think of as the infrastructure of a modern society. Foucault contrasts governance in this sense with sovereignty: the former is about the ways in which power is exercised on and on behalf of the population, while the latter is concerned with the claiming and demonstrating of power by a ruler over a territory. The key difference between the punishments of the absolute monarchies and the new constitutional monarchies, described in *Discipline and Punish* (Foucault 1977), from this point of view is, therefore, that the former is a demonstration of how much power the monarch can, arbitrarily and capriciously, exercise over the bodies of anyone he decides is an enemy, while the latter is a routinized strategy for dealing with illegalities which involves bureaucratization and which is only possible with the acquiescence and participation of the population.

Before the emergence of the governmentality perspective, theorists had concentrated on Foucault's earlier works, and had cherry-picked concepts, using them to characterize contemporary trends as demonstrating continuity with the systems described by Foucault. The spread of control in the community had been documented by Cohen (1979; 1985) who used the proliferation of programmes for delinquents to illustrate the dispersal of discipline from the prison to the neighbourhood. These programmes not only were located physically in the community, in the sense of being run by agencies such as probation and social workers in offices in towns and suburbs (intermediate treatment centres, drop-in centres and the like), but also used community members as befrienders, voluntary supervisors, trainers and monitors.

As crime prevention and community safety became prominent political agendas at central and local level, it looked as though the dispersal of discipline was continuing and broadening (see Hughes 1998, in this series for a comprehensive analytic review of contemporary crime prevention). With the introduction of closed-circuit television systems, private security guards, neighbourhood watch, neighbourhood patrols and gated communities with entry screening devices, it looked as though we were seeing the dispersal of panopticism from the prison throughout the community, with the entire population being under constant surveillance (Lyon 1994; Poster 1990). In addition to surveillance of our physical movements, the citizens of late-modern societies are subject to electronic surveillance of financial transactions, facilitated as electronic transfer of money through credit cards and Internet shopping increases and the use of cash decreases; our preferences for consumer goods, the programmes we watch on television and the newspapers we read, where we take our holidays and the other leisure pursuits we follow, are regularly recorded on a plethora of databases.

As well as the ubiquity of these new forms of control, what is striking, and what fits with aspects of late-modern governance in other spheres, is their impersonality, and their location in agencies other than the central state. We are all caught on closed-circuit television systems; the innocent as well as the guilty are scanned as they seek access to banks, as they shop, and increasingly as they enter residential buildings, whether their own homes or to visit friends and relatives. Individuals become data constructs: collections of items of statistical data, occupants of statistical categories, rather than unique human beings (Hacking 1986). Statistics come to construct people, in the sense that we all become labelled as occupants of categories: creditworthy, middle-brow, high-spending, and of course the acronyms we have become familiar with: DINKY (double income, no kids), for example. These categorizations affect our access to financial services (credit, privileged discount shopping, insurance), and the increasing breadth and penetration of data systems regulate more and more the physical access of statistically defined groups of people to leisure facilities, neighbourhoods and shopping precincts. Under recent curfew by-laws introduced in some towns and cities, categories of people can be denied access to whole town centres.

Many of the new control techniques are operated by or on behalf of private individuals and private institutions, whether individually or co-operatively. Groups of residents form neighbourhood watch schemes and neighbourhood patrols; owners of businesses in a shopping precinct may jointly purchase and operate closed-circuit television systems; a local authority may form a community safety partnership and deploy a range of control tactics. In relation to crime prevention, there has been a rolling back of the state in favour of more local and temporary associations. These associations have shifting and overlapping membership, and come together not because of an ideal of public service but because of a recognition of common interests. Criminologists studying these phenomena have linked them to the governmentality thesis of the 'death of the social' (Rose 1996b), which suggests that functions and sentiments at the level of whole societies are declining, with people relating more to only a narrow range of local and observably similar others.

This decline of state and wider society as a focus for loyalty and for action is also, it is argued, associated with a loss of trust in state government which is part of the general distrust in expert systems and in central authorities that social theorists have proposed as one of the defining characteristics of late modernity (Giddens 1990). On this account, crime control strategies demonstrate a loss of confidence in the state to provide solutions to problems of crime and general degeneration of urban life.

It has been pointed out that the governmentality perspective does not fit as well with developments in punishment as it does with those in crime prevention (Garland 1997; Hudson 1998). Public demand in the period under consideration has been for ever more state action to punish and exclude criminals. This demand has covered property crimes as well as violent and sexual offences: the public is angry about crime as well as afraid of crime (Farrell *et al.* 1997). There has certainly been no rolling back of the state in the sphere of penality, and indeed there has (in the UK at least) been a transfer of power from local to central government. Local authority children's homes have been used less and central state-run youth custody institutions have been used more; the probation service has changed from being run by local management committees of magistrates and elected councillors to being a national service managed by the Home Office; there have been progressive restrictions of judicial discretion; the magistrates courts are in the course of becoming more centrally directed, with a national courts service being introduced on a similar basis to the national probation service.

At first glance there is some lack of fit between the idea of the rolling back of the state to all but a minimum of functions, and the expansion and increased centralization of state punishment and control. This lack of fit is reduced somewhat if punishment is seen as one tactic of crime control rather than as a discrete social phenomenon and if the political content of neo-liberalism, which appears as the taken-for-granted context in many of the governmentality writings, is foregrounded and made explicit. Foucault specifically includes the rise of liberalism in his account of modern governmentality (Gordon 1991: 14–27). Liberalism is concerned with the social good, and recognizes security as involving a delicate balance between freedom and regulation. Under liberalism, the state has to fulfil its part of the social contract: it has to provide security in return for the citizens' acceptance of a regulated life. From the flowering of the industrial revolution to the last quarter of the twentieth century, this interpretation of liberalism supported a widening of state functions, and the installation of the modern welfare state. Foucault documents the deployment of power in this kind of liberal polity, and charts its impact on individual freedom through its ever-widening and ever more sophisticated strategies of control.

At the end of the twentieth century, however, the dominant form of liberalism was that known as neo-liberalism. This allows the state only minimum functions, which are the Hobbesian functions of providing physical security, and not the wider idea of security from want and illness. The leading philosopher of neo-liberalism, Robert Nozick, argues for a withdrawal to a minimum of state functions because social contract liberalism does not warrant the levels of taxation and the degree of state intervention in income distribution that welfare liberalism had established (Nozick 1974, 1981). Relating this to punishment and control, this would allow the state the minimum security functions of repression of the threatening and predatory, so that going to war and punishing people are the residual sovereign powers that neo-liberalism would grant to the state. Repression and exclusion of the dangerous and predatory, on this account, are the function of states in relation to crime, whereas the more positive aspects of crime prevention, which are aimed at creating safer communities, reducing fear of crime and improving quality of life, are more properly located at local and individual levels.

While criminologists and penologists are generally anxious to avoid the reductionism of single explanations for trends in crime and its control, most explanations of contemporary penality include the political context of neo-liberalism, with its combination of economic freedom and social authoritarianism (Hall 1980) in the analytic mix. One prominent theorist of contemporary trends has come to see neo-liberalism and its new right politics as the most significant factor in producing what he sees as 'volatile and contradictory' penal innovations (O'Malley 1999).

Appreciation of the importance of risk in penality is another significant ingredient in explanations of contemporary penal trends. Provision of security means the identification and control of risks, so modern governance is definitionally concerned with risk. Penality is fundamentally bound up with risk: the whole point of criminal law and penal sanctions is to reduce the risk of crime. What is new in contemporary penality is the approach taken to risk: first, risk reduction techniques are concentrated on aggregates rather than individuals; second, risk management has given way to risk control. Risk management accepts risks but tries to make some improvement by reducing the likelihood of feared incidents through education and treatment of offenders, parole assessments and post-release supervision, realizing that some incidents are bound to take place whatever is done. Risk control seeks to avoid incidents altogether through exclusion or elimination of the risk-poser (Clear and Cadora 2001).

As well as distinguishing between sovereignty and discipline, Foucault differentiated discipline and security. Whereas discipline is targeted at an individual, who is to be socialized or reformed into acting normally, security addresses itself to the 'ensemble of a population' (Gordon 1991: 20). Security works through the identification of common risks, and the provision of shared solutions; security's interest in individuals is to place them into categories of risk-posing or risk-vulnerability. As we have seen, contemporary measures of crime prevention are aimed at collectivities in this way, and it has been argued that contemporary penality is a 'new penology' which is consistent with this idea of security power rather than disciplinary power (Simon 1988; Feeley and Simon 1992). Punishment, it is argued, has become impersonal in the way that crime prevention and other strategies of social protection have.

Writing in 1985, Cohen suggested that this aggregate, impersonal approach is the new 'master pattern' in penality:

> For some time now, the few criminologists who have looked into the future have argued that 'the game is up' for all policies directed to the criminal as an individual, either in terms of detection (blaming and punishing) or causation (finding motivational or causal chains).
>
> (Cohen 1985: 147)

In terms of neo-liberalism and governmentality, punishment may be a function that is retained by states, but the form of punishment will be consistent with the general strategies of governmental power. Security is thought to be becoming more dominant than discipline as modernity advances, so the exercise of the power to punish comes to be directed more at aggregates and less at individuals.

The technique for dealing with risks that people pose and face in common is insurance, and insurance is said to be the template which dominates social policy in modern societies (Ewald 1991). Insurance works on actuarial principles for calculating risk; actuarial techniques place people into categories and estimate the 'riskiness' of these groups, rather than looking at individuals as unique cases. For example, car insurance premiums are calculated according to the incidence of road accidents for the age group, car model, and type of area where the driver lives, and the premium will be the same for one person as for others who fall into the same categories – there is no appeal because of one's idea of oneself as a responsible, careful driver. These calculations look to the past – the accident rate for a given group – for aggregates and also for individuals. So premiums may be reduced because of a certain length of time with no reported accidents (the no claims bonus), but not because of individual resolution to do better in future.

Applying actuarial principles to punishment produces the same processes of deciding the riskiness of offenders from their possession of categorical characteristics, and building predictions from past behaviour rather than present and future resolution and change. Categories such as the type of offence, previous record, education and employment history, family size and income, residence, alcohol and addictions, and relationship problems appear on checklists used by probation officers and other criminal justice officials to assess risk of reoffending, and then to make recommendations to the sentencing judge, the case manager or key officer, and other officials at decision points in the penal system. At the time of assessment the offender either possesses these characteristics or does not; the problem of 'false positives' (see Chapter 2) is thereby finessed. The truth or accuracy of these assessments does not lie in whether or not the person assessed commits a further crime in the future or not, but in whether the assessment checklist is filled in correctly: there can be a clerical error or a statistical error, but not a predictive error in the sense identified with earlier incapacitative schemes. The point is not, as in earlier, individually-oriented penal eras, whether this offender among others in the same category will reoffend, but whether this offender is a member of a high-risk or a low-risk group.

Actuarialism in the penal sphere means displacing the idea of danger (which is a category which applies to individuals and which requires validation or refutation by future behaviour) by that of risk (which is a property of aggregates and which needs no such future validation). As Castel (1991: 281) puts it 'The new strategies dissolve the notion of a *subject* or a concrete individual, and put in its place a combinatory [*sic*] of *factors*, the factors of risk' (emphasis in the original). Statistically defined category labels akin to those in other fields enter penality: phrases such as 'high-risk offenders', 'prolific offenders' and 'persistent offenders' become the common currency of penal discourse, rather than the psycho-social categories associated with the rehabilitative era or the straightforward crime categories of the desert era. The aim of the new actuarial techniques of offender risk assessment is to place offenders into the categories of risk, and then isolate and exclude the high-risk, allowing only the low-risk to be punished by proportionate penalties, especially if this means by short sentences or by community penalties.

Jonathan Simon summarizes the emergence of contemporary trends and their difference from the characteristics of disciplinary penality:

> I believe a genealogical analysis of the technologies through which power is exercised today would demonstrate that over the past half century we have been moving away from the disciplines and toward actuarial practices . . .
>
> Disciplinary practices focus on the distribution of a behaviour within a limited population . . . This distribution is around a norm, and power operates with the goal of closing the gap, narrowing the deviation, and moving subjects towards uniformity (workers are to be made more efficient and reliable, prisoners more docile, schoolchildren more attentive and respectful). Actuarial practices seek instead to maximize the efficiency of the population as it stands. Rather than seeking to change people ('normalize them' in Foucault's apt phrase) an actuarial regime seeks to manage them in place.
>
> (Simon 1988: 773)

The move from dangerousness to risk, as Castel describes, is evident in legislation in England and Wales. In the 1991 Criminal Justice Act, there was a twin-track approach with a clear division between violent and sexual crimes, where risk calculations could affect sentence as well as considerations of proportionality, and property crimes, which were very firmly on a proportionality track. As the 1990s progressed, successive White Papers and Acts blurred this division. In the 1996 White Paper *Protecting the Public: The Government's Strategy on Crime in England and Wales*, the public was promised protection from 'dangerous and persistent offenders' (Home Office 1996). This elision of the two terms is illustrative of the new dominance of risk thinking in criminal justice. It also offers at least some explanation of the rise in women's imprisonment rates in recent years. Very few women pose serious risks to public safety, but many of them are persistent property offenders, and a large majority of female offenders possess the characteristics of disadvantage that are identified as 'risk factors' (Carlen 1998; Hudson 2002c).

The society in which actuarialism becomes a key penal technique has been described as the 'risk society' (Beck 1992; Giddens 1990). Although all human societies have been preoccupied with risk, risk-society theorists pinpoint characteristics of modernity which heighten risk awareness. The reflexivity of modernity, it is said, means that inhabitants of modern societies are aware of risks; unlike pre-modern societies, however, risks are not accepted as inevitable. Modernism's belief in progress and the ability to master nature creates expectations that risks will be eliminated, but at the same time the equally characteristic mistrust of governments and experts means that the same citizens who expect risk control have little faith that it will be achieved. The competitive individualism of modern citizens also means that there is a lack of willingness to share risks collectively. Insurance increasingly becomes private rather than social, and risk-sharing is undertaken by persons motivated by *private prudentialism* (O'Malley 1992; 2001) rather than by feelings of social solidarity.

People are only willing to share the costs of risk control with similar others; they are increasingly unwilling to subscribe to collective problem-solving which puts them together with uncategorized others. Even more, they are unwilling to enter social insurance systems with people they blame for the ills of modern society, for the risks they face in their daily lives. Mary Douglas (1992) argued that the nature of punishment systems will bear close relation to the ways in which blame is allocated for risk. Theorists interested in the connection between risk and penality have drawn on her work to demonstrate the connection between late modernism which is not only hyperconscious of risk, but is also a society that always wants to blame someone when risks become realities (Sparks 1997), and harsher, more exclusionary punishments. A system of state-financed exclusion of those characterized as risky or dangerous is the penal system that is demanded for contemporary late modern societies.

Penal policy as problem-solving

These accounts of a new penology (Feeley and Simon 1982) which uses actuarial techniques to manage and contain deviant populations, and of 'post-social' forms of governance (O'Malley 1992, 1996; Rose 2000; Stenson and Sullivan 2001) which examine the exercise of power in neo-liberal, late-modern risk societies, are interesting and informative, but they leave many unanswered questions. Most of these are to do with contradictions: are states becoming more powerful, or less? Are penal systems becoming more rational and bureaucratic, or more irrational and emotional? And they also leave open questions of timing: why did penal sentiments change so abruptly, as evidenced by the abrupt turning away from proportionality towards incapacitation? If risk is a constant preoccupation of modern citizens and security a concomitant constant obligation on governments, what occasioned the change from rational risk management to vengeful risk control? Another question raised by these broad-brush analyses is why criminal justice policy should suddenly have become less influenced by the views of criminal justice professionals, academics and other members of liberal elites.

One thoughtful account of the turning away from proportionality towards incapacitation in the mid-1990s in England and Wales explains that, under the influence of desert theory, the values of criminal justice became internal – consistency and fairness of the system itself. Criminal justice, to use Weber's terminology, became more formally rational, and less substantively rational: it was powered by its own rules and concerns, rather than by outside referents (Bottoms 1995). While professionals and academics – especially legal professionals and academics – attach great importance to due process, proportionality and equality of treatment, the public and the politicians expect criminal justice policy to be concerned with crime (Bottoms 1995). The development of rational criminal justice policy was, therefore, undermined by periodic outbreaks of 'penal populism', policy designed to appeal directly to the public, over the heads of the professional and academic elites.

The work mentioned thus far still does not provide a satisfactory answer to questions about the timing and nature of penal change. Or rather, none of the work by itself provides a full and satisfactory account. Garland (2001a) draws on all the themes introduced so far to explain contemporary penality: risk and actuarialism; governmentality and the demise of the social; authoritarian populism and social authoritarianism – to explain contemporary penality, and fits them into his own overarching framework which brings together the themes of *culture* and *crisis*.

In his earlier work, Garland (1990a, Chapters 9–11) had already introduced a cultural theme into the analysis of punishment, a cultural perspective which goes beyond Pashukanis's hypothesis of the 'equivalence' of wage labour and imprisonment, incorporated by Melossi and Pavarini (see Chapter 7 above). Starting from what he describes as a 'banal' observation found throughout the revisionist histories of imprisonment, that penal practices will reflect wider cultural formations, Garland brings into consideration the cultural resources which criminal justice policy-makers and others have at their disposal. By 'cultural resources' he means, for example, ideas about justice; humanitarian and religious ideals; ideals about the ways in which society ought to operate; and the role of government. These resources form a cultural complex which influences the nature of penal practices. Again, he is giving cultural factors a much more grounded and analytically essential place than theorists of modernist penal systems, for example Ignatieff (1978) in his references to the influence of philanthropists.

Garland (1990a) links his idea of cultural resources to that of Norbert Elias's work on the 'civilizing process' (Elias 1978; 1982) to suggest that in the modern era the cultural complex was such that sensibilities required that the infliction of pain, the carrying out of bodily functions, and the acting out of emotions and impulses should be repressed if possible, but, if unavoidable, carried out in private. To refer to the 'civilizing' process is not to revert to a simple barbarity-to-humanity progressive idea of punishment; it is to point up the importance of culture in that whatever the aims of punishment and whatever the problems and pressures to which penal policy is attuned, policies will be developed that are consistent with the rationalities and sensibilities of their era. The theme of civilization has been taken up by other writers, including Pratt (1998) who describes the trends of the contemporary era as the 'decivilizing' of punishment.

In his more recent work, Garland (1996; 2000) expanded on the theme of culture to talk about the 'cultural preconditions' of the penal trends observed by himself and others. While he incorporates the 'deeper trends' noted by social theorists of late modernity (Giddens 1990; Beck 1992) as well as the middle-range ideas of authoritarian populism, new penology and post-social control, Garland identifies as one of his cultural prerequisites the important social fact of high crime rates becoming accepted as the normal state of affairs. Late-modern societies are, he tells us, high-crime societies (Garland 2000).

He brings this analysis of cultural conditions together with the concept of crisis, which has been a staple of criminal justice writings. Fiscal crisis of the state was invoked by Scull (1977) to explain one change of policy. More recently, crises of prison overcrowding, of the 'toxic mix' in the prison population, of legitimation, and of fear of crime have been prominent criminal justice themes (see, for example, Cavadino and Dignan 1992; Sparks 1994). At the end of the twentieth century, according to Garland, there was a sense of perpetual crisis, creating an insatiable demand for penal innovation, leading to a never-ending stream of plans to tackle offending with new criminal justice legislation almost every Parliament, and constant change in the rules for prisons, probation, the police and the courts. The responses to crisis might appear to be various, to be volatile and contradictory, but they are all influenced by the cultural characteristics of late modernity: patterns of allocation of responsibility for risk; hyperindividualism and distrust of states and expert professionals; the impact of mass media; the social effects of migration; and the dominance of economic rather than social reasoning. The individualism of late-modern societies, the role of the media, and the nature of modern governance acting on behalf of and with the acquiescence of the population means that another cultural precondition for responding to the crisis of high crime rates is that *'the public be protected and its sentiments expressed'* (Garland 2000: 350; emphasis in the original).

In his 1996 paper, Garland introduced a typology of responses to crises, and discussion of these responses is enlarged upon in the subsequent book. He describes three types of responses – adaptive, denial, and 'acting out' – and gives examples of responses of these types to the crisis of high crime rates. Adaptive responses recognize the impossibility of bringing crime rates down to former low levels, while acknowledging both the inevitability and insatiability of demands for complete control of crime. In the face of these impossible demands, adaptive responses in recent years have included non-recording of crimes with little prospect of clear-up; non-prosecution of crimes such as possession of small amounts of drugs for personal use;

community crime prevention programmes; and eschewing crime control goals in favour of values of consistency, fairness and proportionality in punishment. These policies are adapted to high crime rates as something that has to be lived with: they try to make the problem seem manageable; they aim to do what pragmatically can be done and make no further promises. Denial responses take the form of inflated claims by politicians, police and other criminal justice professionals for the effectiveness of their policies, often introduced with slogans such as 'zero tolerance' and 'prison works', and often announced like rabbits being pulled from hats at party conferences, police conferences and other occasions when maximum publicity is afforded. 'Acting out' policies are announced with little careful thought, and are usually responses to public demands and moral panics, often in the aftermath of sensational reporting of horrific crimes, such as Megan's Law in the USA following the murder of Megan Kanka by a sexual offender released after a previous crime, and the introduction of tougher regimes and increased use of custody for young offenders in the UK in the wake of 'one-boy crime wave' and similar stories about prolific young offenders. Acting-out responses are emotional reactions rather than rationally chosen measures.

Garland takes up the issue of why liberal elites, especially criminal justice professionals, have not retained their adherence to adaptive responses but have acquiesced in denial and acting-out responses. He links this change to high crime rates, which, he says, mean that liberal professionals too are victims of crime and fear of crime, and so they too have feelings of anger and outrage alongside other victims. I have suggested that another factor in the changing attitudes of liberal elites is that the emergence of a community safety agenda and the general rise of concern with victims allows them to transfer their traditional stance of solidarity with the underprivileged away from offenders and on to victims and potential victims. These, especially elderly victims, child victims and victims of sexual and violent offending, are identified as the powerless, and liberal professionals have found a cause in their support, a cause which allows them to accept and promote increased repression and exclusion of offenders if this is seen as necessary for the protection of victims. An example of this change is the way in which, after the murder of Sarah Payne and the call for the introduction of a 'Sarah's Law' allowing for notification of the presence in the community of registered sex offenders to residents as well as to the police and appropriate professionals (a replica of Megan's Law), probation and police objections were based on its likely effects in making it more difficult to maintain contact with offenders who might disappear, rather than on the issue of justice to offenders who have paid the penalty for their crimes (Hudson forthcoming).

Adaptive responses need public confidence in governments, and government confidence that their policies will be supported. In late-modern conditions of lack of trust in the state and its professionals and intolerance of the risk of crime inherent in high crime rates, the conditions favourable to them are absent. As well as distrust in government, late-modern societies are peopled by social groups who are mistrustful of each other, and who therefore demand protection and isolation from each other rather than being willing to support policies of inclusion and reintegration. Late-modern societies have been described as manifesting a new 'tribalism', where social groups face each other with hostility and misapprehension (Maffesoli 1996).

The mass imprisonment society

At the beginning of the contemporary period, commentators who sensed a major change in penality coming about did not anticipate the enormous rises in imprisonment; the harshening of regimes, with more prisons becoming carceral warehouses with little or no rehabilitative input; the reintroduction of chain gangs; the emphasis on punishment and control in community penalties; the increasing imprisonment of women, regardless of their responsibilities for children; or the reintroduction and accelerated use of the death penalty. Cohen (1977) and Scull (1977) were not alone in expecting prisons to become peripheral features of the penal landscape, existing only for a 'hard core' of dangerous offenders, with routine offenders dealt with by community sanctions.

Observers of the beginnings of electronic surveillance systems and other community crime prevention techniques thought that the fact that they catch us all in their gaze would reduce the moral distance between offenders and non-offenders, leading to a much reduced use of formal criminal justice as it is replaced by informal and impersonal social control. One commentator, Gary Marx, expected crime prevention to spread to the extent that the criminal justice system 'is perceived as an anachronism whose agents serve only to shoot the wounded after the battle is over' (Marx 1995: 227).

Analysts who noted the rise of the risk theme in criminal justice and observed the development of selective incapacitation, with greater efforts being put into predicting risk and dangerousness, thought that where criminal justice was brought into play, it would use 'smart sentencing' to match the content of sanctions to programmes which would help reduce their offending tendencies. The promise of recidivism prediction was that increased crime control could be achieved without increased public expenditure because high-risk offenders would be imprisoned for very long periods (saving the community the cost of their crimes), but low-risk offenders would stay out of prison, saving the state the cost of their imprisonment (Zimring and Hawkins 1995).

These optimistic possibilities have not been realized, and contemporary penality has brought about the 'mass imprisonment society'. This development is the focus of concern of Garland, Simon and others in a special edition of the journal *Punishment and Society*, subsequently published in book form (Garland 2001b). The cultural accounts discussed so far in this chapter, and the accounts of the rise of modern penal systems examined in previous chapters within this part of the book, generally treated the USA, Canada, Australia, New Zealand and western European countries as a single phenomenon – modern and late-modern societies with modern and late-modern penal systems. All these societies seemed to be experiencing similar trends of helter-skelter penal innovation, a general toughening of penal responses and a spread of community safety programmes, so that the old saying that what happens in California happens in the rest of America the next year and in the rest of the world the year after that, seemed to be borne out (Hudson 2002d). When the US prison population rose to over 2 million for the first time, however, penological attention turned to the USA as a unique and untypical case.

In his editorial introduction to the journal and the book, Garland gives a two-part definition of this new phenomenon of mass imprisonment. The first feature is that the imprisonment rate and prison population size are markedly above the historical norm for societies of the same type, and the second feature is that excessive imprisonment is concentrated on certain groups in the population. Both features are present in the USA in 2002. US imprisonment rates are five times higher than in 1972 and six to ten times higher than in most European countries; mass imprisonment is concentrated among African-Americans and Hispanics.

One of the questions addressed in the volume is 'why did we get it so wrong?' How can we have predicted a reduction in imprisonment but be witnessing mass imprisonment? The answer generally shared by the authors is that earlier, optimistic predictions relied too much on evidence about penal effectiveness, market conditions and fiscal constraints. In other words, they were overly rational, and concentrated on instrumental aspects of punishment and control, at the expense of paying attention to expressive aspects of punishment and emotional elements in the demand for punishment and protection from predatory criminals. Contributors to the mass imprisonment volume share the emphasis of the risk theorists on the selection and political manipulation of risk consciousness, so that risk of crime is elevated as *the* risk to be controlled by the state, the risk that is at the top of the fear list of a majority of law-abiding members of the population. They also all note the substitution of penal policy for social policy according to the received wisdom of the minimum state philosophy of neo-liberalism.

The theme of cultural sensibilities is also present. Mauer (2001) suggests that record numbers of executions, mass imprisonment with hyper-long terms in what Simon has called 'life-trashing' conditions, the return of hard labour and chain gangs with prisoners in identifiable uniforms, only happen because American society has lost its inhibitions about imposing pain on groups it defines as dangerous or wicked. Certain risks are highlighted precisely because they allow blaming of certain kinds of people:

risks of being killed in drive-by shootings, being robbed for the price of a rock of crack, allow for the blaming of black Americans. These groups are regarded with 'fear and loathing' by mainstream white America, which no longer cares to alleviate their fate, merely to exclude and to incapacitate (Simon 2001). Cultural analysis is proving fruitful for illuminating these aspects of punishment as vengeance on people who can be blamed for growing feelings of insecurity and fearfulness, and for showing that the repertoire of responses to high crime rates includes tactics that may be unwelcome and may not have been predicted, but are not inexplicable.

In seeking to explain mass imprisonment in the USA, however, analysts are also returning to the older tradition of seeing punishment as a way of controlling and containing surplus populations and of repressing the poor and marginalized (Reiman 1979; Chapter 7, this volume). This is expressed most clearly and vividly in Wacquant's contribution, which recasts the idea of the equivalence of the prison and the factory by positing the merger of the prison and the ghetto (Wacquant 2001). He says that mass imprisonment is a strategy to contain surplus minority populations, the unemployed inhabitants of 'rustbelt' neighbourhoods, whose labour has been unwanted since the decline of the car industry and other heavy manufacturing industries. The much-lauded recovery in the US economy after the recession of the 1980s was a recovery of profits and dividends rather than of jobs yielding a living wage, which explains the apparent anomaly in terms of the punishment–labour market hypothesis, that of imprisonment rates rising during an economic upturn. Wacquant suggests that as the proportions of black Americans in prisons rise, prisons become ghettos with prisoners associating within their own ethnic groups, and racial stratification negating the possibility of any general inmate solidarity. Simultaneously, on the outside, degenerated neighbourhoods, widespread purposelessness and despair, together with aggressive policing, make minority neighbourhoods, the ghettos, like prisons. Furthermore, Wacquant argues that crime control strategies targeted against minorities, and their consequent disproportionate presence in prisons, confirm a stereotype among white Americans of black Americans as criminals. (Wacquant uses the term 'black', explaining that in apartheid America differentiation into African-Americans, Hispanics and other minority groups is dissolved in favour of a white–black, respectable–criminal dichotomy.)

Wacquant builds on evidence by other criminologists that the 'war on crime' and especially the 'war on drugs', which has fuelled harshening penality, have been conducted against the poor, particularly the minority poor (Tonry 1995). The war on drugs has been waged on the drugs of the minority poor – crack cocaine – and the selectivity of the war suggests that it is more properly understood as an acting-out response to contain loathed and economically surplus minorities than as a rational, adaptive policy to control a drug problem.

Summary and conclusions: punishment in the twenty-first century

The studies of contemporary penality considered in this chapter are post-Durkheim, post-Marx and post-Foucault. Although in many of them Foucault is the most obvious influence and starting point, Durkheimian and Marxist themes are also present. We see the Marxist insistence on the link between economic forms and cultural forms as a taken-for-granted background; in the cultural approach, we see the Durkheimian theme of the influence on penality of forms of social solidarity, the status of governments, and the importance of expressive functions of punishment. These Marxist and Durkheimian themes are especially prominent in the work on mass imprisonment in present-day America, where the existence of minority groups as economic surplus and as objects of fear and loathing is an undoubtedly important factor in the incarceration of so many black people.

In the early years of the twenty-first century, it seems that the USA and UK have an insatiable appetite for punishment, and an insatiable demand for the elimination of risk. Late-modern societies are becoming risk-averse societies, where all risks are expected to be controlled, and they are also risk-blaming societies, where scapegoats must always be found for untoward events. Plane and train crashes result in the search for someone to blame – the driver or pilot, the maintenance worker, the air-traffic controller or signal operator – and then to punish. And punishment means prison: press reports of court proceedings talk of offenders 'walking away free' if they receive a non-custodial sentence; victims and the public feel they are denied justice if an offender is not 'put away'.

We cannot, of course, know, or predict with any confidence, how things will turn out. In the past, penality has been subject to a pendulum effect. There is a constant swing in the balance between due process and crime control at the level of theory and practice; there is a constant swing between individualized and standardized punishments, and there has usually been a swing between eras of incarceration and eras of decarceration. The signs are extremely difficult to interpret at present. In the UK, new prisons continue to be built, and judges call for lengthy prison terms for offences subject to new moral panics (the call by a very senior judge for a standard four-year term for theft from the person of mobile phones, for example), but there is also a renewed encouragement of the use of community penalties. In the USA, while imprisonment rates have now exceeded 2 million, with no sign of reversal, support for the death penalty is falling (although there continues to be a majority in favour), and even right-wing criminologists who urged greater use of imprisonment are now saying that enough is enough (DiIulio 1994; 1999).

What is clear is that the cultural conditions and the perpetual crisis of high crime rates identified by Garland, encompassing as they do the insights on risk and blame, on forms of governmentality, and on the mentalities and social and economic contexts of late modernity, must be considered if contemporary penality is to be understood. It is essential to bring these general analyses of the risk society, of governmentality, of neo-liberal politics and of the condition of late-modernity together with sociological, empirical studies of levels of inequality, of political manipulation of fear, and of degrees of separation and tolerance or intolerance of migrants and minorities, if criminologists and penologists are not to continue to make wrong predictions of future developments and if they are to spot 'surfaces of emergence' on which they can exercise some influence in the direction of a more humane and moderate penality.

part three

Towards justice?

chapter ten

The struggle for justice: critical criminology and critical legal studies

Introduction
Challenges to mainstream penology
  Abolitionism
  Feminist jurisprudence
Concluding comments

Introduction

Criminological knowledge has provided the technical expertise necessary for modern punishment strategies. It is a 'how to' discipline, providing blueprints for operationalizing the different penological aims. The essential starting point of this subservient criminology is an image of the criminal.

The deterrent strategies of classical criminology needed no special knowledge of the criminal personality, for it saw the criminal as acting out of normal motives: *Homo economicus* was the rational, calculating creature of classical criminology as well as classical economics. With the rise of correctionalist, positivist penology in the modern era, however, *Homo criminalis* was born, Foucault's delinquent as object of knowledge. It was describing the psychology, physiology and social milieu of *Homo criminalis* that was the *raison d'être* and the substance of positivist criminology (Garland 1985; Pasquino 1991).

With the decline of correctionalist penal objectives in the 1970s and 1980s, however, *Homo economicus* has reappeared, and in recent years criminological theories which maintain that there is no essential difference between the criminal and the non-criminal have been most influential. Positivist criminology has largely fallen into disrepute (for excellent early critiques of positivist criminology in all its forms, see Matza 1964; Taylor *et al*. 1973), being displaced first by the interactionist/labelling perspective (Rubington and Weinberg 1968) and then by the 'rational choice perspective' (Cornish and Clarke 1986). This latter theory is a return to the older, classical criminology image, depicting an opportunist offender, weighing up the costs and benefits of a potential crime; the rational choice perspective is clearly linked to a move away from rehabilitative penal strategies towards deterrent, neo-classical strategies.

By the 1980s, England and Wales, the USA, and several other Western countries had largely given up correctionalist penal goals, and had adopted the deterrent-retributivist strategies put forward by the new retributivists (Ashworth 1989). The main objective of this 1980s penal policy was to punish fairly; its deeper concern was with restoring legitimacy to criminal justice. It is common currency among sociologists that the 1980s witnessed a 'legitimation crisis' (Cavadino and Dignan 1992); the authority of major social institutions, such as law and parliamentary government, was being challenged on a disturbing scale. These challenges were manifest in political action in the UK such as the miners' strike, anti-nuclear protest action at Greenham Common, street disturbances in London, Liverpool and other cities, and unprecedented levels of criticism of the police and the judiciary.

Reforming offenders through correctionalist penality having apparently failed (Bottoms 1990), and with problems of legitimation being urgent, the target of penological reform and research became the criminal justice system itself. In England and Wales at least, most of the penal innovations in the 1980s – the 1982 Criminal Justice Act which substituted determinate for indeterminate sentences for juveniles; the specification of criteria for imposition of custody; management information systems in criminal justice agencies such as the probation service; training for judges and magistrates, sponsored by the Home Office and the Lord Chancellor's office; sentencing guidelines for judges and magistrates, culminating in the 1991 Criminal Justice Act which made proportionality of sentence severity to offence gravity clearly pre-eminent over other sentencing goals and principles – can be understood as serving this goal of restoring the legitimacy of the criminal justice system.

If the system itself was the target for reform, it is scarcely surprising that the focus of criminological-penological attention shifted from the offender to the system. The largest growth area in research was that which sought to demonstrate whether or not the system was consistent, non-discriminatory and proportionate. This new administrative penology was concerned with criminal justice processes, rather than with outcomes (Ashworth 1988), and therefore posed no real challenges to dominant understandings of 'justice'.

A good example of this trend is given by the research on race and sentencing that appeared during the 1980s and into the 1990s. Most of this was concerned to show whether or not there was 'discrimination' against minority ethnic groups that could not be explained by their criminality. It searched for what Reiner (1993) has called the 'chimera' of pure discrimination, which is to say, the search for differences in treatment by police and courts (in particular) of black and white offenders committing the same offences, with the same criminal records, going through the same criminal justice processes. Such discrimination has been hard to establish by statistical research methods (Hudson 1989), although most people who have any direct contact with the criminal justice system are convinced that justice is racially differentiated, and that the racial disproportion in prison populations (Cook and Hudson 1993) is at least in part due to judicial discrimination as well as to differences in crime rates among various ethnic groups. Two recent studies in England and in the USA have reported some differences in sentencing outcomes which cannot be explained by the crimes or criminal records of the offenders involved, and although both studies stress that even one instance of discrimination is significant, both find that only a small part of racial disproportion in prison populations can be attributed to judicial discrimination (Hood 1992; Blumstein 1993).

None of this research challenges in any fundamental way the penal strategies of the new retributivism. Rather, while often purporting to be investigating discrimination, it presupposes the correctness of new retributivist criteria for punishment by in fact focusing on *disparity*, the consistency with which criteria are applied to cases, rather than *discrimination*, which, properly understood, refers to the legitimacy of the criteria (Blumstein *et al.* 1983). Discrimination occurs when illegitimate criteria are used, and race is a prime example of a criterion which has been recognized as illegitimate. The use of race as a criterion for criminal justice decision-making is proscribed by, for example, the Minnesota Sentencing Guidelines Commission, and implicitly by the 1991 Criminal Justice Act (at Section 95).

Discrimination can also be produced, however, by applying criteria which may appear to be legitimate, but which are brought into question by their systematic disadvantaging of a particular group (for instance, pleading guilty, employment record as a mitigating factor). Some studies of retributive sentencing schemes have challenged their legitimacy on this basis, especially in relation to outcomes for females and minority ethnic groups (Hudson 1987, 1993; Carlen 1989; Daly 1994; Tonry 1995). Even these studies, however, either stop short of radically questioning assumptions involved in basic categories such as 'crime', 'punishment' and 'justice', or, when they do raise these issues (Hudson 1993; Daly 1994), hesitate to go very far in suggesting alternative ways to deal with the social harm that is presently called 'crime'.

Challenges to mainstream penology

More fundamental challenges have come from critical criminologists and critical legal theorists, whose work has already been referred to in Chapter 7. I want here to look at two strands within the wider perspectives of critical criminology and critical legal studies which have particular relevance to an understanding of 'justice': abolitionism and feminist jurisprudence.

Abolitionism

> is based on the moral conviction that social life should not, and, in fact cannot be regulated effectively by criminal law and that, therefore, the role of the criminal justice system should be drastically reduced while other ways of dealing with problematic situations, behaviours and events are being developed and put into practice.
>
> (de Haan 1990: 203)

As de Haan explains, abolitionism is both a theoretical perspective and a political movement. As a political movement, 'at the hard end of the politics of penal dissent' (Rutherford 1994: 285), abolitionism has championed the rights of prisoners, and has taken up issues that are overlooked in more general penal concern with, for example, the effectiveness of prison for the reform of prisoners, prison overcrowding, and prison security. The issues on which abolitionists have campaigned include deaths in custody, control units, the prison medical service, and the use of drugs to control prisoners (Sim 1994). There have also been campaigns, initiated largely by criminal justice practitioners themselves, for the abolition of custody for juveniles. Progress on these issues has ebbed and flowed with the various waves of law and order politics, but abolitionists have maintained what de Haan (1990) has called a 'politics of bad conscience' which has put pressure on legislators to justify any increases in punitive severity against an informed and active lobby for penal deflation.

What most clearly distinguishes abolitionist politics is their strategy of 'negative reform'. Mathiesen's (1974) account of his involvement with the Scandinavian prisoners' rights movement in the 1970s brought to the forefront the dilemma for all who campaign for radical change: any reforms are likely to strengthen the institutions which the campaigners criticize. Thus, reducing disparities in custodial sentencing may make imprisonment seem fairer, and, along with improving conditions in prisons, making prison regimes more constructive may relieve judges' 'bad conscience', thereby encouraging them to impose more prison sentences. Mathiesen's solution was to support only reforms which could reasonably be expected to weaken the institution, or, at least, to weaken the power of the authorities, hence the support for prisoners' rights movements. A crucial tactic is to refuse to say what should be put in place of prisons in advance of their abolition.

The person who famously put this latter abolitionist tactic into practice was Jerome Miller, who, when in charge of juvenile corrections in Massachusetts, insisted on the closure of institutions *before* the development of alternative programmes (Rutherford 1993; 1994). This, he insisted, is the only way to avoid the net widening and net strengthening which, as critics of juvenile justice developments in the 1960s and 1970s repeatedly pointed out, is a near-inevitable consequence of developing 'alternative-to-custody' programmes without institutional closure. Without abolition before programme development, those offenders who, in the absence of the programmes, would be incarcerated are incarcerated anyway, while the new programmes, strengthened in comparison with existing non-custodial programmes in order to 'compete' with custody, are used for minor offenders who would otherwise have received non-strengthened community penalties (Austin and Krisberg 1981; Cohen 1985). In England, social workers and probation officers who formed the Association for Juvenile Justice in the 1980s adopted this abolitionist project, as have penal reform groups such as the Howard League which have campaigned for the abolition of custody for juveniles. For a time in the 1980s, probation officers adopted an anti-custodial stance for all but the most serious offenders, though they have retreated from this in the more punitive 1990s.

Abolitionists have never, as Sim (1994: 280) puts it, 'advocated simply "tearing down the walls" of the penitentiary'. What they do challenge is the taken-for-grantedness, to use Foucault's term, of the prison: they want to break the assumption that prison is the normal response to run-of-the-mill crime. Again, in policy and practice, this was illustrated by debates among probation officers and juvenile justice social workers in the 1980s about the phrase 'alternatives to custody'. The term, they argued, assumed that custody was the expected response to most offences, and that if it was desired to persuade a magistrate or judge to do something else in a case, then an argument would have to be made as to why this case should be excepted from the general rule. An alternative that was in some way punitively equivalent to prison would then have to be proposed. 'Alternative-to-custody' thus reinforces the institution of imprisonment rather than diminishes it.

Most abolitionists grant that there are some offenders who are so dangerous, or whose crimes are so heinous, that they must be separated from the rest of society. Such offenders are, however, very few in number, and they should be treated as exceptions, with special facilities having to be provided, and their incarceration specifically justified, rather than vice versa, with prison being the norm and the non-custodial sentences requiring justification. Since there are so few really dangerous or wicked criminals, the number of prisons required is, so the abolitionists argue, very small, and most penal resources should therefore go to non-custodial programmes rather than into building and maintaining prisons. Carlen (1990) argues this case for the abolition of women's imprisonment: because there are so few women from whom the public really needs protection, women's imprisonment should be rare, and non-custodial facilities rather than custodial institutions should be expanded. I have made a similar case for the abolition of imprisonment for mentally disordered offenders (Hudson 1993).

Some abolitionists, mostly European, have extended their critique of imprisonment to the whole notion of punishment (Christie 1982; Hulsman and Bernat de Celis 1982). There is no point, on this view, in breaking the taken-for-grantedness of prison, without breaking the taken-for-grantedness of punishment. If punitiveness is not diminished but prisons are abolished, then the 'pains of imprisonment' will be infiltrated into the supposed alternatives to custody: Foucault's dispersal of discipline, the carceral archipelago, will truly come into being. Some of the proposals for 'tough' or 'realistic' non-custodial penalties which have been put forward as the remedy for excessive imprisonment would seem to bear this out; electronically monitored home confinement would certainly seem to be turning homes into prisons rather than keeping people out of 'prison' and at 'home' (Hudson 1993).

Feminist jurisprudence

An emphasis on relationships rather than rules is also characteristic of the proposals of the growing body of 'feminist jurisprudence' (see, for example, Daly 1989; Bartlett 1990; Hudson 1993). Feminist jurisprudence has two main premises. The first, which is shared by all its adherents, is that legal categories which are supposedly gender-neutral, are in fact male; the second, which is more controversial among feminists, is that there is a kind of reasoning, characteristic of females, which is being excluded from, or is declining in influence within, criminal justice decision-making.

It is the basis of law's claim to authority that its categories apply to all persons, and that all are equal in the eyes of the law. Feminist scholars and feminist campaigners have demonstrated that legal concepts and assumptions have in mind the 'reasonable man' rather than the 'reasonable woman' or 'the reasonable person'. For example, divorce law and rulings about child custody have assumed that the 'normal' (and desirable) arrangement is for a mother to have care of her child. In criminal law, rape laws have depended upon the stereotype of the male sexual drive and the female responsibility to manage male sexuality by expecting a woman to be careful not to arouse it unless she desires a sexual relationship.

Much controversy in recent years has centred on the idea of provocation in homicide – the provocation defence has been available only to defendants who conform to a male stereotype of instant response to provocation, so that the female strategy of waiting for an opportunity where the man's usually superior physical strength will be neutralized (generally, when he is asleep) before reacting to provocation in the form of abuse which has often been endured for several years, means that women who kill violent partners are convicted of murder and receive life imprisonment, whereas men who kill nagging or adulterous wives can be convicted of manslaughter and receive probation orders. A recent decision (July 1995) has overturned a woman's conviction in such a case on grounds of provocation, indicating that in this instance the male-centredness of law has been recognized, but this has taken several years of vigorous campaigning by women's groups.

In responding to juvenile crime, courts and theorists alike have regarded boys' delinquency as a normal adolescent phase, something which, albeit undesirable, will be grown out of in the normal maturational process, whereas girls' delinquency has been responded to as a sign of maladjustment to the feminine role, something which will get worse unless there is disciplinary, normalizing intervention (B.A. Hudson 1984b; A. Hudson 1989). More generally, female crime has been regarded as abnormal as well as unlawful, and the female offender, whether in theories of crime causation or studies of criminal justice processing, has always been measured against the male 'standard' (Smart 1976; Daly 1994).

The first imperative of feminist jurisprudence is, therefore, what is known as 'asking the woman question', interrogating all laws and procedures to ascertain how they affect women. Work which has 'asked the woman question' about Marxist and Foucauldian analyses of penality has been discussed in Chapters 7 and 8, but the section on the juridical-philosophical theories of punishment did not raise 'woman questions', because these theories have been framed with only the abstract 'legal subject' or 'moral agent' in mind.

The impact of penal rationales on the punishment and control of women has, however, been examined by feminist scholars. As indicated in Chapter 8, there is now a considerable body of literature on the regulation of women during the modernist, rehabilitative era. The general consensus of such studies is that women were treated in a paternalistic way; that their offending was medicalized and sexualized and that its basis in the material conditions of their lives was all too often ignored. Women who conformed to female stereotypes, especially women who were good mothers, were treated comparatively leniently ('chivalrously'), whereas those who were judged as unfeminine or unconventional were treated comparatively harshly.

This pathologizing of the female offender, and the sexualization of the delinquency of young women, led from the 1970s until around the mid-1980s to a call for equality of penal treatment from many critics of the prevailing penal treatment of women. In more recent work, however, this desire for equality has been questioned. This has come about because of the realization that, both in principle and in practice, 'equal' means 'like men'. As punishment has become more severe in the law and order politics climate since the 1980s, especially in England and Wales and the USA, equal treatment with men becomes far less desirable. In England, Carlen (1989) has drawn attention to the harshness and impersonality of the punishment of men, with the emphasis on proportionality and 'making the punishment fit the crime'; while in the USA, Tonry (1993) has noted that the very success of sentencing guidelines in most states has led to increased imprisonment of women as the disparities between sentencing females and sentencing males have been reduced. Daly (1994: 269) notes that an alternative to the 'levelling up' that has generally ensued in the effort to reduce sentencing disparity, is the 'split the difference' policy of California. Average sentences before the determinate sentencing laws passed in the 1980s had been lower for women than for men; the new laws therefore lowered sentences for men and raised them for women.

In states with guidelines rather than mandatory sentences (and in England and Wales), the move towards consistency, equality, and proportionality of punishment to crime has meant that mitigating circumstances, such as childcare or other family responsibilities, ceased to be available (Raeder 1993). The call for 'equality' has therefore largely been replaced by a call for 'appropriateness'. Instead of circumstances more generally applicable to men being built into legislation and policy, and female offenders suffering because of the irrelevance of these circumstances to the lives of most women, what is required is that circumstances appropriate to each person should be considered. Further, some of the considerations that have been taken into account in the sentencing of females before sentencing guidelines and laws, such as childcare or care of elderly relatives, should be available for men in similar circumstances.

Feminist penologists are now arguing for a 'woman-wise' penology (Carlen 1990), which not only takes into account the maleness of supposedly gender-neutral concepts, and requires attention to the lives of female offenders, but also is cognizant of the gendered power relationships in the societies in which women and men are committing crimes and enduring penalties. This 'dominance perspective' asks that the penal regulation of both men and women should not add to women's oppression. Womanwise penality would, therefore, have as its basic requirements:

1 That the penal regulation of female law-breakers does not increase their oppression *as women* still further.
2 That the penal regulation of law-breaking men does not brutalize them and make them even more violently or ideologically oppressive towards women in the future.

(Carlen 1990: 114)

The second premise of feminist jurisprudence concerns the view that women characteristically have a different moral reasoning from men. Women's moral reasoning is, it is claimed, more concerned with finding solutions to concrete, specific problems than is men's, which is more concerned with the application of abstract, general rules. This idea is associated primarily with the work of Carol Gilligan. In her book, *In a Different Voice*, Gilligan (1982) reworked the experiments of the cognitive psychologist Kohlberg, who had claimed that moral development consists in moving from the specific and concrete to the general and abstract. She noticed that all the subjects of his experiments were male, and argued that what he claimed was 'advanced' moral reasoning was in fact 'male' moral reasoning. Gilligan termed the female moral style 'the ethic of care', in contrast to the male 'logic of justice'.

Applied to law, Gilligan argues that the logic of justice is dominant in criminal law, and that the ethic of care is either absent or much subordinated. Others, while agreeing that these two principles can be identified in approaches to crime and punishment, deny that they are specifically male and female. Heidensohn (1986) thus wishes to avoid calling them the 'male voice' and the 'female voice', and designates them the Portia principle (which emphasizes rules and individual responsibility) and the Persephone principle (which places value on relationships and on resolving problems). She associates the Portia principle with the just-deserts, retributivist penal mode, and argues that this has lately become over-dominant, at the expense of Persephone mode. I, too, have argued that the balance between following rules and securing outcomes likely to improve situations became too heavily weighted towards the following of rules during the 1980s (Hudson 1993).

This concept of feminist moral reasoning is controversial, on the one hand because it seems, as Heidensohn makes clear, to be an oversimplification in its dichotomizing of male and female moral concerns, and also, on the other hand, because, as MacKinnon (1989) explains, it suggests, as some sort of essential female characteristic, a mode of being that arises from the position of women in a particular society. Females are encouraged to be caring and think of others, and this encouragement is reinforced by approval for concern for the problems of others and disapproval for (too much) concern with individual achievement; they are encouraged to study 'people' subjects such as literature, history, geography and sociology, and discouraged from studying abstract subjects such as theoretical physics. While endorsing Gilligan's critique of Kohlberg, MacKinnon is wary of endorsing a view of women as somehow essentially different from men.

Feminist scholarship in general, and thus feminist legal scholarship, has lately faced the challenge of postmodernism, which questions the use of all generalizing categories such as 'women'. More pragmatically, feminists have been challenged by minority ethnic women not to imagine that the perspective of white, mainly middle-class academics speaks for 'all women', and their own sympathy with the different dimensions of oppression has encouraged them to move from arguing for ideas of justice to give recognition to the female as well as to the male standpoint, to arguing for a recognition of a multiplicity of standpoints.

Bartlett's (1990: 836) description of 'asking the woman question' thus explains that it 'is designed to expose how the substance of law silently and without justification submerges the perspectives of women and *other excluded groups*' (emphasis added). The accusation that feminist legal scholars make of jurisprudence is that it is not only formulated from a male standpoint but also that it is blind to this fact. By its exclusion of categories of difference between individuals as irrelevant to criminal justice (differences of gender, race and ethnicity, economic circumstances) it assumes it is dealing with individuals who are, by all relevant criteria, the same (Kerruish 1991; Hudson 1993, 1995a). It substitutes procedural equality for substantive inequality, and therefore cannot deliver actual justice to 'real' people.

Concluding comments

It will readily be appreciated that these concerns of feminist jurisprudence to consider relationships and to resolve conflicts and difficulties, as well as its concern to pay attention to all standpoints, to the submerged as well as the powerful voices, have much in common with the principles of restorative justice. There is much that is appealing and valid in these ideas, but it has to be admitted that there are some drawbacks.

If one is convinced, as I am, by the arguments of the Marxists and the Foucauldians that the penal system bears down on the poor and the excluded rather than on the rich and powerful, then the claims of the criminal law to fairness and impartiality – to be able to do 'justice' – are difficult to sustain. The liability of the poor and oppressed to punishment on the benefits-and-burdens theory must be open to question, and proportionality of punishment to blameworthiness would be impractical to calculate if one were seriously to consider the different pressures to which potential offenders are subject. The 'equality' of legal subjects is a myth; what is reality is their social and material differences. The problem of how there can be just deserts in an unjust society is critical for modern retributivists, and, at the very least, indicates that the social facts of each case should be given as much recognition as the legal facts, and that claims to be delivering 'justice' through the imposition of penalties proportionate to the gravity of offences should be muted (Hudson 1995a; Tonry 1995).

On the other hand, attempts to make the individual offender the focus of penal attention, rather than the offence (the Utilitarian approach), have led to excessive punishment because of the prognosis of those with bad employment prospects, with addictions, who have suffered from abuse, who are homeless, mentally ill, unconventional, or from minority communities, as likely to reoffend. The lesson that should be learned from these limitations of the different penal theories is that inflicting punishment (on whatever rationale) can never be the same as delivering justice.

Many of those who are critical of present penal practices and who advocate reductions in penalties, or who argue for adopting parsimony or rights-backed rehabilitation as preferable to proportionality, make clear that they would generally wish to see resort to punishment decline, and for the response to crime to become more restorative (see, for example, Braithwaite and Pettit 1990). Most would concur with the criticisms of the feminist legal scholars that law at present is predominantly reflective of the standpoint of the powerful, property-owning, white male; this seems to me to be irrefutable. Again, then, redress or restoration seems to be the progressive policy.

There are, however, some difficulties with the idea of restorative justice (see Chapter 5). In the first place, it assumes perhaps too readily that in most cases it will be possible to achieve some agreement between offenders, victims and communities. As Garland (1990a; 1990b) has reminded us in his insistence that both Durkheimian expressive functions and the Marxist–Foucauldian instrumental functions of punishment be recognized, punishment relieves the feelings of victims and of the communities in which crimes are committed. If the ceremonies of the criminal law were not enacted, and if penalties were not inflicted, the outcome might be vigilante violence rather than restorative agreements.

More fundamentally, perhaps, if the reach of the criminal law were restricted so that many of the crimes now adjudicated were diverted to restorative processes and only certain especially heinous crimes were dealt with by criminal law, people whose sufferings were dealt with by the restorative meetings might well feel that their troubles were considered of lesser importance than 'proper' crimes. This has been the reasoning used by women's groups campaigning for more frequent prosecution and more severe sentencing for domestic violence, for example, and by those campaigning along the same lines for increased enforcement and penalization in incidences of racial harassment. Criminalization and punishment, as Durkheim explained and as Foucault and Garland have recognized, demonstrate a society's moral boundaries, the limits of its tolerance; the penalization of domestic violence, racial harassment and drunken driving help shape attitudes towards these kinds of behaviour, and show that society in its formal organization is on the side of those who think that racial harassment, wife abuse and drink-driving are wrong (Hudson 1995b).

My own view is that justice should not be so eagerly equated with punishment. Criminal laws and the existence of penal sanctions demonstrate society's moral boundaries; whether punishment should be imposed in a particular case, and to what extent, should have regard to the circumstances of the offender. The pains of punishment are inflicted on the offender, and therefore the severity of punishment should be limited by desert, and also by its likelihood of helping the offender desist from further crime. Like Braithwaite and Pettit, and Tonry, I see parsimony as a principle that should take precedence over proportionality; I would also insist that punishment be oriented to circumstances that are identified as associated with the offence already committed, and that punishment should not be able to be enhanced because of predictions of what the offender might do in the future.

I acknowledge what Garland (1990a) calls the 'tragic quality' of punishment – that it seems to be at the same time both necessary and futile – and because I acknowledge its necessity, I do not foresee its total abolition. The abolitionist critique, however, is salutary: the taken-for-grantedness of punishment should be unsettled. Such necessity of punishment as I allow, is for the existence of penal sanctions, not for their imposition on all offenders (Lacey 1988; Hudson 1993; 1995a). Punishment needs to be justified in general, and in every particular instance, partly because it is imposed differentially on the least powerful groups in society. As Wasserstrom (1980: 112) puts it, a practice that 'intentionally increases human pain or suffering requires justification in a way which many other things that we do to or with other persons do not'. Punishment cannot thus be a synonym for 'justice'. The weaknesses in the philosophical approaches, the insights of the sociological approaches, the challenges of abolitionism and feminist jurisprudence should mean that punishment is restricted and reduced. Rather than imposing penalties with self-righteous confidence, we should always punish with a bad conscience.

Postscript. Beyond modernity: the fate of justice

Introduction
Human rights and the politics of public safety
Justice and postmodernity

Introduction

This book has been about justice in modern society. Although focused on criminal justice rather than other spheres of justice (for instance, the distribution of wealth), the concepts on which theories and practices of punishment are based are essentially the same as those involved in other spheres. 'Justice' in modern society is concerned with the balance between individual freedom and social responsibility; it concerns the fair distribution of the rights and responsibilities of citizenship; it concerns the upholding of rules for distribution of property and physical integrity. In modern society, social institutions are involved in the distribution of such goods as freedom, property, health, wealth; the concept of justice thus has a particular meaning in modern society. Penal justice is, of course, also concerned with the distribution of these social goods. Theories of punishment, in modern times, are not concerned with how to appease the gods or the king, but with upholding the legal distribution of property and freedom; they are concerned with the basis on which, and the extent to which, the state should intervene in the distribution of property and freedom by imposing penalties for crimes.

Chapter 9 suggests that this 'modern' era may now be over. There are strong signs that advanced Western societies have entered a new phase, where their major concerns are not with the distribution of social goods but with management of the risks arising from these very goods themselves (Beck, 1992). As Ulrich Beck explains, the citizens of late-modern societies, while perhaps taking the goods produced by modern knowledges for granted, are ever more aware of their accompanying risks. Increased levels of health care bring the problems of supporting people into advanced old age; the factories that bring us the material goods which make life more comfortable, and which provide employment to enable people to purchase them, also produce pollution; increased opportunities for leisure and travel increase the risk of car or airplane accidents, and so forth. The point made by Beck and others who have highlighted the problems of modernity (Giddens 1990), is not that these negative consequences are new, but that people are more concerned with them than previously. The organizing principle of social life, it is argued, has changed from 'the logic of wealth distribution in a society of scarcity to the logic of risk distribution' (Beck 1992: 19). In this short postscript I address the tensions between this preoccupation with risk and the prospects for our society's commitment to an ideal of justice based on rights.

Human rights and the politics of public safety

At various points in the text, the idea of human rights has been mentioned. For example, in the section on syntheses between desert and consequentialist principles in Chapter 4, and in discussing the debate between retributivists and restorative justice advocates in Chapter 5, it has been suggested that human rights should become the anchoring principle for criminal justice. Ashworth (1995) proposes human rights as the essential criminal justice principle in order to resolve the perennial problem of the right balance between crime control and due process. In the interval between the appearance of the first edition of this book and publication of this second edition, the European Convention on Human Rights has been brought into UK legislation, with the effect that all criminal justice agencies now have to check that their policies and practices are 'convention compliant'. (Canada has gone further than most countries, in revising its penal code in the light of its charter of rights and freedoms.)

Legislation, advocacy by respected academics, and even a strong rights culture, do not, however, guarantee that human rights will be upheld for all citizens. The USA – probably the nation where rights discourse is most culturally embedded – finds no problem in retaining the death penalty, which involves deprivation of the most fundamental right, the right to life. Furthermore, as we all became aware in the presidential election which brought George Bush Jr. to power, in some states offenders are denied the right to vote not just while they are in prison, but for ever.

There is an inevitable tension between rights and risks, and I am concerned that the present politics of safety is tipping this balance far too far away from the protection of the rights of offenders and potential offenders. Old-style incapacitative sentencing (discussed in Chapter 2) recognized the right of offenders not to be a false positive as well as the right of potential victims not to be endangered by false negatives, and, as we saw in Chapter 9, this right is not respected in the new actuarial modes of predicting reoffending. Innovations such as Megan's Law trample the rights of offenders to be left alone once they have paid the penalty for their offence; proposals in the UK to legislate for the possible incarceration of people diagnosed as having severe personality disorders, even if they have not committed an offence, show that the USA is not the only society which disregards rights if they attach to people defined as dangerous (Duff 1998; Gray *et al.* 2002).

Closed-circuit television and other contemporary control measures are often not subject to legislation, and they disregard not only the rights of all people to privacy, but also in many cases (curfews, exclusion from shopping malls and from gated estates) the rights of members of certain groups (usually teenagers and young adults) to freedom of movement and of association. With both crime control measures and incapacitative sentencing, resistance generated by actuarial regimes is, as Simon (1988) has noted and as Garland has shown in his discussion of the support of these policies by liberal elites, less than that encountered by the normalizing regime. This is hardly surprising: who could oppose public safety; who could argue persuasively against policies and practices designed to help people avoid the pain of crime?

The risk society has engendered a new way of thinking about rights. Rights are no longer thought of as inalienable, as due to everyone simply by virtue of their humanity. The new way of thinking about rights links them to responsibilities (Giddens 1999). From this perspective, rights are only available to those who act responsibly; crime is by definition irresponsible (at least socially irresponsible), so there is no firm basis for offenders' rights. This new thinking is extended to prisoners: prisoners need to earn 'rights' by acting responsibly, for example by entering treatment and rehabilitation programmes and by being docile, tractable inmates. Hannah-Moffat's (2000) study of Canadian women's prisons shows that this new rights-and-responsibilities approach triumphs even in a country with an apparently strong commitment to rights, including offenders' rights.

Thinking about criminal justice often yields the view that rights (the right to proportionate punishment, civil rights) ought to be a prime concern for minor offenders, particularly property offenders, and particularly for lightly convicted property offenders. On the other hand, rights are of less concern than risk in the case of repeat offenders, which explains popular support for disproportionate sentences under the California Three Strikes Law, and popular support in the UK for lengthy custodial terms for persistent young offenders. Even more, on this view, sex offenders are not considered worthy of rights. Partly, this is because of widespread belief that they can never be 'cured', so they can never be trusted to behave responsibly, although there are obviously many factors contributing to the special abhorrence felt towards sex offenders.

Alongside the coupling of rights and responsibilities which reduces offenders' claims to rights, there is an entrenched 'zero-sum' thinking about rights which is shared by politicians and professionals as well as media and public. When the issue of offenders' rights is raised, a frequent response is 'I'm interested in victims' rights, not offenders' rights'. This is encountered in thinking about crime prevention, punishment, community notification of sex offenders' whereabouts, and also in some of the formulations of restorative justice.

If justice is not to be overwhelmed by the politics of risk and safety, there will have to be a reassertion of the universalist meaning of human rights: that they inhere inalienably in all human beings, including the most dangerous. While it seems obvious that the rights to physical safety must count more than rights to privacy or to freedom from 'penal marking' after the end of a sentence (Garland 2000), as the legal philosopher Ronald Dworkin (1977) tells us, it cannot be that the one is everything and the other is nothing. If things are of the same category, then there is some equivalence in their value, and it cannot be that one is sacrificed to another – a balance must be struck and maintained between them.

More recently, writing in the aftermath of the terrible events of 11 September 2001, Dworkin (2002) takes issue with the suspension of rights of terrorist suspects held captive. He reminds us that the whole concept of rights is to do with protecting precisely those persons who we think of as terrible. People for whom we have sympathy will be protected by our compassion and our concern for their welfare; it is those for whom we feel no compassion and about whom we do not (or no longer) care who need the protection of rights. The concept of rights does not, he says, mean deciding where our interests (in protection from risk, in the exclusion of the offensive) lie, it means doing what justice requires.

Justice and postmodernity

The new technologies for the management of risk-posing and risk-incurring populations offer many new opportunities for law as an institution (law as a set of rules and procedures, law as a profession). There is much that needs to be regulated (the powers of security guards, the limits of information that may be stored and shared about people, for example), and the increased recognition of victims provides opportunities for establishing rights and claims to compensation. The danger, however, is that the gap between law and justice will be further widened.

Law as an impartial arbiter, as a dispenser of even-handed justice, as a protector of the rights of all, has been heavily challenged by the critical legal studies movement (Fitzpatrick and Hunt 1987) and the feminist legal studies movement, as discussed in Chapter 10. The deconstructionist impulse has shown that, while law may become less male-centred, less white-centred, while the range of rights it protects and of harms it proscribes may be expanded, there must always be a gap between law and justice. Justice is something that must concern individuality, singularity, the precise match of remedy to situation, while law is concerned with generality. Law's rules and remedies can, therefore, at best approximate to the requirements of justice in a situation, but they cannot meet them exactly (Derrida 1990). Justice is an aspiration of law, it cannot be an achievement of law.

Most of the challenges to law by postmodernists, however, are challenges to law's 'imperialism' (Hunt 1993), its colonizing of too many areas of social life (Smart 1989) – the case against law is that it overstates its claims to be a superior voice to that of discourses such as social science; the case is that, in fact, it 'masquerades' as justice (Cornell 1992), when it is in fact ideology (Kerruish 1991) or mythology (Fitzpatrick 1992). These challenges call for acknowledgement of the gap between law and justice, not, as a rule, for the abandonment either of law as an institution or of the aspiration to justice.

So, what is justice? There are probably as many definitions as there are writers on the subject, but the one that is drawn on by many of those who are persuaded by the deconstructionist challenges to the (Durkheimian) claim of an identity between law and justice, is that proposed by the philosopher Levinas (1981). His essential ingredient is respect for the rights of the Other. Justice is recognition of the Other, who is like myself in some ways, and unlike in others; justice involves recognition of the likeness in the sense of shared humanness, but not insistence on reduction or elimination of differences, rather the respecting of differences.

Levinas grounds justice on a face-to-face relationship between myself and the Other. Such dyadic relationships are of the essence of law in its approach to justice: state and individual, judge and judged, male and female, property-owning class and property-less class. Law exists to regulate these relationships of dissymmetry, of Otherness, and justice is approached when the claims of both parties are equitably balanced. The crucial dyad of law is, of course, that between plaintiff and defendant, offender and victim. It is here that the actuarial regime poses its most powerful threat to justice, because of its dissolution of the offender as an Other, as a concrete individual who is like the victim in humanness, and who is like the victim in having rights that should be defended by law.

It might be objected to this anxiety about the fate of justice, that the concepts of law and rights which are threatened – the ingredients of justice – are concepts which have no value beyond the modernist society in which they arose. Certainly, Foucault's powerful critique of the extent of 'unfreedom' allowed in the modern disciplinary regime, and the critiques of the Marxists, the feminists and the deconstructionists do not make it immediately obvious why anyone should want to defend the rule of law, and this apparently inadequate and unobtainable ideal of justice. There are, however, many who wish to learn the lessons of the critiques of justice in modern societies covered here, and who would wish to acknowledge that the confident age of modernity is passed, but who nevertheless seek not to dismiss all the concepts that Enlightenment thought gave to political philosophy and the quest for just societies.

Habermas (1987) wishes to defend the authority of reason against might; Beck (1992) and Giddens (1990) urge a 'reflexive modernity'; Walzer (1983) defends the search for complex equality in a pluralist society: the ideas of rights that differentiate modern liberal society from the Gulag need to be reaffirmed, and must be defended against threats posed by the actuarial technologies of the late-modern era. In relation to debates about crime and punishment, about the balance between the consequentialist and the retributivist, about the balance between the ethic of care and the logic of justice, this means that, as Hunt (1993) puts it, a final choice need never be made, though it may be necessary from time to time to intervene on one side or the other.

Glossary of key terms

(This glossary lists terms which are general to the methods and theories of penology; terms which are specific to certain theories or perspectives are explained in the chapters or sections in which they arise).

Abolitionism The movement in penology and penal reform which seeks to abolish all or part of the penal system.

Actuarialism The calculation of probabilities of risks being realized, used in insurance; applied to forms of contemporary penology which use similar factorial calculations rather than individual diagnostic and assessment techniques.

Consequentialism (in punishment theory) The theory that punishment is justified because of its future consequences (usually, the reduction of crime).

Critical criminology, critical legal studies An approach which examines deficiencies and closures in existing theories and concepts, and which highlights the social origins and the influence of these theories and concepts.

Distributive aim (of punishment) The principles governing who should be punished, and how much punishment there should be.

Feminist jurisprudence An approach which challenges the male-centredness of legal theory and practice, and which seeks to incorporate feminist reasoning into law and legal scholarship.

Functionalism A sociological perspective which assumes that social forms, social institutions and social customs do not survive unless they have some utility for the society in which they occur.

General justifying aim (of punishment) The reason(s) why a system of punitive sanctions for crime should exist.

Governmentality The mode of government of modern societies: the way power is deployed, the uses to which power is put; the roles and functions adopted by government; the management of and provision of security for aggregate populations.

Interactionism The perspective in social science which takes as its prime object of study the shared meanings and understandings that members of society develop, meanings which are developed through social interaction.

Late modernity A term used by some social theorists to describe a period, from approximately 1975 to the present, when all the inherent tendencies of modernism have reached their fullest development. Characterized by extreme individualism, by loss of trust in authorities, and by the dominance of economic rationality over other ways of thinking.

Legitimacy   The agreement of members of a society that its social institutions represent a properly authorized exercise of power.

Modernity   The period (approximately from 1750 to 1970) of industrialization and the establishment of constitutional government and the welfare state. It was characterized by belief in progress, and the solution of problems through science and rationality.

Penality   The complex of ideas, institutions, rules, practices and relationships pertaining to punishment.

Penology   The study of the punishment of crime.

Positivism (in social science)   The belief that social behaviour can be studied by the same scientific methods as natural phenomena, that human behaviour has causes which can be discovered by scientific observation, and that such study can lead to predictive laws.

Postmodernism   An intellectual movement which challenges the claims of scientific thought and rational thought to incorporate fundamental and universal truths.

Postmodernity   A stage in the development of society where belief in the ability of science and reason to achieve progress and to provide solutions to social problems no longer holds.

Realism (in criminology)   A perspective which insists on the reality of crime and sees the major task of criminology as the production of knowledge to reduce the amount of crime.

Reductivism   The theory that punishment is justified if it reduces the amount of crime in society.

Restorative justice   A model of criminal justice which aims to provide redress for victims and offer offenders the chance of reintegration back into communities. Usually involves the offender offering an apology to the victim, some reparative measures and some measures to reduce the likelihood of reoffending.

Retributivism   The theory that punishment is a justified response to a wrong already committed by an offender.

Social contract theory   The idea that the power and authority of government are derived from an (unwritten) contract entered into by members of a society, whereby they surrender some freedom in order to secure protection against the predatory acts of others.

Utilitarianism   The theory that people are motivated by the desire to maximize happiness and minimize pain, and that the duty of government is to promote the maximum amount of happiness (welfare) in society.

Suggestions for further reading

Introduction to penology

Cavadino, M. and Dignan, J. (1992) *The Penal System: An Introduction*. London: Sage. (Second edition 1997)
Garland, D. and Young, P. (eds) (1983) *The Power to Punish*. London: Heinemann.

Part one   The goals of punishment: the juridical perspective

Braithwaite, J. and Pettit, P. (1990) *Not Just Deserts: A Republican Theory of Criminal Justice*. Oxford: Clarendon Press.
Braithwaite, J. and Strang, H. (eds) (2000) *Restorative Justice: From Philosophy to Practice*. Aldershot: Dartmouth.
Duff, R.A. (1986) *Trials and Punishment*. Cambridge: Cambridge University Press.
Hart, H.L.A. (1968) *Punishment and Responsibility: Essays in the Philosophy of Law*. Oxford: Clarendon Press.
Hudson, B.A. (1987) *Justice through Punishment: A Critique of the 'Justice' Model of Corrections*. Basingstoke: Macmillan.
Lacey, N. (1988) *State Punishment*. London: Routledge.
Rotman, E. (1990) *Beyond Punishment: A New View on the Rehabilitation of Criminal Offenders*. Westport, CT: Greenwood Press.
von Hirsch, A. (1976) *Doing Justice: The Choice of Punishments*. New York: Hill and Wang.
von Hirsch, A. (1986) *Past or Future Crimes: Deservedness and Dangerousness in the Sentencing of Criminals*. Manchester: Manchester University Press.
von Hirsch, A. (1993) *Censure and Sanctions*. Oxford: Clarendon Press.
von Hirsch, A. and Ashworth, A. (eds) (1992) *Principled Sentencing*. Edinburgh: Edinburgh University Press.
von Hirsch, A., Roberts, J., Bottoms, A., Roach, K. and Schiff, M. (eds) (2002) *Restorative Justice and Criminal Justice: Competing or Reconcilable Paradigms?* Oxford: Hart Publishing.
Walker, N. (1991) *Why Punish?* Oxford: Oxford University Press.

Part two   Punishment and modernity: the sociological perspective

Box, S. (1987) *Repression, Crime and Punishment*. Basingstoke: Macmillan.

Cohen, S. (1985) *Visions of Social Control: Crime, Punishment and Classification*. Cambridge: Polity Press.

Cohen, S. and Scull, A. (eds) (1983) *Social Control and the State*. Oxford: Martin Robertson.

Donzelot, J. (1980) *The Policing of Families*. London: Hutchinson.

Foucault, M. (1977) *Discipline and Punish: The Birth of the Prison*. London: Allen Lane.

Garland, D. (1990) *Punishment and Modern Society*. Oxford: Oxford University Press.

Garland, D. (2001) *The Culture of Control: Crime and Social Order in Contemporary Society*. Oxford: Oxford University Press.

Garland, D. (ed.) (2001) *Mass Imprisonment: Social Causes and Consequences*. London: Sage.

Howe, A. (1994) *Punish and Critique: Towards a Feminist Analysis of Penality*. London: Routledge.

Melossi, D. and Pavarini, M. (1981) *The Prison and the Factory: Origins of the Penitentiary System*. Basingstoke: Macmillan.

Rusche, G. and Kirchheimer, O. (1968) *Punishment and Social Structure*. New York: Russell and Russell.

Sim, J. (1990) *Medical Power in Prisons: The Prison Medical Service in England 1774–1989*. Buckingham: Open University Press.

Spierenburg, P. (1984) *The Spectacle of Suffering*. Cambridge: Cambridge University Press.

Zedner, L. (1991) *Women, Crime and Custody in Victorian England*. Oxford: Oxford University Press.

Part three   Towards justice?

de Haan, W. (1990) *The Politics of Redress: Crime, Punishment and Penal Abolition*. London: Unwin Hyman.

Fitzpatrick, P. and Hunt, A. (eds) (1987) *Critical Legal Studies*. Oxford: Basil Blackwell.

Giddens, A. (1990) *The Consequences of Modernity*. Cambridge: Polity Press.

Hudson, B. (1993) *Penal Policy and Social Justice*. Basingstoke: Macmillan.

Kerruish, V. (1991) *Jurisprudence as Ideology*. London: Routledge.

Lacey, N. (1988) *State Punishment*. London: Routledge.

Nelken, D. (ed.) (1994) *The Futures of Criminology*. London: Sage.

References

Allen, H. (1987) *Justice Unbalanced: Gender, Psychiatry and Judicial Decisions.* Milton Keynes: Open University Press.

Althusser, L. (1969) *For Marx.* London: Allen Lane.

Althusser, L. (1971) *Lenin and Philosophy and Other Essays.* New York: Monthly Review Press.

American Friends Service Committee (1972) *Struggle for Justice.* New York: Hill and Wang.

Ancel, M. (1987) *Social Defense: the Future of Penal Reform*, trans. T. Sellin. Littleton, CO: Rothman.

Andenaes, J. (1974) *Punishment and Deterrence.* Ann Arbor: University of Michigan Press.

Ashworth, A. (1983) *Sentencing and Penal Policy.* London: Weidenfeld and Nicolson.

Ashworth, A. (1988) Criminal justice and criminal process, *British Journal of Criminology*, 28(2): 241–53.

Ashworth, A. (1989) Criminal justice and deserved sentences, *Criminal Law Review*, May: 340–55.

Ashworth, A. (1993) Some doubts about restorative justice, *Criminal Law Forum*, 4: 277–99.

Ashworth, A. (1995) Principles, practice and criminal justice, in P. Birks (ed.) Pressing Problems in Law, Vol. 1, *Criminal Justice and Human Rights*. Oxford: Oxford University Press.

Ashworth, A. (2002) Responsibilities, rights and restorative justice, *British Journal of Criminology*, 42(3).

Austin, J. and Krisberg, B. (1981) Wider, stronger and different nets: the dialectics of criminal justice reform, *Journal of Research in Crime and Delinquency*, 18(1): 165–96.

Ayres, I. and Braithwaite, J. (1992) *Responsive Regulation: Transcending the Deregulation Debate.* New York: Oxford University Press.

Bachelard, G. (1968) *The Philosophy of No*, trans. G.C. Waterston. New York: Orion Press.

Barlow, D.E., Barlow, M.H. and Chiricos, J.G. (1993) Long economic cycles and the criminal justice system in the U.S., *Crime, Law and Social Change*, 19: 143–69.

Bartlett, K.T. (1990) Feminist legal methods, *Harvard Law Review*, 103: 829–88.

Bean, P. (1976) *Rehabilitation and Deviance.* London: Routledge & Kegan Paul.

Beccaria, C. (1963) *On Crimes and Punishments*. Indianapolis: Bobbs-Merrill.

Beck, U. (1992) *Risk Society: Towards a New Modernity*. London: Sage.

Becker, H. (1963) *Outsiders: Studies in the Sociology of Deviance*. New York: Free Press.

Benn, S.I. and Peters, R.S. (1959) *Social Principles and the Democratic State*. London: Allen & Unwin.

Beyleveld, D. (1979) Deterrence research as a basis for deterrence policies, *Howard Journal*, 18: 135–49.

Blagg, H. and Smith, D. (1989) *Crime, Penal Policy and Social Work*. Harlow: Longman.

Blumstein, A. (1993) Racial discrimination of US prison populations revisited, *University of Colorado Law Review*, 64: 743–60.

Blumstein, A., Cohen, J., Martin, S.E. and Tonry, M.H. (eds) (1983) *Research on Sentencing: The Search for Reform*, Vol. 1. Washington, DC: National Academy Press.

Bottomley, A.K. and Pease, K. (1986) *Crime and Punishment: Interpreting the Data*. Milton Keynes: Open University Press.

Bottoms, A. (1983) Neglected features of contemporary penal systems, in D. Garland and P. Young (eds) *The Power to Punish*. London: Heinemann.

Bottoms, A. (1990) What went wrong? in D. Downes (ed.) *Unravelling Criminal Justice*. Basingstoke: Macmillan.

Bottoms, A. (1995) The philosophy and politics of punishment and sentencing, in C.M.V. Clarkson and R. Morgan (eds) *The Politics of Sentencing Reform*. Oxford: Clarendon Press.

Bottoms, A. and Brownsword, R. (1983) Dangerousness and rights, in J. Hinton (ed.) *Dangerousness: Problems of Assessment and Prediction*. London: Allen & Unwin.

Box, S. (1987) *Recession, Crime and Punishment*. Basingstoke: Macmillan.

Box, S. and Hale, C. (1982) Economic crisis and the rising prisoner population, *Crime and Social Justice*, 17: 20–35.

Braithwaite, J. (1989) *Crime, Shame and Reintegration*. Cambridge: Cambridge University Press.

Braithwaite, J. (1997) On speaking softly and carrying sticks: neglected dimensions of republican separation of powers, *University of Toronto Law Journal*, 47: 1–57.

Braithwaite, J. (1999) Restorative justice: assessing optimistic and pessimistic accounts, in M. Tonry (ed.) *Crime and Justice: A Review of Research, Volume 25*. Chicago: University of Chicago Press.

Braithwaite, J. (2002) *Restorative Justice and Responsive Regulation*. New York: Oxford University Press.

Braithwaite, J. and Daly, K. (1994) Masculinities, violence and communitarian control, in T. Newburn and E. Stanko (eds) *Just Boys Doing Business?* London: Routledge.

Braithwaite, J. and Pettit, P. (1990) *Not Just Deserts: A Republican Theory of Criminal Justice*. Oxford: Clarendon Press.

Brody, S.R. (1976) *The Effectiveness of Sentencing*. London: HMSO.

Burchell, G., Gordon, C. and Miller, P. (eds) (1991) *The Foucault Effect: Studies in Governmentality*. Chicago: University of Chicago Press.

Burnside, J. and Baker, N. (1994) *Relational Justice: Repairing the Breach*. Winchester: Waterside Press.

Carlen, P. (1976) *Magistrates' Justice*. London: Martin Robertson.

Carlen, P. (1983) *Women's Imprisonment: A Study in Social Control*. London: Routledge & Kegan Paul.

Carlen, P. (ed.) (1985) *Criminal Women*. Cambridge: Polity Press.

Carlen, P. (1988) *Women, Crime and Poverty*. Milton Keynes: Open University Press.

Carlen, P. (1989) Crime, inequality and sentencing, in P. Carlen and D. Cook (eds) *Paying for Crime*. Milton Keynes: Open University Press.

Carlen, P. (1990) *Alternatives to Women's Imprisonment*. Milton Keynes: Open University Press.

Carlen, P. (1992) Criminal women and criminal justice: the limits to, and potential of, feminist and left realist perspectives, in R. Matthews and J. Young (eds) *Issues in Realist Criminology*. London: Sage.

Carlen, P. (1998) *Sledgehammer: Women's Imprisonment at the Millennium*. Basingstoke: Macmillan.

Castel, R. (1991) From dangerousness to risk, in G. Burchell, C. Gordon and P. Miller (eds) *The Foucault Effect: Studies in Governmentality*. Chicago: University of Chicago Press.

Cavadino, M. and Dignan, J. (1992) *The Penal System: An Introduction*. London: Sage. (Second edition 1997.)

Cavadino, M. and Dignan, J. (1997) Reparation, retribution and rights, *International Review of Victimology*, 4: 233–53.

Chiricos, J. G. (1987) Rates of crime and unemployment: an analysis of aggregate research evidence, *Social Problems*, 34: 187–212.

Christie, N. (1977) Conflicts as property, *British Journal of Criminology*, 17: 1–15.

Christie, N. (1982) *Limits to Pain*. Oxford: Martin Robertson.

Cicourel, A.V. (1968) *The Social Organisation of Juvenile Justice*. New York: John Wiley.

Clear, T. and Cadora, E. (2001) Risk and community practice, in K. Stenson and R.R. Sullivan (eds) *Crime, Risk and Justice*. Cullompton: Willan Publishing.

Clear, T.R. and Karp, D.R. (1999) *The Community Justice Ideal: Preventing Crime and Achieving Justice*. Chicago: Westview Press.

Cobb, S. (1997) The domestication of violence in mediation, *Law and Society Review*, 31: 397–440.

Cohen, J. (1983) Incapacitation as a strategy for crime control: problems and pitfalls, in M.H. Tonry and N. Morris (eds) *Crime and Justice: An Annual Review of Research*, Vol. 5. Chicago: University of Chicago Press.

Cohen, S. (1977) Prisons and the future of control systems, in M. Fitzgerald, P. Halmos, J. Muncie and D. Zeldin (eds) *Welfare in Action*. London: Routledge & Kegan Paul.

Cohen, S. (1979) The punitive city: notes on the dispersal of social control, *Contemporary Crises*, 3: 339–63.

Cohen, S. (1981) Footprints in the sand: a further report on criminology and the sociology of deviance in Britain, in M. Fitzgerald, G. McLennan and J. Pawson (eds) *Crime and Society: Readings in History and Theory*. London: Routledge & Kegan Paul.

Cohen, S. (1984) The deeper structures of the law or 'Beware the rulers bearing justice', *Contemporary Crises*, 8: 83–93.

Cohen, S. (1985) *Visions of Social Control: Crime, Punishment and Classification*. Cambridge: Polity Press.

Cook, D. and Hudson, B. (eds) (1993) *Racism and Criminology*. London: Sage.

Cornell, D. (1992) *The Philosophy of the Limit*. New York and London: Routledge.

Cornish, D. and Clarke, R. (1986) *The Reasoning Criminal: Rational Choice Perspectives in Offending*. New York: Springer-Verlag.

Cotterrell, R. (1984) *The Sociology of Law: An Introduction*. London: Butterworths.

Couzens Hoy, D. (ed.) (1986) *Foucault: A Critical Reader*. Oxford: Basil Blackwell.

Crawford, A. (1997) *The Local Governance of Crime*. Oxford: Clarendon Press.

Crawford, A. and Newburn, T. (2002) Recent developments in restorative justice in England and Wales: community participation and representation, *British Journal of Criminology*, 42(3): 476–95.

Cullen, F. and Gilbert, K. (1982) *Reaffirming Rehabilitation*. Cincinatti, OH: Anderson.

Daly, K. (1989) Criminal justice ideologies and practices in different voices: some feminist questions about justice, *International Journal of the Sociology of Law*, 17: 1–18.

Daly, K. (1994) *Gender, Crime and Punishment*. New Haven, CT: Yale University Press.

Daly, K. (2002a) Restorative justice: the real story, *Punishment and Society*, 4(1): 55–79.

Daly, K. (2002b) Sexual assault and restorative justice, in H. Strang and J. Braithwaite (eds) *Restorative Justice and Family Violence*. Melbourne: Cambridge University Press.

Daly, K. and Immarigeon, R. (1998) The past, present and future of restorative justice: some critical reflections, *Contemporary Justice Review*, 1(1): 21–45.

de Haan, W. (1990) *The Politics of Redress: Crime, Punishment and Penal Abolition*. London: Unwin Hyman.

Derrida, J. (1990) Force of law: 'The mystical foundation of authority', *Cardozo Law Review*, 11: 919–1045.

Dignan, J. (1999) The Crime and Disorder Act and the prospects for restorative justice, *Criminal Law Review*, January: 48–60.

Dignan, J. (2002) Restorative justice: limiting principles, in A. von Hirsch, J. Roberts, A. Bottoms, K. Roach and M. Schiff (eds) *Restorative Justice and Criminal Justice: Competing or Reconcilable Paradigms*. Oxford: Hart Publishing.

DiIulio, J.J. (1994) Let 'em rot, *Wall Street Journal*, 26 January: A4.

DiIulio, J.J. (1999) Two million prisoners are enough, *Wall Street Journal*, 12 March: A4.

Dobash, R.P., Dobash, R.E. and Gutteridge, S. (1986) *The Imprisonment of Women*. London: Basil Blackwell.

Donzelot, J. (1980) *The Policing of Families*. London: Hutchinson.

Douglas, M. (1992) *Risk and Blame: Essays in Cultural Theory*. London: Routledge.

Downes, D. (1988) *Contrasts in Tolerance: Post-war Penal Policy in the Netherlands and England and Wales*. Oxford: Clarendon Press.

Duff, R.A. (1986) *Trials and Punishments*. Cambridge: Cambridge University Press.

Duff, R.A. (1996) Penal communications: recent work in the philosophy of punishment, in M. Tonry (ed.) *Crime and Justice: A Review of Research, Volume 20*. Chicago: Chicago University Press.

Duff, R.A. (1998) Dangerousness and citizenship, in A. Ashworth and M. Wasik (eds) *Fundamentals of Sentencing Theory*. Oxford: Clarendon Press

Durkheim, É. (1960) *The Division of Labour in Society*. Glencoe, IL: Free Press.

Durkheim, É. (1984) Two laws of penal evolution, in S. Lukes and A. Scull (eds) *Durkheim and the Law*. Oxford: Basil Blackwell.

Dworkin, R. (1977) *Taking Rights Seriously*. London: Duckworth.

Dworkin, R. (2002) The real threat to US values, *Guardian*, 9 March (Review): 3.

Eaton, M. (1986) *Justice for Women? Family, Court and Social Control*. Milton Keynes: Open University Press.

Edwards, S. (1984) *Women on Trial*. Manchester: Manchester University Press.

Elias, N. (1978) *The Civilizing Process, Vol. 1: The History of Manners*. Oxford: Oxford University Press. (Originally published in 1939.)

Elias, N. (1982) *The Civilizing Process, Vol. 2: State Formation and Civilization*. Oxford: Oxford University Press. (Originally published in 1939.)

Ewald, F. (1991) Insurance and risk, in G. Burchell, C. Gordon and P. Miller (eds) *The Foucault Effect: Studies in Governmentality*. Chicago: University of Chicago Press.

Farrell, S., Bannister, J. and Ditton, J. (1997) Questioning the measurement of the 'fear of crime': findings from a major methodological study, *British Journal of Criminology*, 37(4): 658–79.

Farrington, D. and Morris, A. (1983) Sex, sentencing and reconviction, *British Journal of Criminology*, 23(3): 229–48.

Feeley, M.M. and Simon, J. (1992) 'The new penology': notes on the emerging strategy of corrections and its implications, *Criminology*, 30: 449–74.

Feinberg, J. (1970) The expressive function of punishment, in J. Feinberg, *Doing and Deserving*. Princeton, NJ: Princeton University Press.

Ferri, E. (1917) *Criminal Sociology*. Boston: Little, Brown.

Finnis, J. (1972) The restoration of retribution, *Analysis*, 32: 31.

Finnis, J. (1980) *Natural Law and Natural Rights*. Oxford: Oxford University Press.

Finstad, L. (1990) Sexual offenders out of prison: principles for a realistic utopia, *International Journal of the Sociology of Law*, 18: 157–77.

Fitzpatrick, P. (1992) *The Mythology of Modern Law*. London: Routledge.

Fitzpatrick, P. and Hunt, A. (eds) (1987) *Critical Legal Studies*. Oxford: Basil Blackwell.

Flew, A. (1954) The justification of punishment, *Philosophy*, 29: 291–307.

Floud, J. and Young, W. (1981) *Dangerousness and Criminal Justice*. London: Heinemann.

Fogel, D. (1975) *We Are the Living Proof: The Justice Model of Corrections*. Cincinnati, OH: Anderson.

Foucault, M. (1973) *The Birth of the Clinic*, trans. A. Sheridan. London: Tavistock.

Foucault, M. (1977) *Discipline and Punish: The Birth of the Prison*. London: Allen Lane.

Foucault, M. (1978) *The History of Sexuality, Vol. I: An Introduction*, trans. R. Hurley. New York: Random House.

Foucault, M. (1986) *The History of Sexuality, Vol. II: The Use of Pleasure*, trans. R. Hurley. New York: Random House.

Foucault, M. (1991) Governmentality, in G. Burchell, C. Gordon and P. Miller (eds) *The Foucault Effect: Studies in Governmentality*. Chicago: University of Chicago Press.

Frankel, M.E. (1973) *Criminal Sentences*. New York: Hill and Wang.

Fraser, E. and Lacey, N. (1993) *The Politics of Community: A Feminist Critique of the Liberal-Communitarian Debate*. Hemel Hempstead: Harvester-Wheatsheaf.

Friedan, B. (1963) *The Feminine Mystique*. New York: Dell.

Gallo, E. and Ruggiero, V. (1991) The 'immaterial' prison: custody as a factory for the manufacture of handicaps, *International Journal of the Sociology of Law*, 19: 273–91.

Gamble, A. (1988) *The Free Economy and the Strong State: The Politics of Thatcherism*. Basingstoke: Macmillan. (Second edition 1994.)

Garfinkel, H. (1956) Conditions of successful degradation ceremonies, *American Journal of Sociology*, 61: 420–4.

Garland, D. (1983) Durkheim's theory of punishment: a critique, in D. Garland and P. Young (eds) *The Power to Punish: Contemporary Penality and Social Analysis*. London: Heinemann.

Garland, D. (1985) *Punishment and Welfare*. Aldershot: Gower.

Garland, D. (1986) The punitive mentality: its socio-historic development and decline, *Contemporary Crises*, 10: 305–20.

Garland, D. (1990a) *Punishment and Modern Society*. Oxford: Oxford University Press.

Garland, D. (1990b) Frameworks of inquiry in the sociology of punishment, *British Journal of Sociology*, 41(1): 1–15.

Garland, D. (1996) The limits of the sovereign state: strategies of crime control in contemporary society, *British Journal of Criminology*, 36(4): 445–71.

Garland, D. (1997) 'Governmentality' and the problem of crime: Foucault, criminology, sociology, *Theoretical Criminology*, 1(2): 173–214.

Garland, D. (2000) The culture of high crime societies: some preconditions of recent 'law and order' policies, *British Journal of Criminology*, 40(3): 347–75.

Garland, D. (2001a) *The Culture of Control: Crime and Social Order in Contemporary Society*. Oxford: Oxford University Press.

Garland, D. (ed.) (2001b) *Mass Imprisonment: Social Causes and Consequences*. London: Sage.

Garland, D. and Sparks, R. (2000) Criminology, social theory and the challenge of our times, *British Journal of Criminology*, 40(2): 189–204.

Garland, D. and Young, P. (1983) Towards a social analysis of penality, in D. Garland and P. Young (eds) *The Power to Punish: Contemporary Penality and Social Analysis*. London: Heinemann.

Geertz, C. (1978) Stir crazy, *New York Review of Books*, January: 6.

Giddens, A. (1990) *The Consequences of Modernity*. Cambridge: Polity Press.

Giddens, A. (1999) Risk and responsibility, *Modern Law Review*, 62(1): 1–10.

Giller, H. and Morris, A.M. (1981) *Care and Discretion*. London: André Deutsch.

Gilligan, C. (1982) *In a Different Voice*. Cambridge, MA: Harvard University Press.

Gilroy, P. (1987) The myth of black criminality, in P. Scraton (ed.) *Law, Order and the Authoritarian State*. Milton Keynes: Open University Press.

Goffman, E. (1959) The moral career of a mental patient, *Psychiatry*, 22: 2.

Goffman, E. (1961) *Asylums*. Garden City, NY: Doubleday.

Goffman, E. (1963) *Stigma*. Englewood Cliffs, NJ: Prentice Hall.

Gordon, C. (ed.) (1980) *Michel Foucault: Power/Knowledge. Selected Interviews and Other Writings, 1972–77*. New York: Pantheon Books.

Gordon, C. (1991) Governmental rationality: an introduction, in G. Burchell, C.

Gordon and P. Miller (eds) *The Foucault Effect: Studies in Governmentality*. Chicago: Chicago University Press.

Gramsci, A. (1971) *Selections from the Prison Notebooks of Antonio Gramsci*, ed. Q. Hoare and G. Nowell-Smith. London: Lawrence and Wishart.

Gray, N., Laing, J. and Noaks, L. (eds) (2002) *Criminal Justice, Mental Health and the Politics of Risk*. London: Cavendish.

Greenberg, D. (1977) The dynamics of oscillatory punishment processes, *Journal of Criminal Law and Criminology*, 68(4): 643–51.

Greenberg, D. and Humphries, D. (1980) The co-optation of fixed sentencing reform, *Crime and Delinquency*, 26: 206–25.

Greenwood, P. (1983) Controlling the crime rate through imprisonment, in J.Q. Wilson (ed.) *Crime and Public Policy*. San Francisco: Institute for Contemporary Studies.

Habermas, J. (1987) *The Philosophical Discourse of Modernity*, trans. Frederick Lawrence. Cambridge: Polity Press.

Hacking, I. (1986) Making up people, in T.C. Heller, M. Sosna and D.E. Wellerby (eds) *Reconstructing Individualism: Autonomy, Individualism and the Self in Western Thought*. Stanford, CA: Stanford University Press.

Hall, S. (1980) *The Drift to a Law and Order Society*. London: Cobden Trust.

Hall, S. (1988) *The Hard Road to Renewal*. London: Verso/Marxism Today.

Hall, S., Clarke, J., Crichter, C., Jefferson, T. and Roberts, B. (1978) *Policing the Crisis*. London: Macmillan.

Hann, R.G., Harman, W.G. and Pease, K. (1991) Does parole reduce the risk of reconviction? *Howard Journal of Criminal Justice*, 30(1): 66–75.

Hannah-Moffat, K. (2000) Prisons that empower: neo-liberal governance in Canadian women's prisons, *British Journal of Criminology*, 40(3): 510–31.

Hart, H.L.A. (1968) *Freedom and Responsibility: Essays in the Philosophy of Law*. Oxford: Clarendon Press.

Hawkins, D.F. (1986) Trends in black–white imprisonment: changing conceptions of race or changing patterns of social control, *Crime and Social Justice*, 24: 187–209.

Hay, D. (1975) Property, authority and the criminal law, in D. Hay, P. Linebaugh, J.G. Rule, E.P. Thompson and C. Wilmslow (eds) *Albion's Fatal Tree*. Harmondsworth: Penguin.

Headley, B.D. (1989) Introduction: Crime, justice and racially powerless groups, *Social Justice*, 16(4): 1–9.

Heidensohn, F. (1986) Models of justice: Portia or Persephone? Some thoughts on equality, fairness and gender in the field of criminal justice, *International Journal of the Sociology of Law*, 14: 287–98.

Hobbes, T. (1962) *Leviathan*, ed. J. Plamenatz. London: Fontana. (First published in 1651.)

Holdaway, S., Davidson, N., Dignan, J. *et al*. (2001) *New Strategies to Address Youth Offending: The National Evaluation of the Pilot Youth Offending Teams*. London: Home Office.

Home Office (1996) *Protecting the Public: The Government's Strategy on Crime in England and Wales*. London, HMSO.

Honderich, T. (1984) *Punishment: The Supposed Justifications*, rev. edn. Harmondsworth: Penguin.

Hood, R. (1992) *Race and Sentencing: A Study in the Crown Court*. Oxford: Clarendon Press.

Howe, A. (1994) *Punish and Critique: Towards a Feminist Analysis of Penality*. London: Routledge.

Hudson, A. (1989) Troublesome girls, in M. Cain (ed.) *Growing up Good*. London: Sage.

Hudson, B.A. (1984a) The rising use of imprisonment: the impact of 'decarceration' policies, *Critical Social Policy*, 11: 46–59.

Hudson, B.A. (1984b) Femininity and adolescence, in A. McRobbie and M. Nava (eds) *Gender and Generation*. London: Macmillan.

Hudson, B.A. (1987) *Justice through Punishment: A Critique of the 'Justice Model' of Corrections*. Basingstoke: Macmillan.

Hudson, B.A. (1989) Discrimination and disparity: the influence of race on sentencing, *New Community*, 16(1): 23–34.

Hudson, B.A. (1993) *Penal Policy and Social Justice*. Basingstoke: Macmillan.

Hudson, B.A. (1995a) Beyond proportionate punishment: difficult cases and the 1991 Criminal Justice Act, *Crime, Law and Social Change*, 22: 59–78.

Hudson, B.A. (1995b) Restoration, reintegration and human rights: punishment in a socially just justice system. Paper given at Howard League seminar, 'Punishment in the Year 2000', Edinburgh, February.

Hudson, B.A. (1998) Punishment and governance, *Social and Legal Studies*, 7(4): 553–60.

Hudson, B.A. (2002a) Restorative justice and gendered violence: diversion or effective justice, *British Journal of Criminology*, 42(3): 616–34.

Hudson, B.A. (2002b) Victims and offenders, in A. Von Hirsch, J. Roberts, A. Bottoms, K. Roach and M. Schiff (eds) *Restorative Justice and Criminal Justice: Competing or Reconcilable Paradigms*. Oxford: Hart Publishing.

Hudson, B.A. (2002c) Gender issues in penal policy and penal theory, in P. Carlen (ed.) *Women and Punishment*. Cullompton: Willan Publishing.

Hudson, B.A. (2002d) Punishment and control, in M. Maguire, R. Morgan and R. Reiner (eds) *The Oxford Handbook of Criminology*, 3rd edn. Oxford: Clarendon Press.

Hudson, B.A. (forthcoming) *Justice in the Risk Society*. London: Sage.

Hughes, G. (1998) *Understanding Crime Prevention*. Buckingham: Open University Press

Hulsman, L. and Bernat de Celis, J. (1992) *Peines perdues: Le système penal en question*. Paris: Le Centurion.

Hunt, A. (1987) The critique of law: what is 'critical' about critical legal theory? in P. Fitzpatrick and A. Hunt (eds) *Critical Legal Studies*. Oxford: Basil Blackwell.

Hunt, A. (1992) Foucault's expulsion of law: toward a retrieval, *Law and Social Inquiry*, 17: 1–38.

Hunt, A. (1993) *Explorations in Law and Society: Toward a Constitutive Theory of Law*. London and New York: Routledge.

Hutter, B. and Williams, G. (eds) (1981) *Controlling Women: The Normal and the Deviant*. London: Croom Helm.

Ignatieff, M. (1978) *A Just Measure of Pain*. London: Macmillan

Ignatieff, M. (1983) State, civil society and total institutions: a critique of recent social histories of punishment, in S. Cohen and A. Scull (eds) *Social Control and the State*. Oxford: Martin Robertson.

Jankovic, I. (1977) Labour market and imprisonment, *Crime and Social Justice*, 8: 17–31.

Jefferson, T. and Shapland, J. (1994) Criminal justice and the production of order and control, *British Journal of Criminology*, 34(3): 265–90.

Kant, I. (1887) *The Philosophy of Law*, trans. W. Hastie. Edinburgh: T.T. Clark.

Kerruish, V. (1991) *Jurisprudence as Ideology*. London: Routledge.

Kittrie, N.N. (1973) *The Right to Be Different*. New York: Penguin.

Kurki, L. (2000) Restorative and community justice in the United States, in M. Tonry (ed.) *Crime and Justice: A Review of Research, Volume 26*. Chicago: University of Chicago Press.

Lacey, N. (1988) *State Punishment*. London: Routledge.

Laffargue, B. and Godefroy, T. (1989) Economic cycles and punishment: unemployment and imprisonment, *Contemporary Crises*, 13: 371–404.

Lea, J. and Young, J. (1984) *What Is to Be Done about Law and Order?* Harmondsworth: Penguin.

Lemert, E.M. (1967) *Human Deviance, Social Problems and Social Control*. Englewood Cliffs, NJ: Prentice Hall.

Levinas, E. (1981) *Otherwise Than Being or Beyond Essence*, trans. A. Lingis. The Hague: Martinus Nijhoff.

Lewis, C.S. (1971) The humanitarian theory of punishment, in L. Radzinowicz and M. Wolfgang (eds) *Crime and Punishment*, Vol. 2. New York: Basic Books.

Lewis, R., Dobash, R.E., Dobash, R.P. and Cavanagh, K. (2001) Law's progressive potential: the value of engagement with the law for domestic violence, *Social and Legal Studies*, 10(1): 105–30.

Locke, J. (1924) *Two Treatises of Civil Government*, trans. W. S. Carpenter. London: Dent Everyman. (Originally published in 1690.)

Lukes, S. and Scull, A. (1984) Introduction, in S. Lukes and A. Scull (eds) *Durkheim and the Law*. Oxford: Basil Blackwell.

Lyon, D. (1994) *The Electronic Eye: The Rise of the Surveillance Society*. Cambridge: Polity Press.

MacKinnon, C.A. (1989) *Toward a Feminist Theory of the State*. Cambridge, MA: Harvard University Press.

Maffesoli, M. (1996) *The Time of the Tribes*. London: Sage.

Martinson, R. (1974) What works? – Questions and answers about prison reform, *The Public Interest*, 35(Spring): 22.

Marx, G. (1995) The engineering of social control: the search for the silver bullet, in J. Hagan and R. Peterson (eds) *Crime and Inequality*. Stanford, CA: Stanford University Press.

Mathiesen, T. (1974) *The Politics of Abolition*. Oxford: Martin Robertson.

Mathiesen, T. (1990) *Prison on Trial: A Critical Assessment*. London: Sage.

Matthews, R. (1989) Alternatives to and in prisons: a realist approach, in P. Carlen and D. Cook (eds) *Paying for Crime*. Milton Keynes: Open University Press.

Matza, D. (1964) *Delinquency and Drift*. New York: John Wiley.

Mauer, M. (2001) The causes and consequences of prison growth in the USA, *Punishment and Society*, 3(1): 9–20.

Maxwell, G. and Morris, A. (2001) Putting restorative justice into practice for adult offenders, *Howard Journal*, 40(1): 55–69.

McEvoy, K. and Mika, H. (2002) Restorative justice and the critique of informalism in Northern Ireland, *British Journal of Criminology*, 42(3): 534–62.

Mead, G.H. (1918) The psychology of punitive justice, *American Journal of Sociology*, 23: 577–602.

Melossi, D. (1979) Institutions of social control and capitalist organisation of work, in B. Fine, R. Kinsey, J. Lea, S. Picciott and J. Young (eds) *Capitalism and the Rule of Law*. London: Hutchinson.

Melossi, D. (1985) Punishment and social action: changing vocabularies of motive within a political business cycle, *Current Perspectives in Social Theory*, 6: 169–97.

Melossi, D. (1989) An introduction: Fifty years later, *Punishment and Social Structure* in comparative analysis, *Contemporary Crises*, 13: 311–26.

Melossi, D. and Pavarini, M. (1981) *The Prison and the Factory: Origins of the Penitentiary System*. Basingstoke: Macmillan.

Merleau-Ponty, M. (1962) *Phenomenology of Perception*, trans. Colin Smith. London: Routledge & Kegan Paul.

Miller, A.P. (1994) Moving towards humane death technology. Paper given to American Society of Criminology, 46th Annual Meeting, Miami, November.

Miller, P. and Rose, N. (1990) Governing economic life, *Economy and Society*, 19: 1–27.

Minnesota Sentencing Guidelines Commission (1980) *Minnesota Sentencing Guidelines*. St Paul, MN: Minnesota Sentencing Guidelines Commission.

Minow, M. (1990) *Making All the Difference*. Ithaca, NY: Cornell University Press.

Mitchell, J. (1966) Women: the longest revolution, *New Left Review*, December: 11–37.

Mitford, J. (1974) *The American Prison Business*. London: Allen & Unwin.

Morris, A. (2002) Critiquing the critics: a brief response to critics of restorative justice, *British Journal of Criminology*, 42(3): 596–615.

Morris, A. and Gelsthorpe, L. (2000) Re-visioning men's violence against female partners, *Howard Journal*, 39(4): 412–28.

Morris, N. (1982) *Madness and the Criminal Law*. Chicago: University of Chicago Press.

Morris, N. (1992) Desert as a limiting principle, in A. von Hirsch and A. Ashworth (eds) *Principled Sentencing*. Edinburgh: Edinburgh University Press.

Muncie, J. (2000) Pragmatic realism: searching for criminology in the new youth justice, in B. Goldson (ed.) *The New Youth Justice*. Lyme Regis: Russell House Publishing.

Murphy, J.G. (1973) Marxism and retribution, *Philosophy and Public Affairs*, 2: 217–42.

Murphy, J.G. (1979) *Retribution, Justice and Therapy*. Dordecht: Reidel.

Nozick, R. (1974) *Anarchy, State and Utopia*. Oxford: Basil Blackwell.

Nozick, R. (1981) *Philosophical Explanations*. Oxford: Clarendon Press.

O'Malley, P. (1992) Risk, power and crime prevention, *Economy and Society*, 21: 252–75.

O'Malley, P. (1996) Post-social criminologies: some implications of current political trends for criminological theory and practice, *Current Issues in Criminal Justice*, 8: 26–38.

O'Malley, P. (1999) Volatile and contradictory punishments, *Theoretical Criminology*, 1(3): 175–96.

O'Malley, P. (2001) Risk, crime and prudentialism revisited, in K. Stenson and R.R. Sullivan (eds) *Crime, Risk and Justice*. Cullompton: Willan Publishing.

Pashukanis, P. (1978) *Law and Marxism: A General Theory*. London: Ink Links.

Pasquino, E.B. (1991) Criminology: the birth of a special knowledge, in G. Burchell, C. Gordon and P. Miller (eds) *The Foucault Effect: Studies in Governmentality*. Chicago: University of Chicago Press.

Paternoster, R. and Bynum, T. (1982) The justice model as ideology: a critical look at the impetus for sentencing reform, *Contemporary Crises*, 6: 7–24.

Pearson, G. (1977) *The Deviant Imagination*. London: Macmillan.

Philips, D. (1983) A just measure of crime, authority and blue locusts: the 'revisionist' social history of crime and the law in Britain, 1780–1850, in S. Cohen and A. Scull (eds) *Social Control and the State*. Oxford: Martin Robertson.

Piaget, J. (1971) *Structuralism*, trans. C. Maschler. London: Routledge & Kegan Paul.

Pitts, J. (1988) *The Politics of Juvenile Crime*. London: Sage.

Pitts, J. (1992) The end of an era, *Howard Journal of Criminal Justice*, 31(2): 133–49.

Platt, T. (1977) *The Child Savers: The Invention of Delinquency*. Chicago: University of Chicago Press.

Posner, R. (1985) An economic theory of criminal law, *Columbia Law Review*, 85: 1193–1231.

Poster, M. (1990) *The Mode of Information*. Cambridge: Polity Press.

Pratt, J. (1998) Towards the 'decivilizing' of punishment, *Social and Legal Studies*, 7(4): 487–516.

Pratt, J. (2000) The return of Wheelbarrow Man: or, The arrival of postmodern penality, *British Journal of Criminology*, 40(1): 127–45.

Raeder, M. (1993) Gender and sentencing: single moms, battered women and other sex-based anomalies in the gender-free world of federal sentencing guidelines, *Pepperdine Law Review*, 20(3): 905–90.

Rawls, J. (1972) *A Theory of Justice*. Oxford: Oxford University Press.

Raynor, P. (1988) *Probation as an Alternative to Custody: A Case Study*. Aldershot: Gower.

Reiman, J.H. (1979) *The Rich Get Richer and the Poor Get Prison*. New York: John Wiley.

Reiner, R. (1993) Race, crime and justice: models of interpretation, in L. Gelsthorpe and W. McWilliams (eds) *Minority Ethnic Groups in the Criminal Justice System: Proceedings of a Cropwood Conference*. Cambridge: Cambridge University Press.

Robinson, P. (1988) Hybrid principles for the distribution of criminal sanctions, *Northwestern Law Review*, 82(1): 19–42.

Rock, P. (1973) *Deviant Behaviour*. London: Hutchinson.

Rose, N. (1996a) Governing 'advanced' liberal democracies, in A. Barry, T. Osborne and N. Rose (eds) *Foucault and Political Reason*. London: UCL Press.

Rose, N. (1996b) The death of the social? Refiguring the territory of government, *Economy and Society*, 25(3): 327–56.

Rose, N. (2000) Government and control, *British Journal of Criminology*, 40(2): 321–39.

Rotman, E. (1990) *Beyond Punishment: A New View of the Rehabilitation of Criminal Offenders*. Westport, CT: Greenwood Press.

Rousseau, J.-J. (1973) *The Social Contract*, trans. G.D.H. Cole. London: Dent. (Originally published in 1762.)

Rubington, E. and Weinberg, M. (eds) (1968) *Deviance: An Interactionist Perspective*. New York: Collier Macmillan.

Rusche, G. (1978) Labour market and penal sanction: thoughts on the sociology of punishment, *Crime and Social Justice*, 10: 2–8.

Rusche, G. and Kirchheimer, O. (1968) *Punishment and Social Structure*. New York: Russell and Russell.

Rutherford, A. (1993) *Criminal Justice and the Pursuit of Decency*. Oxford: Oxford University Press.

Rutherford, A. (1994) Abolition and the politics of bad conscience: a response to Sim, in A. Duff, S. Marshall, R.E. Dobash and R.P. Dobash (eds) *Penal Theory and Practice: Tradition and Innovation in Criminal Justice*. Manchester: Manchester University Press.

Sabol, W.J. (1989) Racially disproportionate prison populations in the United States: an overview of historical patterns and review of contemporary issues, *Contemporary Crises*, 13: 405–32.

Sartre, J.-P. (1958) *Being and Nothingness*, trans. H.E. Barnes. London: Methuen.

Sartre, J.-P. (1974) *Between Existentialism and Marxism*, trans. John Matthews. London: New Left Books.

Schutz, A. and Luckman, T. (1974) *The Structures of the Life World*, trans. R.M. Zaner and H.T. Engelhardt Jr. London: Heinemann.

Scraton, P. (ed.) (1987) *Law, Order and the Authoritarian State*. Milton Keynes: Open University Press.

Scull, A. (1977) *Decarceration: Community Treatment and the Deviant – A Radical View*. Englewood Cliffs, NJ: Prentice Hall. (Revised edition 1984.)

Shelden, R.G. (1982) *Criminal Justice in America: A Sociological Approach*. Boston: Little, Brown.

Sheleff, L.S. (1975) From restitutive law to repressive law: Durkheim's *The Division of Labour in Society* revisited, *European Journal of Sociology*, 16: 16–45.

Sim, J. (1990) *Medical Power in Prisons: The Prison Medical Service in England 1774–1989*. Buckingham: Open University Press.

Sim, J. (1994) The abolitionist approach: a British perspective, in A. Duff, S. Marshall, R.E. Dobash and R.P. Dobash (eds) *Penal Theory and Practice: Tradition and Innovation in Criminal Justice*. Manchester: Manchester University Press.

Simon, J. (1988) The ideological effects of actuarial practices, *Law and Society Review*, 22(4): 772–800.

Simon, J. (2001) Fear and loathing in late modernity, *Punishment and Society*, 3(1): 21–34.

Skelton, A. (2002) Restorative justice as a framework for juvenile justice reform: a South African perspective, *British Journal of Criminology*, 42(3).

Smart, C. (1976) *Women, Crime and Criminology*. London: Routledge.

Smart, C. (1989) *Feminism and the Power of Law*. London: Routledge.

Snider, L. (1998) Towards safer societies: punishment, masculinities and violence against women, *British Journal of Criminology*, 38(1): 1–39.

Sparks, R. (1994) Can prisons be legitimate? *British Journal of Criminology*, 34: 14–28.

Sparks, R. (1997) Recent social theory and the study of crime and punishment, in M. Maguire, R. Morgan and R. Reiner (eds) *The Oxford Handbook of Criminology* (2nd edn). Oxford: Clarendon Press.

Spierenburg, P. (1984) *The Spectacle of Suffering*. Cambridge: Cambridge University Press.

Spitzer, S. (1975) Punishment and social organization: a study of Durkheim's theory of social evolution, *Law and Society Review*, 9: 613–37.

Spitzer, S. (1979) Notes toward a theory of punishment and social change, *Law and Sociology*, 2: 207–29.

Spitzer, S. (1983) The rationalization of crime control in capitalist societies, in S. Cohen and A. Scull (eds) *Social Control and the State*. Oxford: Martin Robertson.

Steinhert, H. (1986) Beyond crime and punishment, *Contemporary Crises*, 10: 21–38.

Stenson, K. (1996) Communal security as government – the British Experience, in W. Hammerschick, I. Karazman-Morawetz and W. Stangl (eds) *Die sichere Stadt: Jahrbuch for Rechts- und Kriminalsoziologie '95*. Baden-Baden: Nomos.

Stenson, K. (1999) Crime control, governmentality and sovereignty, in R. Smandych (ed.) *Governable Places: Readings in Governmentality and Crime Control*. Aldershot: Dartmouth.

Stenson, K. and Sullivan, R.R. (eds) (2001) *Crime, Risk and Justice*. Cullompton: Willan Publishing.

Sullivan, R.R. (2001) The schizophrenic state: neo-liberal criminal justice, in K. Stenson and R.R. Sullivan (eds) *Crime, Risk and Justice*. Cullompton: Willan Publishing.

Sutherland, E.H. (1939) *Principles of Criminology*. Philadelphia, PA: Lippincott.

Taylor, I., Walton, P. and Young, J. (1973) *The New Criminology*. London: Routledge & Kegan Paul.

Ten, C.L. (1987) *Crime, Guilt and Punishment*. Oxford: Clarendon Press.

Thomas, D. (1979) *Principles of Sentencing*, 2nd edn. London: Heinemann.

Thorpe, D., Smith, D., Green, C.J. and Paley, J.H. (1980) *Out of Care: The Community Support of Juvenile Offenders*. London: Allen & Unwin.

Tonry, M. (1993) Sentencing commissions and their guidelines, in M. Tonry (ed.) *Crime and Justice: A Review of Research, Volume 17*. Chicago: University of Chicago Press.

Tonry, M. (1995) *Malign Neglect – Race, Crime and Punishment in America*. New York: Oxford University Press.

United Nations (2000) *Restorative Justice Handbook*, A/CONF.187/NGO/7. Vienna: United Nations Centre for Crime Prevention and Crime Control.

van Ness, D. (1993) New wine and old wineskins: four challenges of restorative justice, *Criminal Law Forum*, 4: 251–76.

van Ness, D. (2002) Proposed UN basic principles on the use of restorative justice: recognizing the aims and limits of restorative justice, in A. von Hirsch, J. Roberts, A. Bottoms, K. Roach and M. Schiff (eds) *Restorative Justice and Criminal Justice: Competing or Reconcilable Paradigms*. Oxford: Hart Publishing.

van den Haag, E. (1975) *Punishing Criminals: Concerning a Very Old and Painful Question*. New York: Basic Books.

von Hirsch, A. (1976) *Doing Justice: The Choice of Punishments*. New York: Hill and Wang.

von Hirsch, A. (1985) *Past or Future Crimes: Deservedness and Dangerousness in the Sentencing of Criminals*. Manchester: Manchester University Press.

von Hirsch, A. (1990) The politics of just deserts, *Canadian Journal of Criminology*, 32: 397–413.

von Hirsch, A. (1993) *Censure and Sanctions*. Oxford: Clarendon Press.

von Hirsch, A. and Ashworth, A. (eds) (1992) *Principled Sentencing*. Edinburgh: Edinburgh University Press.

von Hirsch, A. and Ashworth, A. (1993) 'Dominion' and censure, in A. von Hirsch, *Censure and Sanctions*. Oxford: Clarendon Press.

von Hirsch, A. and Jareborg, N. (1992) Gauging harm to others: a living standard analysis, in A. von Hirsch and A. Ashworth (eds) *Principled Sentencing*. Edinburgh: Edinburgh University Press.

von Hirsch, A. and Maher, L. (1992) Should penal rehabilitation be revived? in A. von Hirsch and A. Ashworth (eds) *Principled Sentencing*. Edinburgh: Edinburgh University Press.

von Hirsch, A., Roberts, J., Bottoms, A., Roach, K. and Schiff, M. (eds) (2002) *Restorative Justice and Criminal Justice: Competing or Reconcilable Paradigms?* Oxford: Hart Publishing.

Wacquant, L. (2001) Deadly symbiosis: when ghetto and prison meet and merge, *Punishment and Society*, 3(1): 95–134.

Walgrave, L. (1999) Community service as a cornerstone of a systematic restorative response to (juvenile) crime, in G. Bazemore and L. Walgrave (eds) *Restorative Justice: Repairing the Harm of Juvenile Crime*. Monsey, NY: Criminal Justice Press.

Walgrave, L. and Aertsen, I. (1996) Reintegrative shaming and restorative justice: Interchangeable, complementary or different? *European Journal of Criminal Policy and Research*, 4: 67–85.

Walker, N. (1985) *Sentencing: Theory, Law and Practice*. London: Butterworths.

Walker, N. (1991) *Why Punish?* Oxford: Oxford University Press.

Walker, N. and Marsh, C. (1988) Does the severity of sentences affect public disapproval? An experiment in England, in N. Walker and M. Hough (eds) *Public Attitudes to Sentencing: Surveys from Five Countries*. Aldershot: Gower.

Walzer, M. (1983) *Spheres of Justice: A Defense of Pluralism and Equality*. New York: Basic Books.

Walzer, M. (1986) The politics of Michel Foucault, in D. Couzens Hoy (ed.) *Foucault: A Critical Reader*. Oxford: Basil Blackwell.

Wasik, M. and Taylor, R.D. (1991) *Guide to the Criminal Justice Act 1991*. London: Blackstone Press.

Wasserstrom, R. (1980) *Philosophy and Social Issues: Five Studies*. Notre Dame, IN: Notre Dame University Press.

Weber, M. (1930) *The Protestant Ethic and the Spirit of Capitalism*. London: Allen & Unwin.

Weber, M. (1978) *Economy and Society*, G. Roth and C. Wittick (eds). Berkeley: University of California Press.

West, D.J. and Farrington, D. (1973) *Who Becomes Delinquent?* London: Heinemann.

Wicharaya, T. (1985) *Simple Theory, Hard Reality: The Impact of Sentencing Reforms on Courts, Prisons and Crime*. New York: State University of New York Press.

Williams, B. (1993) Bail bandits: the construction of a moral panic, *Critical Social Policy*, 37: 104–12.

Wilson, J.Q. (1975/1983) *Thinking about Crime*. New York: Basic Books.

Wootton, B. (1963) *Crime and the Criminal Law*. London: Stevens.

Worrall, A. (1990) *Offending Women: Female Lawbreakers and the Criminal Justice System*. London: Routledge.

Young, I.M. (1990) *Justice and the Politics of Difference*. Princeton, NJ: Princeton University Press.

Young, J. (1986) The failure of criminology: the need for a radical realism, in R. Matthews and J. Young (eds) *Confronting Crime*. London: Sage.

Young, J. (1988) Radical criminology in Britain: the emergence of a competing paradigm, *British Journal of Criminology*, 28(2): 289–313.

Young, J. and Matthews, R. (1992) Questioning left realism, in R. Matthews and J. Young (eds) *Issues in Realist Criminology*. London: Sage.

Young, R. (2001) Just cops doing 'shameful' business, in A. Morris and G. Maxwell (eds) *Restorative Justice for Juveniles: Conferencing, Mediation and Circles*. Oxford: Hart Publishing.

Zedner, L. (1991) *Women, Crime and Custody in Victorian England*. Oxford: Oxford University Press.

Zedner, L. (1994) Reparation and retribution: are they reconcilable? *Modern Law Review*, 57: 228.

Zehr, H. (1990) *Changing Lenses: A New Focus for Crime and Justice*. Scottdale, PA: Herald Press.

Zimring, F.E. (1976) Punishing homicide in Philadelphia: perspectives on the death penalty, *University of Chicago Law Review*, 43(2): 227–52.

Zimring, F. (2001) Imprisonment rates and the new politics of criminal punishment, *Punishment and Society*, 3(1): 161–6.

Zimring, F. and Hawkins, G. (1995) *Incapacitation: Penal Confinement and the Restraint of Crime*. New York: Oxford University Press.

Index

abolition, of capital punishment, 111, 117, 153
abolitionism, 12–13, 75–6, 83, 178–80, 185, 186
actuarial practices in criminal justice, 9, 87, 161–4, 165, 191
administrative criminology, 10–11, 176
Aertsen, I., 82
Agnew, Spiro, 60
Allen, H., 129, 151
Althusser, L., 113, 123–4, 130
American Friends Service Committee, 39, 40, 69
Ancel, M., 36, 101, 145
Andenaes, J., 21
Ashworth, A., 19, 24, 25, 43, 46, 57, 58, 88, 89, 91, 107, 176, 188
Attica, prison riots, 39
Austin, J., 40, 42, 179
authority, forms of, 2, 9, 96, 105–6, 107, 132
Ayres, I., 87

Bachelard, G., 134, 144
Baker, N., 121
Barlow, D.E., 121
Bartlett, K.T., 180, 183
Bean, P., 27
Beccaria, C., 19–20, 28, 66, 119, 141
Beck, U., 3, 163, 166, 187–8, 192
Becker, H., 140
Benn, S.I., 1
Bentham, J., 18–20, 25, 40, 66, 101, 136, 141, 150
Bernat de Celis, J., 13, 180
Beyleveld, D., 23

bio-power, 135
Blagg, H., 22, 30, 32
Blumstein, A., 177
Bottomley, A.K., 22
Bottoms, A., 35, 68, 69, 145, 165, 176
Box, S., 11, 66, 118, 121, 122, 124, 125, 126
Braithwaite, J., 3, 20, 57, 60–1, 70–2, 76, 77, 81–2, 86, 87, 88, 89, 90, 91, 92, 109–10, 184, 185
Brody, S.R., 30
Brownsword, R., 35, 68, 69
Burchell, G., 141, 157
Burgess, A., 31
Burnside, J., 81
Bynum, T., 49

Cadora, E., 80, 161
California Determinate Sentencing Laws, 44, 154, 182
Canberra model, of restorative justice, 79, 82
capital punishment, abolition of, 63, 111, 117, 153
   see also death penalty
carceral archipelago, 141, 149–50, 180
cardinal proportionality, 45
Carlen, P., 11, 12, 52, 65, 67, 69, 109, 129, 146, 151, 152, 163, 177, 179, 181, 182
Castel, R., 162, 163
Cavadino, M., 3, 6, 8, 18, 67, 68, 72, 90, 103, 105, 125, 166, 176
censure, as purpose of punishment, 47, 54, 84, 88, 101

Children and Young Persons Act,
      1969, 42
Chiricos, J.G., 125
Christie, N., 12, 76, 77, 180
Cicourel, A.V., 108
Clarke, R., 176
classical criminology, 11, 19, 141, 175,
      176
Clear, T., 80, 161
Cobb, S., 85
Cohen, S., 10, 31, 36, 40, 66, 133,
      145, 150, 151, 152, 157, 161,
      168, 179
communitarianism, 73
community justice, 80
community punishments, 11, 34, 42–3,
      58, 86, 154, 158, 163, 168, 171
      see also non-custodial penalties
community safety, 157, 167, 169
conflict
      between penal purposes, 4, 57–8, 73
      of interest groups, 103, 104
conscience collective, 98–9
consequentialism, 3, 5, 52, 56, 66, 73,
      77, 89
Contemporary Justice Review, 77
Cook, D., 177
Cornell, D., 191
Cornish, D., 176
Cotterrell, R., 105, 106
Court of Appeal, 43, 44
Couzens Hoy, D., 149
Crawford, A., 80, 157
Crime and Disorder Act, 1998, 80
crime prevention, 158–9, 160, 161,
      167, 168
Criminal Justice Act
      1982, 42, 154, 176
      1991, 23, 42, 43, 45, 54, 58, 67,
            154, 163, 176, 177
      1993, 55, 61
      and Public Order Act, 1994, 61–2
critical legal studies, 9, 13, 81, 127
critical penology, 9–11
Cullen, F., 30, 62–4, 67, 73
culture and collective sentiments,
      punishment as expression of, 97,
            111, 157, 165, 170, 171

Daly, K., 75, 77, 84, 85, 86, 87, 90,

91, 177, 180, 181
Damiens, the regicide, 134
dangerous offenders, 3, 4, 12, 55, 69,
      88, 160, 163, 164, 168
Darwin, C., 103
death penalty, 12, 19, 23, 27, 32, 46,
      63, 135, 153, 155, 156, 168, 171,
      188
deconstruction, and law, 13, 190–1
decrementalism, 20, 72
definitional stop, 25, 41
de Haan, W., 12, 76, 178
delinquency, as category, 137–9, 141,
      147, 175
Derrida, J., 191
Dignan, J., 3, 6, 8, 18, 67, 68, 72, 80,
      87, 89, 90, 91, 103, 105, 125,
      166, 176
DiIulio, J.J., 171
disparity of sentences, 8, 24, 40, 106,
      177
dispersal of discipline, 137, 142, 145,
      157, 180
distribution of punishment, principles
      of, 6, 31, 46–7, 49, 52–4,
      73
division of labour, 98, 113
Dobash, R., 151
Donzelot, J., 145, 150
Douglas, M., 164
Downes, D., 145
Duff, R.A., 29, 47, 49, 50, 54, 87, 90,
      189
Durkheim, E., 8, 96, 97–104, 105,
      107, 109, 110, 112, 113, 115,
      116, 117, 118, 128, 131, 132,
      133, 134, 135, 147, 152, 153,
      171, 185
Dworkin, R., 68, 190

Eaton, M., 129, 146
economic determinism, *see* economic
      reductionism
economic reductionism, 9, 117, 121,
      147
Edwards, S., 40, 129
Elias, N., 110, 165
enforcement pyramid, 87–8, 89
Engels, F., 130
Enlightenment, the, 20, 192

equality of law and justice, 13, 60–1, 122, 127, 135, 140, 181, 182, 183–4
European Convention on Human Rights, 91, 188
European Court of Human Rights, 74
Ewald, F., 162
exchange of equivalents, 119–20, 121, 130, 165

fairness
  as principle of justice, 48–9, 86, 156, 167, 176
  of law, 13, 49, 183, 184
Farrell, S., 159
Farrington, D., 33, 129, 146
Faucher, Leon, 134
Feeley, M.M., 161, 164
Feinberg, J., 47
female reasoning, 180, 182–3
feminist jurisprudence, 81, 178, 180–4, 186
Ferri, E., 28, 33, 36
Finnis, J., 47
Finstad, L., 85
Fitzpatrick, P., 127, 190, 191
Flew, A., 1
Floud Committee, 35, 36
Floud, J., 35
Fogel, D., 40
Foucault, M., 7, 9, 11, 103, 132–52, 153, 155, 156, 157–8, 160, 161, 163, 171, 175, 180, 185, 191
Frankel, M.E., 39, 40, 106
Fraser, E., 81
free choice, 20, 27, 31, 52, 53, 54
free will, *see* free choice
Friedan, B., 124
functionalism, 9, 97, 117, 143, 148

Gallo, E., 64
Gamble, A., 126
Garfinkel, H., 108–9, 134
Garland, D., 6, 9, 10, 28, 96, 102, 103, 104, 108, 111, 112, 130, 133, 134, 143, 144, 146, 147, 148, 150, 151, 156–7, 159, 165–9, 171, 175, 185, 189, 190
Gaylin, W., 150
Geertz, C., 149

Gelsthorpe, L., 85
general justifying aim of punishment, 6, 31, 47, 50, 54, 68, 73, 186
'get tough' politics, 20–1, 39, 40, 50, 54, 73, 124, 155
Giddens, A., 159, 163, 166, 188, 189, 192
Gilbert, K., 30, 62–4, 67, 73
Giller, H., 40
Gilligan, C., 182–3
Gilroy, P., 127
Godefroy, T., 128
Goffman, E., 7, 140
Gordon, C., 147, 157, 160, 161
governmentality, 9, 141, 157–60, 161, 165, 172
Gramsci, A., 122
Gray, N., 189
Greenberg, D., 54, 67, 118, 121, 122, 124
Greenwood, R., 33

Habermas, J., 149, 192
Hacking, I., 159
Hale, C., 66, 118, 121, 122, 124
Hall, S., 126, 161
Hann, R.G., 34
Hannah-Moffat, K., 189
harm to living standard, as measure of crime seriousness, 44–5
Hart, H.L.A., 3, 6, 25, 31, 47
Hawkins, D.F., 119
Hawkins, G., 168
Hay, D., 123
Headley, D.B., 11
Heidensohn, F., 183
Hobbs, T., 7
Holdaway, S., 80
Honderich, T., 39
Hood, R., 177
Howard, Michael, 61
Howe, A., 128, 129, 133, 143, 145, 148, 151
Hudson, A., 181
Hudson, B.A., 2, 13, 23, 29, 30, 44, 52, 54, 62, 67, 73, 75, 76, 85, 86, 89, 106, 125, 127, 128, 139, 150, 151, 154, 159, 163, 167, 169, 177, 179, 180, 181, 183, 184, 185, 186

Hughes, G., 158
Hulsman, L., 13, 180
Humphries, D., 54, 67
Hunt, A., 124, 127, 141, 190, 191, 192
Hutter, B., 145

ideological functions, of punishment, 115, 123, 130
ideology
  law and order, 124–5, 126
  liberal, 127
Ignatieff, M., 9, 148, 165
Immarigeon, R., 75, 86, 90
imprisonment, as dominant form of punishment, 27, 100–1, 112, 116, 118–21, 153, 154
indeterminate sentences, 29, 30, 39, 62, 69, 154
innocent, punishment of the, 25, 41, 46, 52, 67

Jankovic, I., 117, 121
Jareborg, N., 44, 90
Jefferson, T., 126
Judicial Studies Board, 43
juvenile justice, 40, 42, 79–80, 83, 84, 144–5, 150, 151, 155, 176, 179, 181

Kant, I., 51, 53–4, 57
Karp, D.R., 80
Kerruish, V., 13, 49, 127, 191
Kirchheimer, O., 116–17, 118, 120, 132, 133, 136, 143, 153
Kittrie, N.N., 30
Kohlberg, L., 182–3
Kozol, L., 35
Kinsberg, B., 40, 42, 179
Kurki, L., 77

labelling theory, 108, 140
labour market, and punishment, 115–18, 130, 136, 170, 145
Lacey, N., 29, 49, 52, 73, 81, 186
Laffargue, B., 128
law
  and social solidarity, 8, 9, 99
  as source of authority, 8, 99
Lea, J., 126, 127

legitimacy, 8, 73, 78, 111, 176
Lemert, E.M., 108
lesser eligibility, 116–17, 120, 121
lesser intensity, of punishments, 100, 110
Levinas, E., 191
Lewis, C.S., 29, 31
Lewis, R., 84
lex talionis, 38, 40
limiting retributivism, 59–60
Locke, J., 7
Lombroso, C., 28
longue durée, as historical perspective, 110, 144
Luckman, T., 21
Lukes, S., 102, 103, 104
Lyon, D., 158

McEvoy, K., 78
MacKinnon, C., 129–30, 131, 183
Maffesoli, M., 168
Maguire, M., 11
Maher, L., 29
Marsh, C., 23
Martinson, R., 30
Marx, G., 168
Marx, K., 96, 113, 114, 130, 150, 153, 171
mass imprisonment, 168–70, 171
Mathiesen, T., 9, 12, 76, 138, 139, 148, 178
Matthews, R., 55, 65, 66, 151
Matza, D., 108, 176
Mauer, M., 169
Maxwell, G., 84
Mead, G.H., 104, 110
Megan's Law, 167
Melossi, D., 10, 112, 118, 119–20, 121, 122, 125, 127, 129, 133, 135, 141, 153, 165
Merleau-Ponty, M., 134
Mika, H., 78
Miller, A.P., 135
Miller, J., 178
Miller, P., 157
Minnesota Sentencing Guidelines Commission, 46, 177
Minow, M., 81
Mitchell, J., 124
Mitford, J., 40

modernism, *see* modernity
modernity, 1–2, 26, 161, 164, 192
    late, 156–7, 158, 159, 164, 166,
        167, 169, 171, 172, 187–8
Morris, A., 40, 77, 84, 85, 129, 146
Morris, N., 59–60, 61, 68, 69, 71
Muncie, J., 80
Murphy, J.G., 47, 49

negative reform, 178–9
neo-liberalism, 156, 160, 161, 164,
    169, 172
Newburn, T., 80
new penology, 161
new rehabilitation, 62–4
New Zealand model, of restorative
    justice, 79, 80, 82, 83
non-custodial penalties, 10, 24, 27, 30,
    46, 73, 142, 154, 171, 180
    see also community punishments
normalization, 140–1, 142, 145, 146,
    148, 151, 154, 163
Nozick, R., 50, 160

O'Malley, P., 155, 156, 161, 164
ordinal proportionality, 45, 46

panopticon, 27, 136–7, 142, 149
parsimony, 60–1, 71, 185
Pashukanis, E.B., 119, 120, 130, 165
Pasquino, P., 132, 145, 175
Paternoster, R., 49
Pavarini, M., 112, 119–20, 133, 141,
    153, 165
Pearson, G., 145
Pease, K., 22
Peters, R.S., 1
Pettit, P., 3, 20, 57, 60–1, 70–2, 184
phenomenology, 108–9, 134
Philips, D., 107
Piaget, J., 123
Pitts, J., 30, 145
Platt, T., 145
political obligation, 7, 18, 49, 126
positivist criminology, 11, 28, 33, 36,
    101, 138, 150, 175
Posner, R., 52, 128
Poster, M., 158
postmodern penality, 156
power, 103, 104, 105, 109, 111, 135,

    143, 147, 161, 163
    –knowledge, 140–2
    technologies of, 134, 142, 143, 147,
        163
    see also bio-power
Pratt, J., 156
presumptive sentences, 40–1, 44
Protecting the Public, 1996, White
    Paper, 163
protection, against crime, 5, 10, 32,
    35–6, 60, 156, 166
public executions, 110–12, 134, 135,
    143
Punishment and Society, 169

race, and criminal justice, 11, 12,
    47, 127, 170, 171, 176–7,
    183
Raeder, M., 182
rationality
    forms of, 105, 106, 107, 110
    penal, 132
rationalization, of punishment, 107
Rawls, J., 47–9, 51, 71
Raynor, P., 30
Reagan, Ronald, 126
'real' purposes of punishment, 8–9,
    101, 138–9, 148
reduction
    of crime, 3, 4, 5, 17, 60, 62, 157
    of prisons, 5, 27
    of punishment, 60, 72
regulatory functions, of law, 115
Reiman, J.H., 9, 123, 170
Reiner, R., 176
reintegrative shaming, 81–2, 109–10
repressive functions of punishment, 9,
    99, 102, 109, 115, 123
republican criminal justice, 70–2
'revisionist' histories of punishment,
    102, 148, 165
rights, 13, 72, 78, 88–9, 91, 92, 127,
    135, 137, 142, 153, 188
    human, 21, 67, 68–70, 73, 78, 89,
        91, 188–90
    of offenders, 3, 21, 35, 39, 63, 64,
        69, 70, 71, 88–9, 91, 92, 96, 155,
        178, 188–9, 190
    of victims, 3, 35, 69, 71, 78, 91, 92,
        96, 189, 190, 191

risk, management of, 87, 161–4, 165, 168, 169, 171, 172, 187–8, 190
Robinson, P., 58–9, 61, 62, 66, 67, 71
Rock, P., 108
Rose, N., 157, 159, 164
Rotman, E., 30, 62, 64, 66, 69, 73
Rousseau, J.-J., 7
Rubington, F., 108, 140, 176
Ruggiero, V., 64
rule-enforcement, as justification for punishment, 51
Rusche, G., 116–17, 118, 120, 133, 136, 143, 153
Rutherford, A., 178

Sabol, W.J., 11
Sarah's Law, 167
Sartre, J.-P., 134
Schutz, A., 21
Scraton, P., 126
Scull, A., 102, 103, 104, 166, 168
sentencing guidelines, 43–5, 46, 55
severity of punishments, 26, 36–7, 45–6, 47, 53, 69, 100, 103, 116, 121, 136, 185
Shapland, J., 126
Shelden, R.G., 128
Sheleff, L.S., 102
Sim, J., 150, 178, 179
Simon, J., 161, 163, 168, 169–70, 189
Skelton, A., 78
Smart, C., 13, 181, 191
Smith, D., 22, 30, 32
Snider, L., 85
social contract theory, 7, 48, 51, 52, 160
social defence, 36, 101, 145
social justice, 73
social solidarity, 9, 98, 101, 102, 108, 110, 111, 164
South Australia model, of restorative justice, 80, 83, 84, 85
Sparks, R., 156, 164, 166
Spencer, H., 96, 103
Spierenburg, P., 110, 111, 112, 143, 144, 151
Spitzer, S., 102, 103, 107, 119, 122
state-obligated rehabilitation, 64–6, 70
Steinhert, H., 12
Stenson, K., 164

Straw, Jack, 89
Sullivan, R.R., 156, 164
surveillance, 136–7, 158–9
Sutherland, E.H., 112

tariff, of penalties, 19, 24, 39, 40, 43, 53, 154
Taylor, I., 176
Taylor, R.D., 54
technicist penology, 10–11, 13
Ten, C.L., 60, 62
Thames Valley model, of restorative justice, 79, 80, 83
Thatcher, Margaret, 126
Thomas, D., 43
Thorpe, D., 42
three strikes, law, 32, 36, 54, 126, 155, 189
Tonry, M., 44, 170, 177, 181, 184
tragic quality of punishment, 104, 185

unfair-advantage, justification for punishment, 47–51
United Nations, 73, 76, 78, 89
Utilitarianism, 3, 7, 17, 18, 20, 25, 48–9, 51, 52, 53, 56, 57, 58, 59, 67, 70, 73, 184

van den Haag, E., 40
van Ness, D., 77, 78, 88
von Hirsch, A., 3, 19, 24, 25, 29, 35, 40, 44, 46, 47, 54, 55, 57, 58, 60, 73, 87, 88, 90, 150

Wacquant, L., 170
Wagga model of restorative justice, 79, 80
Walgrave, L., 82, 90
Walker, N., 2, 3, 18, 23, 29, 32, 35, 38, 53, 61, 67, 70, 73
Walzer, M., 149, 150, 192
Wasik, M., 54
Wasserstrom, R., 186
Weber, M., 8, 104–8, 113, 114, 151, 155
Weinberg, M., 108, 140, 176
West, D.J., 33
Wicharaya, T., 155
Williams, B., 34
Williams, G., 145

Wilson, J.Q., 33, 40, 126, 157
woman-wise penology, 182–3
women, control and punishment of,
    11, 39–40, 128–30, 145–6,
    151, 163, 179, 181–2, 189
Wootton, B., 29
Worrall, A., 146

Young, I.M., 81

Young, J., 10, 28, 66, 126, 127, 157
Young, P., 6, 10
Young, R., 80, 83, 86
Young, W., 35
Youth Justice and Criminal Evidence
    Act, 1999, 80
Zedner, L., 90, 151
Zehr, H., 81, 88
Zimring, F.E., 44, 76, 168

UNDERSTANDING CRIMINOLOGY
Current Theoretical Debates
Second Edition

Sandra Walklate

- What does contemporary criminological theory look like?
- What impact does it have on policy?
- What might its future be?

This substantially revised and updated text provides the student with an accessible understanding of the current nature of criminological theory. Its main focus is on development in criminological theorizing over the past twenty five years paying particular attention to 'right realism', 'left realism' and developments arising from the influence of theorizing around gender. The relationship of criminological theory and knowledge to current policy agendas is given particular attention in this second edition, and a key concern of the text is to paint a picture for the student of the complex interplay between criminology, criminal justice, social justice and politics. The author concludes by offering an insight into some of the theoretical concerns that might better inform the future development of criminological theory. In all, this represents an ideal theoretical text for students of criminology and trainees in criminal justice, including clear summaries, an expanded glossary and suggestions for further reading.

Contents
Series foreword – Preface – Introduction: some key problems in criminology – Perspectives in criminological theory – Understanding 'right realism' – Understanding 'left realism' – Gendering the criminal – Crime, politics and welfare – Criminal victimization, politics and welfare – Conclusion: new directions for criminology? – Glossary – Bibliography – Index.

192pp   0 335 20951 3 (Paperback)   0 335 20952 1 (Hardback)

UNDERSTANDING COMMUNITY PENALTIES
Probation, Policy and Social Change

Peter Raynor and Maurice Vanstone

- What are community sentences for?
- How has the theory and practice of community supervision developed?
- What kind of impact has research evidence had on policy and practice?
- Can community sentencing help offenders and protect the public at the same time?

Understanding Community Penalties provides a concise and critical understanding of community sentences in relation to policy, practice and research. Coverage of these three contexts is a distinguishing feature of the book, which takes a comprehensive approach informed by the authors' long involvement in this field. It begins by examining the role and function of community sentences, and how they challenge the framework of thinking about punishment in the criminal justice system. The book then traces the historical development of the theory and practice of community supervision, and shows what impact the first wave of research into its effectiveness has had on policy and practice.

In the context of the penal crisis in recent years and the construction of crime as a political issue, a critical assessment is made by the authors of the achievements of, and problems facing, community sentencing, and they address the questions facing sentencers, politicians, policy makers and practitioners. In particular, they consider whether current organizational structures and divisions are appropriate for the purposes of punishing and helping in the community those who offend. In all, this authoritative text will be essential reading for students of criminology and criminal justice, and an invaluable reference for researchers and practitioners in the criminal justice system.

Contents
Series editor's foreword – Introduction – The origins of community sentences – Good intentions and probation practice – Does anything work? the emergence of an empirical critique – Too soft on criminals? community sentences and populist punitiveness – More punishment or more effectiveness? how some things work – Community penalties today – Conclusion: a future for community sentences? – References – Index.

160pp   0 335 20625 5 (Paperback)   0 335 20626 3 (Hardback)